RETAIL EMPLOYMENT

Edited by

GARY AKEHURST
and
NICHOLAS ALEXANDER

FRANK CASS • LONDON

First published in Great Britain by
FRANK CASS & CO LTD
Newbury House, 900 Eastern Avenue
London IG2 7HH, England

and in the United States by
FRANK CASS
c/o ISBS
5804 N.E. Hassalo Street, Portland, Oregon 97213-3644

Library of Congress Cataloging-in-Publication Data
Applied for.

British Library Cataloguing in Publication Data
Applied for.

ISBN 0-7146-4177-4

This group of studies first appeared in *The Services Industries Journal*, 1984–95,
published by Frank Cass & Co. Ltd.

Printed in Great Britain by
Antony Rowe Ltd., Chippenham, Wilts

Contents

Introduction

Retail textbooks stress the importance of service provision. At the beginning of their discussion of personnel issues in retailing, Lewison and DeLozier [1989] reproduce an observation on the importance of the sales function and hence the role of the retail employee: 'In a product's long journey from the producer to the customer, the last two feet are the most important' [Kurtz *et al.*, 1985: 365]. Few retail managers would disagree with the philosophy which lies behind the observation, but the manner in which the last two feet is managed varies considerably between retail sectors, between retail operations, and inevitably within retail organisations, despite the best efforts of those organisations to ensure conformity of service provision.

The customer's perceptions of retail organisations are not established by head office or external marketing activity. Images may be enhanced, and misconceptions addressed through actions such as advertising campaigns, but the day-to-day contact that customers have with store personnel will fundamentally effect the customer's attitude toward the retail outlet. As Anderson [1993: 430] notes: 'Strategic plans could not be made nor strategies executed without people.' The three most important retail issues may often appear to be 'location, location and location', but the service provided by personnel in store will fundamentally affect the customer's perceptions.

Even in the superstore environment, where personal service has not been emphasised, the advent of post-saturation competitive conditions [Duke, 1991] will place a new emphasis on retailers' employment policies, their training programmes, and the attitudes of their staff toward customers; in other words, the last two feet. As McGoldrick [1990: 322] has remarked: 'Even in retail settings dominated by self-service, the services provided by the store staff can exert a major influence upon patronage decisions and retail images.'

However, despite the importance of personnel issues in the context of retail management, employment is a comparatively under-researched area. This is in part a result of the intellectual framework in which retailing has been studied. It is perhaps not surprising that employment issues *per se* and the public policy context in which retail employment issues are enmeshed, have not enjoyed the spotlight given to management and delivery issues by a marketing perspective which has been an important influence on retail studies in recent years. As Kirby [1992: 19] suggests, 'for scholars of marketing such issues [public policy] differed markedly from those with which they were accustomed' because '...research in marketing traditionally confined itself to subjects which were relatively easy to define.' However, the retail employee and employment policy issues within retailing have been, and to some extent continue to be, an under-researched area. That is not to say that official bodies and enquiries have not at specific times considered the position of the retail employee in some depth. The 'Sunday trading' question clearly illustrates the debate which will at times rage around this issue when it enters the political agenda. However, it is in such contexts that judgement of social issues is required to balance what may at times be perceived as opportunity and at others as exploitation [Walsh, 1989]. In this context, Kirby's [1992] dilemma is evident.

The issue of Sunday trading has received considerable media coverage and raises important social questions. But within retailing, Sunday trading is apart of a wider development leading to extended opening hours and a response by retailers to the needs of the consumer in a rapidly changing socio-economic environment. Therefore, Sunday trading and its impact on employment conditions cannot be seen simply as a means by which retailers are going to affect their employees' quality of life, but it is in itself a reflection of change. Changes in the structure of retailing have been, in part at least, a response to changing consumer needs. Despite the fact that time pressures make it difficult for consumers to access service outlets for extended periods during the working week, the demand for fixed-store provision has remained. Research suggests that for working women non-store retailing does not provide an alternative to the benefits derived in-store [Lavin, 1993]. Therefore, social change has stimulated the need for the extension of opening hours and hence the need for retailers to adopt new working practices, such as part-time working, to serve consumers' new shopping habits. At the same time, and as part of those broader social changes, there has been a demand for working hours which reflect changing social conditions and expectations. Therefore, Sunday trading is as much a measure of social change as a harbinger of it.

Changes in employment characteristics in retailing have been caused by changing needs in society both in terms of the effects of such change on purchasing behaviour but also on the supply of labour created by the same social changes. Sunday trading highlights certain fundamental changes which have been the result of structural change within the retail environment, which in itself is a response to economic development and social change.

RETAIL STRUCTURE

Change in the retail structure has had a considerable impact on employment within retailing. In the UK, the changes in the retail structure which occurred from the 1950s to the 1980s heavily influenced the number of staff employed per outlet, the owner-manager's role in retail provision, the technical skills and training required by staff, and the operational role of individual employees. It was a period of rapid and radical change that was particularly evident in the food sector which saw the development of self-service and the introduction of retail formats such as the supermarket, superstore and the hypermarket.

Therefore, as major changes have occurred in respect of the retail structure itself, it is also possible to identify changes in the structure of retail employment. Reynolds [1983], while recognising the limitations of the statistical sources, has suggested that structural changes are recognisable in employment within the distributive trades and has proposed a periodisation of changes in retail employment. The 1950s, he suggests, was a period in which expansion within retailing saw a general increase in the level of employment within the sector. This was followed by a period of a decade and a half when, as a result of fundamental changes in the economics of distribution, due to fundamental shifts in social and economic factors, and the concomitant decline in the number of retail outlets, there was an innovative use of labour resources, such as part-time female labour.

These changes led to a change in the spatial dimensions of store operations and the service levels expected within the store. Like Reynolds [1983], Sparks [1983] acknowledges that the considerable changes in retail employment have been stimulated by changes in the structure of retailing and the wider socio-economic environment. In Sparks words: 'Shopworkers have been transformed and de-skilled from assistants, who were expected to give customers personal service and have a detailed knowledge of the goods, into checkout operators' [Sparks, 1983: 63]. The structural changes in the food sector had an impact on the number of operators able to compete in the new and highly competitive environment, the number of outlets, the spatial dimensions of those outlets, the support systems associated with those outlets, the behaviour and role of customers within those outlets, and the staffing levels and staff skills required to operate the new operations.

An examination of employment statistics from member states of the European Union (EU) illustrates the dramatic changes which have occurred in markets such as the UK, Germany, the Netherlands and Denmark in the comparatively recent past, and the effect structural change has had on employment. Similarly it shows how employment figures may be used as an indicator of development and sophistication within a retail structure.

Modern retail formats introduced into the UK at the end of the 1960s have more recently made an impact in some EU markets. In the UK there were 13 superstores for every one million inhabitants by 1991, in Greece there were only two [Eurostat, 1993: 24]. The superstore has had a major impact on the store employment characteristics [Sparks, 1981, 1982a,b, 1983, 1987, 1991, 1992; Dawson et al., 1986a,b, 1987; Penn and Wirth, 1993; Freathy, 1993].

In relatively undeveloped European markets such as Portugal and Greece there are a high number of retail enterprises per inhabitant: there were more than 170 per 10,000 inhabitants at the beginning of the 1990s [Eurostat, 1993]. In contrast, in the Netherlands and the UK there were less than 70 outlets per 10,000 inhabitants. The former markets of Portugal and Greece display a structure that would be familiar to UK consumers a generation or more ago: smaller enterprises both in terms of the business itself, but also the outlets through which the business was managed by the owner and a significant number of full-time male staff. By the beginning of the 1990s Greece had on average 1.9 individuals employed per retail outlet; in the UK the figure was 8.7 [Eurostat, 1993]. Wage and salary earners constituted only 28.9 per cent of those engaged in retailing; in the UK the figure was 84.2 per cent [Eurostat, 1993]. In Greece 43.6 per cent of the retail labour force were female and only 3.3 per cent were part-time: in the UK the figures were 58.1 per cent and 40.7 per cent respectively [Eurostat, 1993].

These national figures illustrate the differences which exist within retail employment within the EU. However, it should also be recognised that considerable regional differences exist and that trends within national markets should also be considered. There is a tendency to perceive changes in employment to be reflected across the country, but as Reynolds [1983] points out, the aggregation of figures serves to 'conceal very significant local variations' [p.355]. Shifts in population, for example, have had an impact on regional retail employment figures. For example, in food retailing a significant decline in the numbers employed in London in the 1970s was balanced by a significant rise in the numbers employed in retailing in the rest of the South East.

INFORMATION SOURCES

A major problem associated with the analysis of retail employment is the quality of information available to the researcher [Reynolds, 1983]. In Britain there is 'a fundamental lack of a consistent, reliable and comprehensive statistical base from which analysis may proceed' [Reynolds, 1993: 344]. Reynolds [1993] has outlined the problems associated with using the different data sources available to the researcher and the information available to the researcher for different periods, lamenting that the Census of Distribution for 1971 'has come to represent the high point of statistical survey work' [Reynolds, 1993: 345].

The lack of data in the area of retail employment has considerable implications for research in retailing and analysis of retail development. Guy [1992] has observed that the lack of employment information makes the assessment of new retail developments difficult. Researchers have, therefore, various approaches to data gathering, in order to build a picture of retail employment conditions.

RESEARCH METHODS

Some of the important articles concerned with retail employment are repro-duced in this volume. The research methods employed by the researchers indicate the variety of research issues and the reliability of information.

Robinson [1993] sets the scene by considering the debate which has emerged from North America. The service sector is a major employer of labour in advanced economies and is the principal source of employment growth. In the US and Canada the service sector proportion of total employ-ment is now around 70 per cent.

Coupled with this growth has been a change in labour market structure, showing a strong and significant growth in what can be called 'non-standard' employment, that is, 'the creation of jobs which do not involve a full-time and continuous relationship between employer and employee' [Robinson, 1993: 2]. Different modes of employment have emerged, primarily part-time, tem-porary and self-employed. Robinson [1993] reminds us that part-time work-ers are the principal and most rapidly expanding component of this non-stan-dard workforce. What we are witnessing is the dramatic growth of a contin-gent workforce.

There is no universally recognised definition of part-time employment, with the only official definition available being that used in compiling labour force statistics [Robinson, 1993: 2] Generally part-time work is considered to be employment for shorter than usual, collectively agreed or statutory work-ing hours. For survival, service activities must be in tune with fluctuations in customer flows and demands. Computerisation of systems allows the identi-fication of peak and trough trading periods so that labour input can be more closely matched to needs.

The emerging debate centres on the conflicting views that part-time work is a threat to full-time jobs, a precarious form of employment and a source of unequal treatment of women workers, but at the same time, it reconciles worker needs and preferences with corporate operational requirements. There is unquestionably the profound implications of the divergent treatment of part-time workers compared with their full-time counterparts. In the US and Canada it is being demonstrated 'that part-time work does not appear to afford an equitable or mutually satisfactory reconciliation of the interests of workers and their employers' [Robinson, 1993: 3]; see also Thurman and Trah [1990]. Furthermore, this imbalance is quickening labour market seg-mentation, which may generate short-term cost savings for employers but at the expense of long-term productivity growth. The concern is that service industries already have lower measured rates of productivity growth compared with the manufacturing sector [Stanback and Noyelle, 1990].

Reynolds [1983] provides a useful introduction to later chapters when he discusses the merits of, and problems associated with, alternative research opportunities. He notes that questionnaires, for example, provide 'a detailed insight' [Reynolds, 1983: 359], but there is a danger that the results provide little insight into change over time unless follow-up surveys are carried out. However, in the absence of comprehensive data he observes: 'governmental statistical sources are of particularly limited use in the area relating to the internal employment policies of firms, and some of the most interesting and revealing aspects of employment change are those which are occurring at the establishment or business level, rather than at the aggregate national or regional scale' [p.359]. Reynolds sets a research agenda in this second chapter which is taken up in subsequent chapters.

Recognising the neglected nature of employment within retailing and superstore employment in particular, Sparks [1983], through survey findings, discusses the characteristics of employment within the superstore environment. His survey results are based on 71 responses from superstores. The respondents provided details of levels of employment with respect to such factors as the job performed, the hours worked, and the employee's gender. Using these data, Sparks discusses superstore size and employment characteristics and the relationship between the two. This chapter provides a useful introduction to the issue of employment within the superstore environment and was a ground- breaking exercise when it was carried out, providing as it did a more detailed examination of the issues than had previously existed.

Dawson, Findlay and Sparks [1986a] consider the operations of three superstore operators: ASDA, Fine Fare and Tesco. The information used is based on a total of 175 superstores operated by these companies and represents nearly a third of all grocery superstores operating in the UK at that time. This and the previous chapter are therefore instructive not only in the results they report but also in terms of the methodologies employed.

Dawson *et al.* [1986a] clearly show the value of survey work, but as they note both in terms of the qualification this research made to previous work and also the evolving policy of one superstore operator, there is a dynamic of time here which Reynolds [1983] in an earlier chapter recognises as significant but also notes is not easily overcome through the use of 'surveys...of the "snapshot" variety' [Reynolds, 1983: 359].

As the abstract to Sparks [1991a] notes: 'Employment patterns in food superstores have received much research attention in recent years. Employment in non-food superstores has, however, been inadequately researched' [Sparks, 1991a: 304]. This chapter helps to redress the balance.

The research focuses on store level issues, with information gathered on working hours, gender, and the categories within which staff were employed. Reference may be made here to Sparks' [1983] earlier work reprinted below and the work of Dawson *et al.* [1986a] also reprinted below. Results are presented which provide a contrast for the results of Dawson *et al.*'s [1986a] earlier findings. There is an appendix to this chapter in the form of an update.

The results of survey work carried out by the EDC's Part-Time Employment Group are discussed in Robinson's article [1984]. The survey carried out considered the issue of part-time working in retailing and these findings are used to discuss training needs.

Penn and Wirth [1993] have provided a useful update and development of specific themes raised by Sparks in an earlier chapter, as well as an interesting exploration of the dynamic of employment patterns. Further, Penn and Wirth [1993] provide a stimulating coverage of the context in which changes in retail employment may be seen as far as numerical, functional and pay flexibility is concerned. The issue of part-time employment is taken as a central theme. This chapter focuses on five stores in Lancaster: Sainsbury, Marks and Spencer, E.H. Booth, Asda and Littlewoods. The authors were particularly conscious of the social context which had influenced the use of, and increase in, part-time female workers. They propose that the social issue is far more complex than the literature often suggests.

Penn and Wirth's [1993] work provides a comparison with the survey approach favoured by Sparks [1983], and also by Dawson *et al.* [1986a] and the aggregated figures discussed by Reynolds [1983]. Thurik [1984] provides an international perspective to the issue of superstore employment as well as providing a statistical test of information derived from data gathered.

Much of the work discussed in the chapters below considers the situation which has developed within retailing and the factors which brought about that development. Freathy [1993] considers the applicability of segmentation theory to the retail labour market. Continuing a theme of earlier papers he considers the situation in superstores. The author provides a useful discussion of the literature on superstore employment, before addressing the research he carried out in the Manchester area on employment relations.

In a further drive towards understanding the nature of retail employment Freathy and Sparks [1994] recognise and welcome the variety of methodological approaches to studying employee relations in food retailing. They provide a very useful commentary upon developments within food retailing, within the context of a more dynamic framework than that traditionally provided by labour market theories and consequent segmentation theory. Such an approach needs to be supplemented by more case studies, such as those provided by Sparks [1990].

NATURE OF EMPLOYMENT

It has been suggested that there have been four main trends in retail employ-ment in recent decades: a steady decline in employment numbers, the reduc-tion in the numbers of self-employed; an increase in the proportion of the workforce accounted for by women; and an increase in the proportion of the workforce accounted for by part-time employees [Sparks, 1992]. The rela-tively small decline in the numbers employed in retailing, the major decline in the number of self-employed in retailing, has been a direct result of the changing structure of retailing as illustrated above. The 'feminisation of the workforce' [Sparks, 1992: 13] and the increasing importance of part-time employment has been the product of both considerable social change but also the nature of in store operations. While retailers may on the one hand be accused of asking their employees to work unsocial hours, they have also pro-vided employees with flexible work opportunities and have thereby drawn on a growing pool of labour. The feminisation of retail employment through part-time working has provided those employees concerned with supplementary household income, and a degree of financial independence: the two most fre-quently cited reasons for working in stores registered by female retail employ-ees in Kirby's [1992] research on retail employment.

Broadbridge [1995] has demonstrated that female sales assistants and checkout operators in retailing earned just under 80 per cent of their male counterparts' gross weekly wage in 1992. Using New Earnings Survey data, differentials between male and female earnings in retailing persistently remain.

Sparks [1992] identifies a further four characteristics of employment in retailing: the relative youth of retail employees, the rapid rate of employee turnover in retailing, the lack of unionisation and relatively low pay. These four characteristics are closely related, as are the factors of feminisation and part-time working. Retailers have required particular workforce characteris-tics and been prepared to accept the benefits, and also the problems associat-ed with such employee characteristics.

The significance of, and concomitant issues associated with, modern retail employment profiles are discussed below and in the articles reproduced in this volume.

PART-TIME EMPLOYEES

There has been a shift away from full-time male employees to part-time female employees. This has been encouraged by the selective employment tax (SET) and operational changes [SET,1966], for example. Part-time working has provided retailers with a more flexible workforce [Walsh, 1989] and allowed retailers to be more responsive to the peaks in shopper demand and has provided opportunities for the workforce, to address both pressures of financial necessity and opportunities for increased social interaction [Feldman and Doerpinghaus, 1992].

At the time of Dawson *et al.*'s [1986a] research Tesco was considered to have a relatively high number of full-time and male employees, although at the time of the survey a corporate drive toward greater efficiency was recognised as leading to a change in the role of employees and the balance in the composition of the staff.

Part-time staffing has proved useful to retailers but there are fundamental questions to be considered. Robinson [1984] suggests that the use of part-time labour as unskilled staff may be detrimental, in the long term, to the retailer, as well as the employee, if for no other reason than the service provided by the retailer will suffer and will illicit a negative customer response.

In the minds of retailers, advancement in career terms for store employees means a switch to full-time working for part-time operatives. There are clear operational problems in supervisory staff being employed on a part-time basis but the attitude of retailers that part-time staff did not wish to develop their careers further is not borne out by the attitudes of part-time staff [Robinson, 1984].

However, even where the majority of employees are part-time the proportion of the staff in part-time employment and the age and family circumstances of employees may vary considerably. In Penn and Wirth's [1993] research, while more than half the workforce in all the stores they surveyed were part-time, the figure at Sainsbury's was 58 per cent whereas at ASDA it was 78 per cent. Marks and Spencer's use of married female staff stands out: 90 per cent of Marks and Spencer's full-time staff were married. The store operator clearly has an impact on selection procedures and the subsequent composition of staff. Although other factors will also have their effect so that, for example, as the size of stores increases, so will the number of sales staff and so will the proportion of sales staff operating on a part-time basis [Sparks, 1983].

GENDER

As it is not possible to discuss part-time working without reference to gender it is not possible to discuss gender without reference to social change and the increasing participation of women in the workforce. In the light of demographic changes, the attitude of retail management toward the employment of married women is significant in that it highlights the reliability, commitment, flexibility and loyalty that greater life experience can bring to a part-time employee's work [Penn and Wirth, 1993]. However, as Penn and Wirth [1993] recognise, even where there exists the same evaluation by management of employee characteristics this will not necessarily lead to the same approach to recruitment, so that, as was the case in their study, while one store favoured the recruitment of married women, another tended to employ younger women, although both recognised the benefits of the former group.

DE-SKILLING AND TRAINING

De-skilling has been a notable characteristic of the changes which have occurred in the retail sector, particularly the food sector [Robinson, 1984]. However, the increasing significance of technological innovation within the retail working environment, which implies the need for greater training input by retailers [Robinson, 1984], may help to reverse this trend. Indeed, this change points to a further development in retailing which may prove as important in demanding a new type of skilled retail employee different from but comparable with the old type of pre-retail revolution employee. However, if such is the case then as Robinson [1984] suggests retailers will have to adopt a fundamentally new approach to training.

The decline in the number of owners active in their own business reflects the increasing concentration levels within the retail sector and the fundamental shift toward salaried employment [Reynolds, 1983]. This has led to an increase in graduate recruitment within retailing and the subsequent development of degrees in retail management within the University sector supported by major retailers.

Penn [1995] examines British retailing employment patterns during the 1980s, focusing on the flexibility thesis and theories of skill and technical change using an economic sociological perspective. His analysis, based upon a random sample of 72 retail establishments (which had been investigated as part of the Economic and Social Research Council's [ESRC] Social Change and Economic Life Initiative) reveals that technological change has not produced much in the way of de-skilling but has rather enskilled the work of already qualified employees. Such a view is of course, contentious and no doubt other researchers will return to this in the future.

Retailers have also recruited younger employees, but changing demographic conditions have encouraged some retailers to consider again the older employee [Eure, 1991]. Retailers such as Tesco have responded by targeting the 55s and over as potential employees [Heaton, 1988]. This has implications for retailers in terms of the technical skills and social skills the older worker may bring to the retail environment.

However, retailers' training policies and retailers training practices have been found to differ markedly [Robinson, 1984]. Retailers are often aware of what is required but do not successfully implement the necessary practical training objectives.

The structural changes in the industry should not be used as an excuse for a lack of training provision [Robinson, 1984]. Training for retail employees in the UK does not compare with that provided in Germany. Germany can not be excused as possessing a backward retail structure. Again, as with Sunday trading, retail employment move into the area of public policy and such specific issues as the 'social chapter'. Training practices in retailing can strongly reflect changing social mores and attitudes. The Woolworth Corporation's subsidiary Kinney Shoe has recognised the issues of cultural diversity its store manages face and has consequently developed a training programme which seeks to build awareness of such differences and their importance in employee relations [Santora, 1991].

OPERATOR

Sparks [1983] suggests that store size rather than operator has the greatest impact on employment levels within the store. Although, he notes the importance of other variables such as the importance of space allocation, the turnover of the operation and the characteristics of the operator will influence staffing issues.

Dawson et al. [1986a] built on previous work, including Sparks [1983]. However, previous research concentrated on issues of employment levels and categories, such as gender, hours worked, and staff grading, and the relationship of such factors to spatial considerations. This left further questions to be answered, particularly the importance and role of the individual operator. The question of operator influence was to prove important. The research findings from this survey qualify considerably the findings of previous research. Here the operator was found to be of major importance and there were recognisable differences between male/female and part/full-time ratios within the stores operated by specific retailers. As the authors acknowledge, this may in part have been the result of the changing use of staff and, therefore, the nature of employment within stores, but also the result of methodological issues. Nevertheless, these results should be considered when reference is made to earlier findings.

Further work by Sparks [1991] has also produced results which show that the operator has an important impact on the structure of employment within the stores studied. Although, it is also noted, and this harks back to Sparks' [1983] initial work on food superstores, there are similar discernible trends across company boundaries.

Penn and Wirth's [1993] findings are interesting in the light of the work carried out by of Dawson *et al.* [1986a]. Again operators' policies were found to be important in determining the structure of employment with the retail store. Again the operator was found to be of major importance when gauging the level of female and part-time employment although similar general similarities could be determined.

INTERNAL LABOUR MARKET

With reference to the retail employment sector, Freathy [1993] has considered the internal labour market, where the organisation ties the employee in to the organisation in return for company-specific benefits and career advancement. He discusses the primary and secondary elements which the literature suggests exist within the labour market. He draws here on the classic work of Doeringer and Piore [1971].

Freathy also notes the segmented nature of employment in respect of gender. Sparks [1983] illustrates a polarisation within the workforce between those in the sales function and those in managerial roles where the sales function is performed, as it frequently is, by female part-time staff. Conversely, he found male workers characteristically filled managerial positions.

The results of Freathy's [1993] research into employment relations in stores reveal that in contrast to 'traditional approaches to segmentation theory...it was found that a degree of access did exist between' [p.76] different employment groups. Therefore it was possible for individuals to move from the secondary labour market as defined by Doeringer and Piore [1971] to the primary labour market. This is noteworthy in the light of Robinson's [1984] findings.

Within the context of their secondary labour market, retailers are faced with the rapid turnover of staff. Indeed while there are problems attached to this issue, there are also benefits for the retailer in a natural turnover of staff, although a level which is too high will result in increased training costs in certain areas. The reasons why retail employees leave their jobs is an important aspect of employment. Fields and Nkomo's [1991] research has highlighted the importance of the expectations which have not been met in the retail work environment, while Heetderks and Martin [1991] have investigated employee perceptions of and satisfaction with a two-tier system of remuneration.

CONCLUSIONS

Retail employment enjoys a complex and curious mixture of imagery and perception. Retailing has not been seen as a high status occupation. Shopkeeping has often been a response to unemployment. Not surprisingly, therefore, shop-keeping has been seen as a last resort occupation and shop assistants have not enjoyed high social status. This reputation of retail employment has to some extent survived the radical changes which have occurred in the industry in recent decades. Despite the increase in managerial opportunities for graduates, public perceptions have lagged behind reality. To some extent this is changing. Within the UK with the establishment of retail degree courses and modules on retailing within business or management courses the role and importance of retailers is better understood and appreciated, not least in the sense that a career in retailing may provide significant rewards.

Retail employment has received limited academic attention in recent years, but given the importance of personnel in the provision of retail service it is surprising that this important area has not received greater attention. However, with the paucity of information available and the problems of gathering information from organisations, and the methodological issues raised in the study of this area, it is perhaps not surprising that limited research has been possible and considerable research opportunities remain.

Changes in retail employment in recent years, however, have been considerable, reflecting and contributing to structural and functional changes in retailing. It is not possible to understand changes within retail operations without an understanding of the changing role of retail personnel. Similarly the socio-economic conditions to which retailers have responded is in part measured by the changing composition of retail staff.

As Sparks [1992] has recognised, an increase in the proportion of the workforce accounted for by women working part-time and the reduction in the number self-employed has been fundamental to an understanding of retail employment in recent years. Similarly, as Sparks [1992] notes, other factors, such as the youth of employees, higher labour turnover, low pay and low unionisation, have also characterised retail employment. These features have marked the last two decades of rapid evolution or revolution [Thomas, 1991] in retailing within the UK and in developed global markets. It would nevertheless be a mistake to assume that this dynamic area of retailing will retain these characteristics in the future. The structure of retailing is continually changing and its employee needs evolving. Similarly the supply of labour is itself changing and a product of socio-economic conditions. With, for example, demographic changes, it may be increasingly older employees who enter the retail workforce and contribute to fundamental changes in employment characteristics and the overall provision of service in retailing.

REFERENCES

Anderson, C., 1993, *Retailing: Concepts, Strategy and Information*, St Paul MN: West Publishing Company.

Broadbridge, A., 1995, 'Female and Male Earnings Differentials in Retailing', *Service Industries Journal*, Vol.15, No.1, pp.14–34.

Dawson, J., A. Findlay and L. Sparks, 1986a, 'The Importance of Store Operator on Superstore Employment Levels', *Service Industries Journal*, Vol.6, No.3, pp.329–61.

Dawson, J., A. Findlay and L. Sparks, 1986b, 'Anatomy of Job Growth: Employment in British Superstores', *Institute for Retail Studies, Working Paper*, 8601, Stirling: University of Stirling.

Dawson, J., A. Findlay and L. Sparks, 1987, 'Employment in British Superstores: Summary of Project Findings', *Institute for Retail Studies, Working Paper*, 8701, Stirling: University of Stirling.

Doeringer, P. and M. Piore, 1971, *Internal Labour Markets and Manpower Analysis*, Massachusetts: Heath.

Duke, R., 1991, 'Post-saturation Competition in UK Grocery Retailing', *Journal of Marketing Management*, Vol.7, No.1, pp.63–75.

Eure, J., 1991, 'Toward the New Century in Retailing: Survival; Strategies for an Industry in Turmoil', *Business Forum*, Vol.16, No.4, pp.24–8.

Eurostat, 1993, *Retailing in the Single European Market 1993*, Brussels: Commission of the European Communities.

Feldman, D., and H. Doerpinghaus, 1992, 'Missing Persons No Longer: Managing Part-Time Workers in the '90s', *Organizational Dynamics*, Vol.21, No.1, pp.59–72.

Fields, D., and S. Nkomo, 1991, 'Examining the Role of Job Attribute Preferences in the Rapid Turnover of Newly Hired Retail Employees', *Journal of Applied Business Research*, Vol.7, No.4, pp.28–35.

Freathy, P., 1993, 'Developments in the Superstore Labour Market', *Service Industries Journal*, Vol.13, No.1, pp.65–79.

Guy, C., 1992, 'Estimating Shopping Centre Turnover: A Review of Survey Methods', *International Journal of Retail and Distribution Management*, Vol.20, No.4, 1992, pp.18–23.

Heaton, S., 1988, 'Bridging the Skills Shortage', *Industrial Society*, Dec., pp.13–17.

Heetderks, T., and Martin, J., 1991, 'Employee Perceptions of the Effects of a Two-Tier Wage Structure', *Journal of Labor Research*, Vol.12, No.3, pp.279–95.

Kirby, D., 1992, 'Employment in Retailing', *International Journal of Retail and Distribution Management*, Vol.20, No.7, 1992, pp.19–28.

Kurtz, D., H. Dodge and J. Klopmaker, 1985, *Professional Selling*, 4th edition, Plano TX: Business Publications, p.365

Lavin, M., 1993, 'Wive's Employment, Time Pressure, and Mail/Phone Order Shopping – An Exploratory Study', *Journal of Direct Marketing*, Vol.7, No.1, pp.42–9.

Lewison, D., and M. DeLozier, 1989, *Retailing*, Columbus: Merril.

McGoldrick, P., 1990, *Retail Marketing*, Maidenhead: McGraw-Hill.

Penn, R., and B. Wirth, 1993, 'Employment Patterns in Contemporary Retailing: Gender and Work in Five Supermarkets', *Service Industries Journal*, Vol.13, No.4, pp.252–66.

Reynolds, J., 1983, 'Retail Employment Research: Scarce Evidence in an Environment of Change', *Service Industries Journal*, Vol.3, No.3, pp.344–62.

Robinson, O., 1984, 'Employment Policies in the Service Sector: Training in Retail Distribution', *Service Industries Journal*, Vol.10, No.2, pp.284–305.

SET, 1966, *Selective Employment Tax*, CMND 2986.

Santora, J., 1991 'Kinney Shoe Steps into Diversity', *Personnel Journal*, Vol.70, No.9, pp.72–7.

Sparks, L., 1981, 'A Note Upon Retail Employment and Superstore Development', *Service Industries Journal*, Vol.1, No.3, pp.44–58

Sparks, L., 1982a, 'Female and Part–time Employment within Superstore Retailing', *European Journal of Marketing*, Vol.16, No.7.

Sparks, L., 1982b, 'Employment in Hypermarkets and Superstores', Reading: *URPI Information*

Brief, 82/7.

Sparks, L., 1983, 'Employment Characteristics of Superstore Retailing', *Service Industries Journal*, Vol.3, No.1, pp.63–78.

Sparks, L., 1987, 'Employment in Retailing: Trends and Issues', in G. Johnson (ed.), *Business Strategy and Retailing*, Chichester: Wiley.

Sparks, L., 1990, 'Spatial–Structural Relationships in Retail Corporate Growth: a Case Study of Kwik Save Group Plc', *Service Industries Journal*, Vol.10, No.1, pp.25–84.

Sparks, L., 1991a, 'Employment in DIY Superstores', *Service Industries Journal*, Vol.11, No.3, pp.304–23.

Sparks, L., 1991b, 'Retailing in the 1990s: Differentiation through Customer Service', *Irish Marketing Review*, Vol.5, No.2, pp.28–38.

Sparks, L., 1992, 'Restructuring Retail Employment', *International Journal of Retail & Distribution Management*, Vol.20, No.3, pp.12–19.

Thomas, A., 1991, 'Leadership and Change in British Retailing 1955–84', *Service Industries Journal*, Vol 11, No 3, pp.381–92.

Thurik, A., 1984, 'Labour Productivity, Economies of Scale and Opening Time in Large Retail Establishments', *Service Industries Journal*, Vol.4, No.1, pp.19–29.

Thurman, J.E. and G. Trah, 1990, 'Part-time Work in International Perspective', *International Labour Review*, Vol.129, No.1, Geneva.

Walsh, T., 1989, 'Part-Time Employment and Labour Market Policies', *National Westminster Bank Quarterly Review*, May, pp.43–55.

1
Employment in Services: Perspectives on Part-time Employment Growth in North America

OLIVE ROBINSON

Service industries are the major employers of labour in the advanced market economies and generally the principal source of employment growth. They also account for the significant expansion of the numbers of part-time workers, who form the main component of the 'non-standard' or 'flexible' workforce. Over 40 per cent of the estimated 50 million part-time workers in these economies are found in the United States and Canada, the bulk engaged in service sector activity. Part-time employment growth is the subject of extensive discussion and it is the purpose of this article to consider the debate that has been emerging recently in North America. It is concluded that the advantages of labour force flexibility widely seen as conducive to productivity improvement and profitability in the labour intensive services sector may not be fully realised unless employers appreciate the longer-run implications of their increasing utilisation of labour on a part-time basis.

INTRODUCTION

It is a distinguishing feature of the advanced industrial economies that the labour intensive services sector accounts for a major and increasing proportion of employment. In the United States and Canada this proportion is now approximately 70 per cent. At the same time the labour market structure has been changing, exhibiting a significant growth in non-standard employment, the creation of jobs which do not involve a full-time and continuous relationship between employer and employee. Although such jobs encompass differing employment modes, represented chiefly by part-time, temporary and self-employment, part-time workers are commonly the principal and most rapidly expanding component of the non-standard workforce. In 1991 the OECD Employment

Outlook reported that 'the proportion of part-time workers in total employment was increasing virtually everywhere over the 1980's', confirming the results of the ILO's 1988 international survey which showed that in the industrialised market economies alone part-time work had increased by some 30 per cent over the decade, reaching a total of some 50 million workers. Over 40 per cent of these are employed in North American labour markets, some 20 million in the United States and 2 million in Canada.

There is no universally recognised definition of part-time work, and often the only official definition available is that used in compiling labour force statistics. In practice part-time work is regarded as employment for shorter working hours than statutory, collectively agreed or usual/normal working hours. In the United States part-time employment relates to working hours of up to 34 and in Canada 30 hours per week, the latter figure the same as that used in the United Kingdom [EIRR, 1990]. The strong association of part-time employment growth with the broad sectoral shift in employment from manufacturing to services reflects the 'uneven' labour requirements of service industry employers [ILO, 1988]. Expansion of service industries in both the private and public sectors of advanced economies where wages typically form a higher proportion of overall costs than in the more highly capitalised manufacturing sectors, leads to the creation of new jobs with a working week geared to fluctuations in customer/client flow, resulting in the offer by employers of jobs requiring fewer than normal full-time hours. Computerised systems allow employers to identify precisely peak trading periods and to match labour input more closely to needs, notably in retailing, hotels and catering, and leisure services. The ability to hire labour on a less than full-time basis has also facilitated profitable exploitation of new technology in banking and insurance, business services, education and health care, where incremental labour use may be achieved by additions of less than one full-time worker [ILO 1988; Robinson, 1985, 1991].

The variously described non-standard, atypical, flexible or contingent labour force is in North America, the subject of increasing debate. In the United States, labour market analysts are directing attention to the dramatic growth of the contingent workforce, which 'consists of workers who do not have a long-term attachment to their employers, comprising distinct as well as overlapping groups, but dominated by part-time workers'. Part-time jobs which are heavily concentrated in service industries are not only a sizeable portion of total employment but are growing faster than full-time jobs. [Belous, 1989; Christopherson, 1990]. In Canada, part-time employment growth attracts attention because it has been the subject of a Commission of Inquiry in the early 1980s, and has accounted for over one quarter of all employment growth during the last decade. All industries in the country now rely more on part-time work than they did in the past, but it continues to predominate in the services sector, the source of the bulk of employment growth [Lévesque, 1987; Coates, 1991].

The essence of the debate about part-time employment growth is comprehended in the antithetical views recorded in the ILO survey: 'part-time work is widely condemned as a threat to full-time jobs, a precarious form of employment and a source of unequal treatment of women workers; it is a regular, well-protected way to reconcile the needs and preferences of workers with the operational requirements of enterprises, to create jobs, and to benefit workers with family responsibilities, workers approaching retirement and other special groups'. Underlying these opposing assessments is the substantive problem of the implications of the divergent treatment of part-time workers compared with their full-time counterparts, a divergence involving inferior labour market treatment of workers who do not enjoy full-time permanent and continuing employment contracts. Within the labour markets of the European Community, for example, where the incidence of part-time work has increased rapidly in recent years, rising at almost twelve times the rate of full-time employment growth, to approximately 15 million or over 14 per cent of the total labour force, the lack of 'parity between part-time and full-time work' has fuelled successive proposals for legislative intervention. In 1982 a draft Directive sought 'to guarantee part-time workers the same rights as full-timers with due regard to the special nature of part-time employment'. Despite progress in narrowing this gap following unilateral action by governments and employers in individual member states, the unadopted Directive has been recently revived in the European Commission's proposals for Council Directives on non-standard or atypical work, which are among the first of the social action programme proposals under the Community Social Charter. The proposed Directives are promoted on equity grounds and as a necessary step 'to avert the danger of the development of terms of employment, such as to cause problems of social dumping or even distortions of competition at Community level' [EIRR, 1990].

This article seeks to examine the labour market circumstances pertaining to part-time employment in North America, and to review the ensuing debate surrounding its increasing utilisation by service sector employers. It will be seen that in the United States and Canada also, part-time work does not appear to afford an equitable or mutually satisfactory reconciliation of the interests of workers and their employers

[Thurman and Trah, 1990]. Rather this imbalance is exacerbating segmentation of the labour market, a process which may be generating short-term cost savings for service sector employers at the expense of longer run productivity growth in industries already generally characterised by rates of measured growth lower than those recorded for industrial sector productivity [Stanback and Noyelle, 1990].

A GROWING LABOUR FORCE: STATISTICAL EVIDENCE

In 1989 about 20 million people employed in the non-agricultural sectors of the United States economy worked part-time, comprising almost one-fifth of all employees; an 'overwhelming 90 per cent' of part-time employment occurs in the generally labour intensive service industries. While some estimates of employment growth in the 1980s claim that the strong rate of growth has not been due to a disproportionate growth in part-time jobs, the significant feature of the part-time employment growth is its gradual but persistent upward trend since the late 1950s, rising from 12.1 per cent in 1957 to 18.1 per cent in 1989. While in the short run the incidence of part-time employment 'climbed during economic recessions and dipped during expansions', over the long term increases exceeded decreases so that on average the fraction of the workforce employed part-time trended upward at roughly 0.19 percentage points per annum. At the same time these statistical estimates under report the rate of expansion of part-time employment as the numbers of workers rather than jobs are counted: the number of multiple job-holders, of whom 85 per cent work 24 hours per week or less on their second job increased from 4.9 per cent in 1979 to 6.2 per cent in 1989. The United States has a lower percentage of workers in part-time jobs than the United Kingdom or Sweden, for example, where it is approaching a quarter of the labour force, but with work of up to 34 hours per week classified as part-time the share of total labour input [in terms of hours] by part-time workers is higher [Belous, 1989; Christopherson, 1990; EIRR, 1990; Tilly, 1991].

In the case of Canada, while the proportion of the workforce employed part-time is at just under 16 per cent, lower than its share in the United States, the trend in part-time work is not only persistently upward since the early 1950s, but since the mid-1970s some 30 per cent of the increase in employment has been due to the growth of part-time work. By the end of the last decade, 1.9 million people were employed part-time, usually for fewer than 30 hours per week on a regular and continuing basis. With no trend change anticipated, it is estimated that the part-time employment figure, the fastest growing element of service sector employment, will reach 2 million or almost 20 per cent of total employment during the latter part of the present decade. More liberal definitions of part-time work, such as counting people who were employed part-time at any time during the year, would almost double official estimates of part-time employment in Canada [Coates, 1988, Statistics Canada 1990].

THE CAUSES OF PART-TIME EMPLOYMENT GROWTH

Explanations of the growth of part-time employment cite its attractions for both workers and employers. The 1988 ILO report on part-time work in industrialised economies summarised the 'many' reasons put forward by workers seeking part-time employment:

> students may wish to use their spare time to help pay for their personal or educational expenses, workers with family responsibilities may need to limit their hours of work; workers entering or re-entering the labour market may prefer to work shorter hours at first; older workers may wish to leave working life gradually or to supplement their retirement income; in an era of increasingly varied lifestyles, some workers may simply prefer shorter hours or reduced incomes so that they can devote more time to other activities. [Thurman and Trah, 1990, p. 25].

This list indicates the potentially wide appeal of part-time work, yet in market economies its growth is associated not only with service sector expansion but with increased participation of women in the labour force. While there are variations in rates of female labour force participation, the number of part-time women workers ranges from two to five times the number of part-time men, depending on the country, and these ratios have not varied much over time. The proportion of women working part-time now approaches half of all women workers in a few countries, and overall about one in four working women is a part-timer. This latter proportion is typical of the female labour force in Canada and the United States, and in both countries with female labour force participation rates on a sharply upward trend over the last two decades, rising to well over 60 per cent, women account for the majority of part-time employees: 72 per cent in Canada and 67 per cent in the United States, proportions somewhat lower than in several European countries with substantial part-time employment, such as the Netherlands, Sweden, Germany (west) and the United Kingdom, where they range from more than 80 per cent to over 90 per cent [Dex, 1988; OECD, 1989; Thurman and Trah, 1990].

Regarding employers' reasons for hiring labour part-time, the report found that those

> who favour part-time work tend to see its greatest advantages in terms of enterprise flexibility . . . part-time work permits adjustments to operational requirements, particularly when there are high and low points in staffing requirements during the day or week . . . it can allow increases in operating hours without the need for a full additional shift and can cover gaps between normal weekly hours of work and desired operating hours . . . this has become especially important as normal hours have declined in many countries . . . other advantages include the higher productivity and lower absence rates of the workers concerned . . . ; experience seems to have been very convincing: almost all part-time work systems have been expanded and made more flexible over time. . . [Thurman and Trah, pp. 24–5, 1990].

That part-time work presents an 'attractive' choice for both workers and employers is confirmed by labour force analysts researching the changing employment structure in North America. Discussing implications of the growth of the contingent workforce in the United States, they discern a variety of reasons why individuals may prefer contingent arrangements. A 1989 study reported that many workers

> in order to meet family, school or other non-work responsibilities, need more flexible schedules than can typically be found in permanent work arrangements. Parents of young children may wish to work only during school hours or during the school year . . . students may want to work when school is not in session . . . other workers may need flexible schedules so they can care for elderly parents. [Polivka and Nardone, 1989, p. 18].

In Canada the 1982 Commission of Inquiry predicted that

> the supply of part-time workers will continue to increase, mainly because today's workers are beginning to demand more flexibility in the work place – the old life cycle in which a person finishes school, works full-time for the next 40 years and then retires to do nothing until he dies is on the way out . . . workers now want to be able to move from full-time to part-time and back again at different periods in their lives, depending upon their responsibilities and financial requirements. [Commission of Enquiry, 1983, p. 27].

The nature of the choice underlying employers' decisions to engage labour on a part-time rather than on a full-time basis was apparent from surveys of private and public sector service industry employers. In the early 1980s Canadian employers

> utilized part-time workers because it makes good business and economic sense to do so . . . they are at least as productive, if not more productive than full-time workers, are more energetic, work more quickly, are more enthusiastic about their jobs and do not suffer from fatigue and burnout . . . they also have less absenteeism and sick leave because they are able to schedule their personal appointments on days off and cover for each other during periods of sickness. [Commission of Inquiry, 1983, pp. 26, 119–26].

By the close of the decade employers' attempts to achieve competitive cost structures, improve productivity and product quality in response to pressures arising from the 'new competitive environment' were beginning to transform the world of work and employment relationships in Canada, signalling that in the 1990s flexibility would be a key requirement for effective human resource utilisation [Kumar and Coates, 1991].

Similarly, assessment of the reasons for employment of contingent workers by American employers emphasised the cost savings – from a decline in the number of paid idle hours, lower wages, decreased liability for benefits, reduced personnel and training costs:

> from 1969 part-time jobs have expanded primarily because more employers view them as a means to cut labour costs, and not because more workers want them [Tilly, 1991, p.10; cf. Belous, 1989].

Through the 1980s the human resource systems at many American corporations were reported to be undergoing 'vast change': managements were under pressure to gain greater control over labour costs because of the severe recessions of the early years of the decade, the rise in international competition in many manufacturing industries, and the deregulation of domestic transportation, communication and finance industries [Belous, 1989; Polivka and Nardone, 1989].

THE ISSUES

It is clear that demand for part-time employment emanates from both sides of the labour market. Contemporary discussions of the implications of its persistent and sustained growth in North America are focused, as elsewhere, on the distribution of the advantages between workers and employers.

The evidence relating to the benefits accruing to employers in the service industries in the United States, where part-time employment 'was greatest and growing fastest', indicates both the association of part-time jobs with employers' needs for flexibility in labour utilisation and the significant role of increased part-time/full-time employment ratios in controlling labour costs. American employers throughout the 1980s were operating under increasingly competitive pressures : the shift to part-time employment was 'neither in response to technical imperative nor an outright anti-labor measure – rather companies have shifted because they have decided that cutting labor costs and enhancing staffing flexibility are more important' [Tilly, 1991, p.16; cf. Belous, 1989].

In the retail food industry, for example, most notably in supermarkets where part-time employment rose from 35 per cent of the workforce in 1962 to 60 per cent in 1987, the initial impetus for the use of part-time workers came from the extension of store hours, the emergence of a 'time-scarce' American consumer exacerbating the variability of peak and non-peak periods of demand going back several decades; 'because the oscillations in demand are somewhat predictable, the retailer can gain flexibility by using part-time labour to meet the demand at any given time' [Haugen, 1986, p.13]. However, in this industry

> from at least the late 1950's the key to part-time employment was not simply the pursuit of flexibility but cost, a strategy facilitated by technological changes that permitted greater boosts in part-time employment . . . supermarket operators moved towards stores that are larger both in floor size and sales volume . . . they maintain a full-time core of department managers and one or two full-timers per department; this core does not grow proportionately with store employment, so that larger stores have higher rates of part-time employment [Tilly, 1991, p.16].

In the insurance industry in the 1980s, through the applications of new technology, companies increased part-time ratios from less than 7 per cent to 24 per cent in five years, a drive described by managers as 'very cost effective: computerisation of claims processing simultaneously reduces skill requirements and enhances the productivity differential between part-time and full-time work' [Tilly, 1991]. The association between cost-cutting and part-time employment was also evident in the airline industry, where management responses to volatile demand and deregulation led not only to job losses, but to the accelerated introduction of part-time working; much of the growth in employment of flight attendants in the last decade is in part-time jobs [Gil, 1990].

Surveys of employer behaviour in Canada in the 1980s concluded that the belief that part-time work is a valid choice open to employees was not widely held and certainly was not as significant a factor in determining part-time work patterns as were the work loads and staffing requirements of employers [Robinson, 1991]. While employers claimed that the disproportionate number of females in part-time positions compared with full-time positions in the same organizations resulted primarily from women applying for part-time positions more frequently than men, research analysts seeking to elucidate the reasons for part-time employment growth were unconvinced. They considered that this supply side phenomenon was related to the types of positions employers were seeking to fill. Moreover, the cost savings arising from hiring labour on a part-time basis were implicitly acknowledged by the large majority of employers in retailing, tourism, hotels and food services, in banking and insurance and in health care, the principal users of part-time labour: both survey and structured interview responses showed that they did not believe that the imposition of mandatory benefits for part-time workers would affect their hiring practices, despite contrary views often expressed by employers' associations at public hearings. The transportation industry (urban transit, trucking and railways), which made the least use of part-time labour because of union resistance, saw its extension as 'an important solution to the increasing costs of providing services, and in some cases as critical to operating success or failure' [Commission of Inquiry, 1983, pp. 119–31; Coates, 1988].

Contrasting with the evidence that employers enjoy substantial benefits from using labour on a part-time rather than full-time basis, employees appear to be disadvantaged by working part-time. Classification of the jobs held by part-time workers in the United States identified two distinct categories in the service industries, responsible for 90 per cent of all part-time work. The first comprised secondary or part-time jobs with 'low pay and benefits, low productivity, lack of advancement opportunity and high turnover' – jobs constituting the secondary segment configured in the dual labour market model. The other category, containing 'retention' part-time jobs – 'good jobs in terms of pay, skill requirements, advancement opportunity', are created to retain (or in some cases attract) valued employees whose life circumstances prevent them from working full-time, particularly women with young children. Unlike secondary part-time employment, 'retention' part-time work tends to be offered only to workers in relatively skilled jobs, with high

compensation, high productivity and low turnover, characteristics associated with the upper tier of the dual labour market. However, the
distribution of part-time workers in the services sector points to secondary part-time employment as 'the most common type of part-time job in
America' [Tilly, 1991].

In 1987 three sectors, restaurants and hotels, retail trade, and education provided less than 25 per cent of all jobs in the economy but more
than 44 per cent of part-time jobs. Of the 6.6 million part-time workers
in retail trade, 71 per cent were employed in sales clerk or service
worker occupations; in restaurants and hotels 79 per cent of part-timers
were employed in service worker occupations; in education nearly half
were in clerical and service worker jobs. Opportunities for part-time
work were thus clearly restricted to a narrow range of jobs, 'virtually
assuring that part-time employment will continue to be unattractive to
men who might otherwise prefer a reduction in hours, older workers
desiring partial retirement, for example' [Appelbaum and Albin, 1990].

The compensation attached to part-time jobs is also restricted, falling
decisively at the lower end of the United States wages spectrum. In 1985
part-timers made up 65 per cent of workers at or below the minimum
hourly wage of $3.35, and one half of all minimum and sub-minimum
wage workers were engaged in the retail trade; in the restaurant trade
most employees worked less than 20 hours per week, and 'most were
relatively badly paid'. In 1987 median hourly wages of persons who
usually worked part-time were $4.24 compared with $7.24 for full-time
wage and salary workers paid by the hour; the average weekly earnings
of all full-time wage and salary workers was $369 or approximately $9.22
an hour. In 1991 a Pittsburgh supermarket chain with over four fifths of
its labour force part-time was paying the national minimum hourly rate
of $4.25, raised by 40 cents following industrial action. Where a trade
union has been certified as a bargaining agent, employers are obliged to
bargain collectively on wages, hours of work and other terms and conditions for part-timers; their earnings reflect however, the lower hourly
and weekly earnings of industries where unionisation is relatively weak
– with the exception of communications, education and public administration, union membership in the United States service industries is well
beneath even the comparatively low national labour force average of 17
per cent.

Part-time employees are also much less likely to receive major fringe
benefits than full-timers. In 1985 more than three quarters of individuals
who worked full-time full-year received health insurance coverage from
their employers, compared with 'roughly one third or fewer of part-time
workers'. While part-timers may be covered by other employers under a

spouse's plan, or under non-employer plans, 'many part-timers must be without medical coverage', and only 42 per cent have paid sick leave as against almost all full-time employees. Employers are required by statute to make social security contributions for part-timers, and grant the same retirement benefits they give to full-timers to those who work a minimum of 1,000 hours per year; entitlement to unemployment benefit which is governed by a dual system of federal and state law, is widely curtailed by earnings thresholds, and claimants may be required to accept full-time jobs [Alpert, 1986; Belous, 1989; OECD, 1989; Applebaum and Albin, 1990; Christopherson, 1990; Kilborn, 1991].

As in the United States, part-time employment in Canada is characterised by a preponderance of part-time jobs with low pay and widespread total or partial exclusion from employer-provided fringe benefits, regarded as the major symptoms of the 'unfair treatment' of part-time workers [Commission of Inquiry, 1983]. In 1987 some 18.5 per cent of 'mostly part-time women workers' and 31.6 per cent of part-time male employees had annual earnings of under $4,000, compared with 3.4 per cent and 2.2 per cent of 'mostly' full-time female and male workers, in a year when the average statutory minimum hourly wage for employees aged over 18 was $4.00 and the median annual earnings for full-time men and women were $29,779 and $19,822 respectively. A study of wages and jobs in the 1980s estimated that 'almost three quarters of all part-time jobs created between 1981 and 1986 paid $5.24 an hour or less, the lowest wage category'; the share of part-time jobs paying £5.24 or less was up from 26 per cent in 1981 to 33.4 per cent in 1986, with the share of full-time employment in the lowest paying job category increasing from 8.2 to 10.4 per cent [Kumar and Coates, 1988]. The full-time/part-time differences in hourly wage rates were also greater between non-unionised and unionised workers, producing an 88 per cent pay ratio for the unionised and 63 per cent for non-unionised part-time employees [Robinson, 1991].

In a 1989 report on employment in the service economy, 'the source of over 70 per cent of the country's jobs and of virtually all net job creation in the preceding ten years', the Economic Council of Canada noted that 'the increasing appearance of part-time and part year jobs suggests that the labour market may be providing less economic security for Canadians'. In its 1990 labour market review the Council made recommendations aimed at 'promoting the economic security of workers while maintaining the flexibility needs of employers and employees'. Proposals included adoption of legislation by all jurisdictions to provide employee-benefit programmes on a pro-rated basis to part-time employees with a continuing employer attachment, design of public benefit programmes to ensure inclusion of workers in 'non-standard' employment, and an evaluation by governments of private and public pension systems in light of recent trends in employment growth in small firms and in non-standard types of work [Coates, 1991]. These proposals were largely reiterative of those advocated by the 1982 Commission of Inquiry and the 1986 Parliamentary Committee on Equality Rights; with the exception of the amendments to the pension Benefits Standard Act in 1987, 'which had minimal effects because of high earnings and salary floors that excluded a high proportion of part-time employees from benefit', none had been accepted by the federal government [Robinson, 1991].

The nature of the issues arising from part-time work in North America is manifest therefore from the circumstances pertaining to part-time employment growth in major service industries. It is evident that these industries are expanding in conditions of intensifying competitive pressures, which impose on employers a need for more stringent control over labour costs. The utilisation of labour on a part-time rather than full-time basis allows employers to match more precisely the hiring of labour with their actual requirements, a process increasingly facilitated by technological and organizational innovations in services delivery. Employment growth in the services sector is generating jobs which not only offer employees fewer weekly hours of work than full-time employment, but for the majority of workers terms and conditions of employment which are not pro-rated with their full-time counterparts.

THE DEBATE

The issues highlighted in the debate surrounding part-time work in North America differ little from those identified in other industrial countries. Part-time employment is assessed in relation to the standards associated with the normal employment form of full-time work. This 'norm' is represented by full-time wage employment of indefinite duration with one employer. It has its origins in the advent of large-scale manufacturing industry and has provided the framework within which national labour laws, collective bargaining and social security systems have evolved. Workers employed full-time have progressively enjoyed statutory protection entitling them to substantial guarantees and benefits, while the law has imposed obligations on the employer and the State [Cordova, 1986]. The use of such terms as atypical, non-standard or flexible to distinguish part-time workers derives from their different employment status *vis-à-vis* full-timers and does not connote either their labour force numbers or their working hours, other than as noted earlier, shorter than usual/normal working hours. Despite the diversity of the employment circumstances of part-time workers within and between countries, in the United States and Canada, the available evidence, though quantitatively and qualitatively variable, points clearly to differentiation in the labour market treatment of part-time and full-time employees. These differences mark inferior treatment of part-timers, and place the apparent balance of advantage from the utilisation of labour on a part-time basis with employers, the voluntary nature of most part-time work notwithstanding.

There is disagreement about the nature and extent of this imbalance and its implications, and the outcome of the debate is far from consensual. There is a view that although the growth of a contingent workforce in the United states may denote 'a degree of segmentation', it does not lead to a split labour market but to a more complex model in which different groups of employees occupy varying positions with regard to wage rates, job security and social benefits; membership of the contingent workforce thus helps some people to join the labour force and can serve as a prelude to permanent employment [Rojot, 1989; Thurman and Trah, 1990]. While this view of the American labour market as constituting a continuum or queue of job seekers in a single market appears plausible in the light of claims that the workforce stands out as being more flexible ('more responsive to changes in supply and demand in the market') than its counterparts in other industrialised countries [Christopherson, 1990], it is not supported by the evidence concerning the circumstances of the part-time labour force adduced above. Closer consideration of labour market change has led analysts to see the growth of part-time employment as an extension of the secondary labour market, a discernible manifestation of substantial labour market segmentation. Part-time jobs, concentrated as they are in the services sector, are characterised by low pay and benefits, little job security and poor promotion prospects; these attributes are those of jobs found in the secondary segment of the dichotomous labour market conceptualised in dualism, the theory formulated to explain the distinguishing features of urban American labour markets in the 1960s. Permanent full-time employees are in the primary sector, in the higher skilled/graded jobs, with relatively better wages and benefits, good working conditions, promotion prospects and employment security.

Alternatively, a 'new labour market segmentation' is posited to explain the diversity in employment relationships arising from the proliferation of contingent work forms, as firms in response to competitive pressures endeavour to minimise the number of workers to whom they are committed. It is suggested that labour markets are being reorganised around three major segments: a segment of core workers, permanently attached to the firm or employing organisation, responsible for developing, carrying out and communicating to others the strategic message of the organisation; a segment of skilled contingent workers, and a segment of low-skilled contingent workers. Part-time workers, it is argued, may be found in the skilled contingent segment which has been extending its occupational spectrum in recent decades to include, for example, para-professional skills, but it is nonetheless the case that a growing proportion of the low-skilled contingent work is structured to accommodate part-time employment, with youth, women and low-skilled immigrants providing the bulk of its labour force; these workers have also suffered deterioration in their labour market status because of the inability of unions to develop a strategy to shelter jobs once structured as entry positions on a firm's employment ladder [Noyelle, 1990].

The value of this attempt to delineate more sharply the contours of labour market segmentation in face of a complexity of non-standard work forms pervading American labour markets, lies in the concept of a distinctive segment for the relatively higher skilled contingent workers; they are filling jobs categorised in the dualistic approach cited earlier as 'retention' part-time jobs, those with higher compensation, higher productivity and low turnover. It does not invalidate the argument that there is imbalance in the distribution of the benefits accruing from part-time work to the detriment of the majority of part-timers [Tilly, 1992].

In the Canadian context, the debate about the implications of part-time employment growth was quite specifically focused on labour market inequality issues from the early 1980s, with the establishment of an official Commission of Inquiry. This inquiry was prompted by the 'mounting' pressure to do something about 'what many perceive to be unfair treatment of part-time workers – their low pay, lack of fringe benefits and pensions, and the fact that most are working in job ghettos with little chance of training or promotion'. In its findings, the result of comprehensive in-depth investigation of the labour market circumstances of part-time workers, the Commission advanced conclusive evidence to support the view that part-time workers in the Canadian labour force are treated unfairly compared to full-time workers: 'every group in the workforce – employers, governments, unions and even individual full-time workers – have been guilty of treating part-time workers unfairly'. Its proposals for change, while included on federal employment policy agenda until 1987, remained largely unadopted [Robinson, 1991]. They continue to be evoked by the Economic Council of Canada which has called for reconciliation of the requirement for flexibility and equity in the changing labour market. In the light of the increasing contribution of part-time work to the Canadian economy, the Council endorsed the Commission's belief that the promotion of labour market equity was not incompatible with demands stemming from both workers and employers for greater flexibility in employment re-lationships. However, the likelihood of a positive official response may, as in the late 1980s, recede in line with the federal government's in-creasingly non-interventionist, market oriented approach to the labour market, an extension of its growing commitment to trade liberalisation, deregulation, privatisation and other free market policies [Coates, 1991].

CONCLUSION

It is evident then that part-time work in the United States and Canada shares the attributes of this atypical employment form commonly observed in other industrial economies. The debate there, however, has not yet impacted strongly on policy questions. For more than a decade within the European Community, bridging the gap between atypical and standard employment relationships has been widely seen as an employ-ment policy goal essential both to the achievement of social equity and extension of competition, to be achieved through modifications to social security, employment protection and discrimination laws at national or Community levels. In the United States, the attention of employers and governments has only more recently been drawn to the social equity problems of increased human resource flexibility, exemplified in the continuing rigidity of federal and state social welfare systems. Neither the public programmes covering social security and unemployment in-surance, nor the pensions, health benefits and savings plans representing the 'major areas of the private sector's growing role in the social welfare system' are adapting to match the increasing flexibility of the labour market – the system continues to relate mainly to the full-time worker. However, there are signs that employers are recognising that differential treatment of a substantial section of their workforce, while reducing at least indirect wage costs, does not guarantee lower unit labour costs. 'Some major corporate employers' have adjusted their systems, introducing pro-rated employee benefits and portable pen-sions, and 'a few' have taken steps to ensure that affirmative action goals associated with commitments to equal employment opportunity are still obtained under a more flexible human resource environment [Belous, 1989].

That the latter developments are appearing shows awareness amongst American employers that the benefits from increased human resource flexibility could in the long term be eroded by failure to ensure that the gains are more equitably shared between workers and employers. They begin to confront arguments that both internal and external labour market policies directed to redressing the imbalance between the rewards available to part-time and full-time workers must raise unit labour costs and threaten profitability of service industries in particular. This is the general basis for example, of the United Kingdom's opposition to the European Commission's proposed Directives on non-standard or atypical work under the Community Social Charter, and consequent unwillingness to be bound by qualified majority voting on social policy measures under the Single European Act; it led to the 'opting out' compromise reached at the European Community's Maastricht Summit of December 1991 [IDS, 1992]. Opposition to the introduction of mandated benefits for non-standard workers in the United States and Canada is also grounded in the belief that it may cause less rather than more social equity and be in effect employment-retarding [Coates, 1988; Siebert and Addison, 1991]; it rejects views that unregulated labour markets 'can yield unacceptable consequences for productivity, income distribution and security' [Walsh, 1991]. Although the merits of extending mandatory benefits are the subject of continuing Congressional discussion, in an increasingly deregulatory environment shaped by intensifying competition and recessionary influences, intervention is problematical. In Canada the last decade witnessed in a similar environment, a dilution if not extinguishing of policy interest as the federal government virtually turned its back on earlier aspirations to 'improve the employment position of part-time workers consistent with the optimal utilization of both part and full-time labour' [Commission of Inquiry, 1983; Bakker, 1991].

In the absence then of official policy interventions and with only tentative indications of systematic change in employer practices, it is doubtful if the gains achievable through part-time employment growth in North America are being fully realised. It is not in question that there are substantial cost savings accruing to service industry employers from utilising labour on a part-time basis, but there are costs entailed in the further segmentation of labour markets through the expansion of non-standard forms of employment. It is of course difficult for employers to assess these costs, depending heavily on their ability to predict workforce behaviour as employees respond to low pay, lack of job security and benefits, training and promotion opportunities, etc. [Christopherson 1990; Hunter and MacInnes, 1991]. Nevertheless, they are responses which can raise unit labour costs, and it is probable that they may assume greater significance as service sector firms and organisations become increasingly reliant on the development by all their workers of client-oriented skills necessary to sustain and enhance productivity [Bengtsson, 1988]. This is an objective difficult to attain if responsibility for developing, carrying out and communicating to others the strategic message of the organisation is left to a core segment of workers to the exclusion of those with a non-standard relationship with their employer (cf. p.14 above). Moreover, as service sector employers in North America enter a period of projected slowdowns in labour force expansion affecting particularly the numbers of women and young people seeking work [Carey, 1991; Coates, 1991], the need is pressing for employment policies more informed by appreciation of such longer run implications of increased flexibility in labour use.

ACKNOWLEDGEMENT

The author's research was supported by the Nuffield Foundation, Social Sciences Small Grants Scheme.

REFERENCES

Addison, J. T. and W. S. Siebert, 1991, 'The Social Charter of the European Community: Evolution and Controversies', *Industrial and Labor Relations Review*, Vol. 44, No. 4.
Alpert, W. J., 1986, *The Minimum Wage in the Restaurant Industry*, New York: Praeger.
Appelbaum, E. and P. Albin, 1990, 'Shifts in Employment, Occupational Structure and Educational Attainment', in T. Noyelle (ed.), *Skills, Wages and Productivity in the Services Sector*, Colorado, Oxford: Westview.
Belous, R. S., 1989, 'How Human Resources Systems adjust to the Shift towards Contingent Workers', *Monthly Labor Review*, Vol. 112, No. 3.
Bengtsson, J., 1988, 'Human Resource Development in the Service Sector: The Need for More Research', *Service Industries Journal*, Vol. 8, No. 2 (April).
Carey, M. L. and J. C. Franklin, 1991, 'Industry Output and Job Growth Continues Slow in the Next Century', *Monthly Labor Review*, Vol. 114, No. 11.
Christopherson, S., 1990, 'Emerging Patterns of Work', in T. Noyelle, (ed.), *Skills, Wages and Productivity*.
Coates, Mary Lou, 1991, *Industrial Relations in 1990: Trends and Emerging Issues'*, in *The Current Industrial Relations Scene in Canada 1990*, Kingston, Ontario: Industrial Relations Centre, Queen's University.
'Commission of Inquiry into Part-time Work', Report, 1983, Labour Canada, Ottawa.
Córdova, E., 1986, 'From Full-time Wage Employment to Atypical Employment: A Major Shift in the Evolution of Labour Relations?', *International Labour Review*, Vol. 125, No. 6, Geneva.
Dex, S. and P. Walters, 1989, 'Women's Occupational Status in Britain, France and the USA: Explaining the Difference', *Industrial Relations Journal*, Vol. 20, No. 3.
Ehrenberg, R. G. *et al.*, 1988, 'Part-time Employment in the United States', in R. A. Hart, (ed.), *Unemployment, Employment and Labour Utilisation*, Boston: Unwin Hyman.
European Industrial Relations Review, 1990, 'Non-standard forms of Employment in Europe', EIRR Report, Number Three.

Employment Outlook, 1989, Paris: OECD.

Haugen, S.E., 1986, 'The Employment Expansion in Retail Trade, 1973–85', *Monthly Labor Review*, Vol. 109, No. 8.

Hunter, L.C. and J. MacInnes, 1991, *Employers' Labour Use Strategies – Case studies*, Employment Department Research Papers, No. 87, London.

ILO, 1989, *Conditions of Work Digest, Part-time Work*, Vol. 8, No. 1, Geneva.

ILO, 1990, *The Hours We Work – New Work Schedules in Policy and Practice*, Vol. 9, No. 2, Geneva.

Incomes Data Services, IDS Brief 460, January 1992.

Kilborn, Peter T., 1991, 'Part-time Work Force Increases in U.S.', *International Herald Tribune*, 18 June.

Kumar, P. and M. L. Coates, 1991, *Industrial Relations in 1991: Trends and Emerging Issues, Current Industrial Relations Scene*, Kingston, Ontario: Industrial Relations Centre, Queen's University.

Maxwell, J., 1989, 'Flexibility in Canadian Labour Markets: A Challenge for Management and Labour', in G. Laflamme *et al.* (eds.), *Flexibility and Labour Markets in Canada and the United States*, Geneva: ILO.

Noyelle, T., 1990, 'Toward a New Labor Market Segmentation', in T. Noyelle, (ed.), *Skills, Wages and Productivity*.

Polivka, A.E. and T. Nardone, 1989, 'On the Definition of "Contingent Work"', *Monthly Labor Review*, Vol. 112, No. 12.

Robinson, O., 1991, 'Atypical Workforce: Raising the Status of Part-time Employment – Canada, Industrial Relations Journal', Vol. 22, No. 1.

Robinson, O., 1985, 'The Changing Labour Market: The Phenomenon of Part-time Employment in Britain', *National Westminster Bank Quarterly Review*, November.

Rojot, R., 1989, 'National Experiences in Labour Market Flexibility, in Labour Market Flexibility', Paris: OECD.

Rosenberg, S., 1989, 'From Segmentation to Flexibility', *Labour and Society*, Vol. 14, No. 4.

Stanback, Jr., T.M. and T. Noyelle, 1990, 'Productivity in Services: A Valid Measure of Economic Performance?', in T. Noyelle, (ed.), *Skills, Wages and Productivity*.

Statistics Canada, 1987, 'Earnings of Men and Women', Ottawa.

Statistics Canada, 1990, 'Labour Force Annual Averages', Ottawa.

Thurman, J.E. and G. Trah, 1990, 'Part-time Work in International Perspective', *International Labour Review*, Vol. 129, No. 1, Geneva.

Tilly, C., 1991, 'Reasons for the Continuing Growth of Part-time Employment', *Monthly Labor Review*, Vol. 114, No. 3.

Tilly, C., 1992, 'Dualism in Part-Time Employment, Industrial Relations', *Journal of Economy and Society*, Vol. 31, No. 2.

Walsh, T., 1991, 'The Reshaping of "Flexible" Labour?: European Policy Perspectives', in Blyton, P. and J. Morris (eds.), *A Flexible Future?, Prospects for Employment and Organisation*, Berlin: de Gruyter.

This study first appeared in *The Service Industries Journal*, Vol.13, No.3 (1993).

2
Retail Employment Research: Scarce Evidence in an Environment of Change

by

J. Reynolds

National trends in retail employment show that considerable structural change has already taken place within a now stable workforce; future change may be no less radical. As a by-product of research designed to reveal the detailed characteristics of change, this article aims to review the extremely variable quality and usefulness of both official and alternative sources of information on retail employment and to present a summarised analysis of the most significant components of this change both nationally and regionally. The conclusions are that considerable problems both in terms of data availability and definition will make it increasingly difficult to recognise the effects of forthcoming medium- and long-term employment impacts.

INTRODUCTION

The call for more work in a relatively under-examined area of retail research, that of retail employment [NEDO, 1974], would seem to conflict with what is, in Britain at least, a fundamental lack of a consistent, reliable and comprehensive statistical base from which analysis may proceed. The need for analysis is apparent in the retail trade no less than in any other service sector, or indeed in any part of the economy. It is perhaps especially so, for retailing, after all, is an industry which accounted in Great Britain in 1981 for 8.8 per cent of total employment in all industries and services (14.2 per cent in all service industries) [Department of Employment, 1982] and has traditionally employed up to 20 per cent of school leavers [DITB, 1981].

Such investigation in the UK is also particularly important in the wider context of the contribution of the service sector as a whole, in terms of both output and employment, to the national economy. It is a contribution which may be in need of considerable reassessment in the light, for example, of the differential impact of the recession upon different sectors of the economy.

The author's own research into retail employment was prompted by the examination of recent aggregate national trends in the retail labour force. These, together with recent economic analyses [e.g. NEDO, 1981], seem to indicate not only that considerable structural change has already taken place within a now relatively stable workforce, but also that future change shows signs of being no less radical. Yet, for the retail trade, in particular, amongst the service industries, even simple exploratory and descriptive work on employment is remarkably thin on the ground. That which exists has tended to rely upon alternative research strategies, such as the selective use of retailer surveys, as well as upon official sources of information. This article is an attempt, therefore, both to explain the shortfalls in analysis, through the examination of the available data sources, and to make a general assessment, as far as is possible, of the detailed employment restructuring which has already taken place in the industry. This is presented as a by-product of the work the author is currently undertaking into the emerging employment characteristics of innovatory forms of retail trading in the North East of England.

GOVERNMENT STATISTICAL SOURCES

It is instructive initially to explore the official sources of information which are available to the interested researcher and examine their quality and usefulness in analytical work. Table 1 outlines the main characteristics and certain of the limitations of those data sources which address themselves in some degree to the retail trade.

As is evident, and is perhaps to be expected, the most striking feature of the table is the poor level of both spatial and business disaggregation in all the data-sets presently available for public examination and analysis. Access to the considerably more useful establishment-based data of the Census of Employment ERI and the Distributive Industries Training Board's levy surveys is restricted by the Statistics of Trade Act 1947, other than to the CE for certain public authorities – including local planning authorities – under the 1973 Employment and Training Act. The 1947 Act prohibits the disclosure, without the consent of the owner, of any information relating to an individual undertaking, (s.9[1]). In addition, it permits government to impose further restrictions upon the disclosure of such information as it thinks fit (s.9[3]]. The guarantee of confidentiality is, of course, an important consideration in all employment-related survey work; yet the 1947 Act which enforces this confidentiality is an inflexible and unsophisticated means of achieving such an end.

That which remains accessible is poorly spatially disaggregated, with only the Census of Population offering anything below the regional unit of the Quarterly L-Return estimates – and this is but a ten per cent sample based on Enumeration Districts (available for 1981 from late 1983). This is far from the achievements of the 1971 Census of Distribution which now, it seems, has come to represent the high point of statistical survey work in the distributive trades. There has been no means since 1971, for example, of distinguishing between the amount and structure of employment in retailing in central urban areas and that in peripheral or suburban sites. Reaggregation of ERII Employment Office Area data is possible

TABLE 1

CURRENT SOURCES OF INFORMATION ON RETAIL EMPLOYMENT

Data-set	Description	Access	Spatial Class	Business Class	Statutory	Sample	Sample Size	Dis-continuities	Comments
Census of Employment	Count of employees in Employment	Y	1,4-6[a]	3,4	Y	N	1m	1981	99% of PAYE points. Triennial from 1978
Quarterly Estimates of Employees	Survey of Employees in Employment	Y	5,6	3,4	N	Y	37500	1974	Service Industries series started only in 1974
Census of Population	Survey of Employees by Private Household	Y	3	1,3,4	Y	Y	2m	1971 1981	Definitions changed at each Census year
Labour Force Survey	Survey of Employees by Private Household	Y	6	1,4	N	Y	90000	1981	Only selected occupations analysed. 1981 new SIC
Retail Inquiry	Persons employed by Establishment	Y	6	2	Y	Y	20000	1978-1980	KOBs redefined 1980; turnover threshold adopted
New Earnings Survey	Survey of Employees in Employment by PAYE PP	Y	6	1	N	Y	9000	-	Random 1% survey drawn from PAYE pay points
DITB Levy Returns	Survey of Employees in "assessable" firms	N	2	5	Y	Y	11000	1981	Board wound up in 1982; Levy exempt excluded

Spatial Classification - (most disaggregated available)
1. DE 'Census Unit' (establishment, business or part of business)
2. Business
3. Enumeration District/Ward
4. Employment Office Area
5. Standard Economic Region
6. Great Britain

Business Classification - (types employed)
1. CODOT Order (Occupational classification)
2. Kind-of-Business (Industry classification)
3. Minimum List Heading (Industry classification)
4. Standard Industrial Classification Order
5. DITB Occupational Categories

Notes: a.   Only levels 5 and 6 publically available without DE permission

subject to Department of Employment permission, but these areas have poor spatial coincidence with local authority areas or other strategic levels.

Similarly, there are inadequacies in business classification. Of course, changing classification mid-stream considerably reduces the value of a data-set for time-series analysis. Yet the increasingly dynamic nature of change in the retail trade rapidly renders existing functional classifications of businesses, occupations and other employment characteristics obsolete. Just as much, the diversity of kinds-of-business (KOB) and forms of organisation in retailing is likely to give rise to a number of significant differences of interpretation in any attempt at classification. Consequently, there are functional discontinuties both within and between all the data-sets under discussion. For example, the Retail Inquiry has undergone changes in KOB definitions in every year since 1977, and in 1983 a major new Standard Industrial Classification is being introduced for all Government employment series.

The collection of statistics at such a scale (2.3 million persons engaged in 350,000 retail outlets in 1980) and from such a diverse population (from self-employed grocers shops to variety store businesses employing more than 10,000 persons) presents a number of dilemmas, not least in the amount of detail requested. This will be both inversely related to the potential response rate in a non-statutory survey and will vary in relevance for the wide-ranging characteristics of the establishments concerned. Whilst, therefore, there would appear to be seven main data sources described in Table 1, only three of these show more than what can only be described as a partial and inconsistent interest in the retail industry (the CE, the Retail Inquiry and the DITB levy returns). For the others, retailing figures only as one amongst many other sectors competing for attention.

As a result, all the surveys under discussion here, with the exception of the Census of Employment, are in some way sample surveys. (Census of Employment surveys, based at present on PAYE – point addresses supplied by the Inland Revenue, are intended to be comprehensive assessments.) The biennial Labour Force Survey is conducted on a stratified 0.5 per cent sample of private households; the New Earnings Survey on a random one per cent of employees selected through PAYE numbers. The Quarterly Estimates (L-Returns) present particular problems in that they are subject to cumulative errors in between the now triennial Censuses of Employment. Some 7,500 'census units' are surveyed each quarter, but these are derived from the previous CE Register. Whilst 'deaths' amongst firms can be relatively easily established from this, the estimates fail to take into account 'births' – a particularly significant consideration in the retail trade. The Census of Employment in 1981 revealed gross underestimations in the equivalent quarterly figures (see Table 2).

The underestimation derives from a broader problem which gives cause for concern: the decreasing frequency of the most important statistical series. Inherent inadequacies apart, the Census of Employment and

TABLE 2

EMPLOYMENT CHANGE 1978-81 – THE L-RETURN UNDERESTIMATION

GB:Retail Distribution of Food and Drink (MLH 820) (Thousands)

Year	Male			Female			Male/Female	
	Full	Part	Total	Full	Part	Total	TOTAL	
1978	184.9	40.2	225.9	160.2	222.0	382.1	607.4	1(Census 1978)
1981	n/a	n/a	221.7	149.2	216.7	365.9	587.6	2(L–Return 6/81)
1981	185.0	46.0	231.0	154.0	232.0	386.0	617.0	3(Census 1981)*
Diff	n/a	n/a	−9.3	−4.8	−15.3	−20.1	−29.4	4(3 − 2)

GB:Other Retail Distribution (MLH 821) (Thousands)

Year	Male			Female			Male/Female	
	Full	Part	Total	Full	Part	Total	TOTAL	
1978	327.3	84.6	411.8	397.5	451.0	848.6	1260.5	1(Census 1978)
1981	n/a	n/a	380.5	375.2	434.4	809.6	1190.1	2(L–Return 6/81)
1981	323.0	67.0	390.0	402.0	454.0	856.0	1246.0	3(Census 1981)*
Diff	n/a	n/a	−9.5	−26.8	−19.6	−46.4	−55.9	4(3 − 2)

*Provisional 1981 Census of Employment results

Source: Department of Employment *Gazette*

Retail Inquiry during the late 1970s at least had the guarantee of consistent annual collection. The Rayner Review of the Government Statistical Services [HMSO, 1981] marked the end of this guaranteed continuity. It remarked that,

> In general, there is no more reason for Government to act as universal provider in the statistical field than in any other ... Information ... should be collected primarily because Government needs it for its own business. [HMSO, 1981: ss.8,17]

The government has accepted Rayner's recommendations, with the result that the Retail Inquiry is now biennial and the once annual Census of Employment is now triennial (although this is subject to review 'depending on the overall employment situation and prevailing circumstances' [HMSO 1981: 513]). Current planning is for a considerably more sophisticated Employment Statistics System (ESS) which will rely upon a more accurate establishment data-base (derived from the Inland Revenue Collector's Register). However, loss of detail is possible since the new ESS is likely to abandon the idea of a full census in favour of a sampling strategy weighted particularly towards the smallest firms. The retail trade, with its still significant number of small independent outlets, would be especially vulnerable to such a strategy.

It is possible to undertake a certain amount of analysis of the statistical material which is available, provided that, not surprisingly, considerable caution is exercised in drawing firm conclusions from it. What follows offers a very general overview of the detailed components of change within the retail workforce. The reader is recommended to the work particularly of Tucker [Tucker, 1978] and more recently of Moir [Moir, 1982] which present more detailed and painstaking analyses through the reconciliation of divergent statistical series than is possible, for reasons of space, here. What becomes rapidly apparent is that whilst the contemporary economic situation demands ever more reliable assessments of the structure of employment change in the UK, the capacity for robust and incisive analytical work derived from official sources has diminished markedly since 1971.

Assessment depends on an appreciation of the longer-term processes working both within and outside the retail industry as a whole. As a consequence, research must take into account both external changes in the retail environment, as well as the evolving internal policies of firms, and seek to relate these to the available data. Conceptual work, especially in the first of these areas, is relatively advanced [Davies, 1976; Guy, 1979], although less so in the latter. The assessment which follows reveals many gaps which may need to be filled by alternative research methods.

AN ASSESSMENT OF RETAIL EMPLOYMENT CHANGE

The evolution of economic influences upon and within the trade nationally during the last three decades and, as a result, the evolution of employment structure, can reasonably be divided into three phases (of which the significant trends are summarised in Figure 1).

Access to government statistical sources carries with it advantages in that observations are possible over an extended time-scale, even if the required detail is not present. It enables us to observe that, in absolute terms, employment in retailing has been remarkably stable over 30 years. However, this stability conceals significant shifts in the composition of the workforce. The 1950s encompassed a period of general expansion in which a link between entrepreneurial growth and an increasing level of

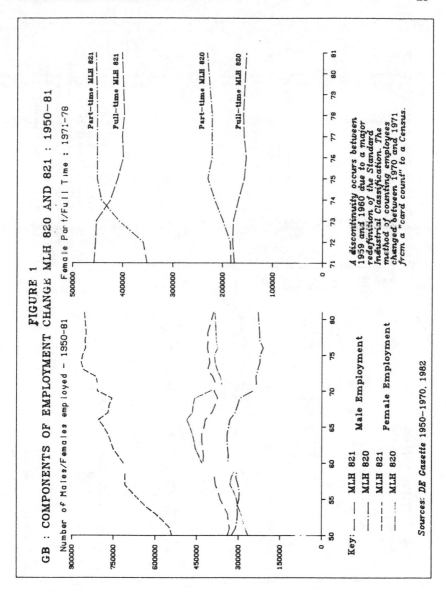

FIGURE 1

GB : COMPONENTS OF EMPLOYMENT CHANGE MLH 820 AND 821 : 1950-81

overall employment can be established. Between 1960 and the mid-1970s there occurred a further expansion of trade, but in this instance it was allied with a decline in the number of retail outlets, largely as a result of the penetration of multiple store groups and a shift in the economics of operations.

A growing sophistication in the operating sphere is reflected in a greater flexibility and planning in the use of the retail workforce; made

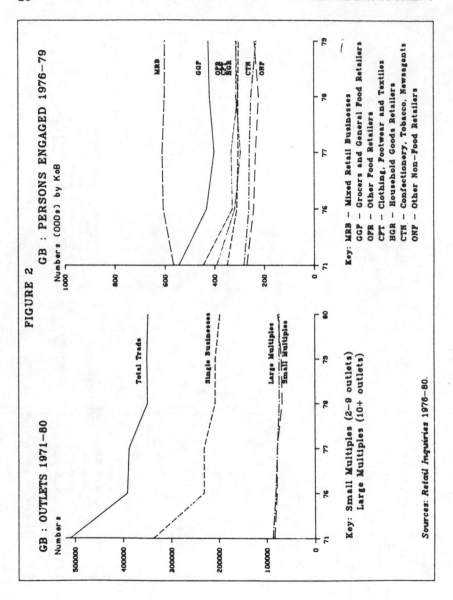

FIGURE 2   GB : PERSONS ENGAGED 1976–79

GB : OUTLETS 1971–80

Key: Small Multiples (2–9 outlets)
     Large Multiples (10+ outlets)

Key: MRB – Mixed Retail Businesses
     GGF – Grocers and General Food Retailers
     OFR – Other Food Retailers
     CFT – Clothing, Footwear and Textiles
     HGR – Household Goods Retailers
     CTN – Confectionery, Tobacco, Newsagents
     ONF – Other Non-Food Retailers

Sources: Retail Inquiries 1976–80.

particularly remarkable in a move towards increasing part-time, and especially part-time female, labour. This has undoubtedly been the most widely recognised and well-documented element of structural change in retail employment in the UK as elsewhere [Bluestone and Huff Stephenson, 1981; Robinson and Wallace, 1976] connected as it is to discussions of innovations in retail trading such as self-service and the considerably larger-scale enterprises of the food superstore and retail warehouse.

These in turn, of course, have been the result of broader social and economic changes which have been reflected in altered consumer behaviour throughout the 1960s and early 1970s. Increasing car ownership and rising living standards have prompted in the retailer an initiatory role, in which the most enterprising organisations have been able to identify and cater for particular markets in innovative ways (such as the emergence of the large, out-of-town, one-stop superstore). Equally, more liberalised attitudes and opinions expressed, for example, through the emergence of the more discriminatory and sophisticated consumer, have forced retailing organisations to respond to changing fashions and demands in a much more flexible way (in providing extended opening hours, or adapting to periods of peak demand, or providing credit card facilities). All of these factors will have detailed and inter-related effects on the amount and structure of retail employment.

As one of the consequences, at the Minimum List Heading level – the most disaggregated business classification for which data is available – the proportion of female part-time employment, in terms of the absolute numbers employed in retailing, increased from 20.2 per cent in 1961 to 36.2 per cent in 1975. Female part-time employment in the food sector would seem to have risen to a peak of 230,000 in 1975 before falling slightly the following year, whilst the same type of employment in the non-food sector climbed slightly during the early 1970s to a peak in the same year of 450,000 before beginning to level off. Because of the more general stability, this growth has been at the expense of full-time employment, which has declined roughly in proportion to it.

This part-time growth can itself be disaggregated through the availability of a limited amount of data from the Census of Distribution for 1971, together with a comparable question (not repeated for successive years) in the 1976 Retail Inquiry (see Table 3).

TABLE 3

PERSONS ENGAGED 1971–76 BY STATUS AND HOURS WORKED
(TOTAL RETAIL TRADE)

% Change	Owners working in firm				Paid Employees			
	Total	+30	8–30	–8	Total	+30	8–30	–8
Persons 71–76	–21.8	–17.0	–31.0	–56.9	3.6	–2.0	25.0	–10.5
Males 71–76	–15.2	–11.4	–27.6	–59.1	1.3	4.4	14.2	–17.9
Females 71–76	–29.5	–25.1	–32.5	–55.5	4.8	–7.2	26.3	–6.3

Sources: Census of Distribution 1971, Retail Inquiry 1976.

This shows that, much as one would expect, there has been a decline (for all categories of hours worked) in the number of owners working in their businesses – in line with the decline in single-outlet retailers over the same period. More interestingly, the data reveals a differential shift in terms of hours worked by paid employees: a severe fall in the number of male casual workers (working less than eight hours in the week) is balanced by an increase in those working between eight and 30 hours. Conversely, a much less noticeable fall in female casual labour is more than compensated for by a 26 per cent increase in numbers working between eight and 30 hours. Such information (from official sources) is not available after 1976.

It is not clear how the economic changes discussed above have affected the age and occupational characteristics of the retail workforce. Such evidence as there is, for example, points to the emergence from the general category of 'sales assistant' of the part-time 'checkout operator' and from the 'ancillary' category of the 'shelf filler' required by the more efficient, higher turnover operations in the convenience goods sector. The most disaggregated material currently available at the time of writing (until the 1981 10 per cent SAS Population data becomes available) is from the New Earnings Survey for selected occupations only, and for the country as a whole. From this partial material, therefore, it is not possible to develop a detailed analysis of the changing age structure of the workforce at this level; nor to speculate upon the specialised nature of these tasks, their substitutability and the relationships with both age and sex.

The assessment of productivity changes has also proved extremely difficult since 1971, when the Census of Distribution enabled the calculation of several significant productivity indices: notably sales per employee by unit of floor space, and sales per employee by size of establishment. This is the material which prompted some of the carefully analytical work of Ward [Ward, 1973] and George [George, 1966]. It can only be suggested that there will have been a differential effect as a result of the varying operating scales both within and between different kinds-of-businesses, [NEDO, 1976] but with a generally recognised trend towards a more efficient and sophisticated use of personnel:

> Retailing has emerged as one of the centres of productivity growth in the British economy [Livesey and Hall, 1981: 48].

This is an effect which is likely to be equally evident as between individual firms. However, there is no reliable evidence from government sources to support this detailed proposition after 1971, except the rate of increase in sales volume growth per employee which appears to have been maintained into the 1970s, despite the recession.

Robust statistical material for the third phase, the period between 1975 and the present day, is less in evidence than that for the early 1970s. Consequently, analysis of contemporary trends in the composition of the retail workforce using governmental sources has proved less easy.

Contrary to the trends revealed in the L-Returns, preliminary indications from the 1981 Census of Employment are that the trade as a whole has borne up remarkably well to the impact of the recession [Department of Employment, 1982: 504]. As one would expect given the differential nature of retail markets, the relatively more elastic non-food sector has fared marginally worse in terms of overall employment change than the more resilient food sector. In both, the extent of full-time male employment has emerged as the most vulnerable element in the picture. We can hypothesise that the still atomistic and dynamic nature of the trade, even given the increasing dominance of multiple organisations, has helped to sustain employment levels (the continued entry of new firms counteracting the decline which the L-Returns would have indicated).

Just as much, the surprising buoyancy of sales in specific kinds-of-business will have helped to sustain levels of employment in the larger organisations, but not necessarily to have led to an increase in such levels. For generally it is the case that employers tend to be less willing to take on new staff in relatively buoyant trading conditions than they are to cast off staff in an adverse trading environment. But again, this is an hypothesis which we are unable to test by reference to government statistical sources alone; evidence to support this general belief has come rather from more detailed research work conducted in particular case-study areas [Scottish Office, 1982].

Another dimension of the problem is revealed through the examination of unemployment and vacancy rates. Figure 3 shows a considerable increase in that number of unemployed who were previously employed in the retail industry, between 1978 and 1982. This is in line with what one might expect, given more general trends in unemployment. The unemployment to vacancy ratio for Great Britain (that is, the numbers previously employed in the trade competing for each notified vacancy) has also grown, for example in Minimum List Heading 821, from a low point of 2.7 in May 1979 to a high point of 15.3 in February 1981. Clearly, the role of strongly seasonal influences can be identified here: many vacancy peaks are occurring towards the end of each year, whilst unemployment peaks occur in the slack trading months following the busy Christmas and Sales period. As might be anticipated, these peaks are less pronounced in the food sector.

But such rates alone are particularly misleading in retailing for a number of reasons. Perhaps the most important of these is that the figures in this form take no account of new entrants to the labour market, who are also competing for notified vacancies. Nor is it possible to ascertain the status of those unemployed who were previously employed in retailing: whether or not, for example, they were the chief wage-earners of the household or whether they were more casual participants in the workforce. This factor may also account for a degree of underestimation of job shedding amongst casual (particularly seasonal) ex-retail labour, which either does not need or does not wish to register as unemployed. (Mature married females, who form an important element in the workforce, are an example.) The retail industry is also a particularly substitutable one

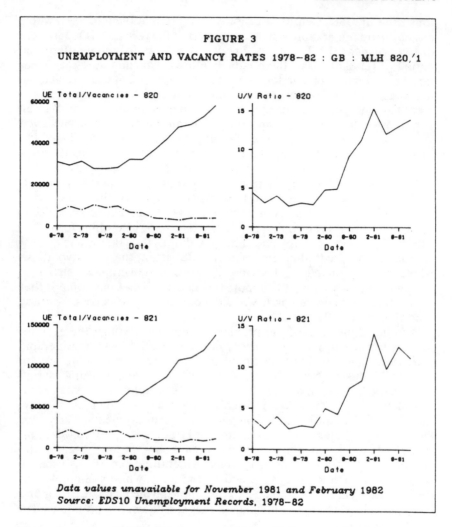

FIGURE 3

UNEMPLOYMENT AND VACANCY RATES 1978–82 : GB : MLH 820,'1

Data values unavailable for November 1981 and February 1982
Source: EDS10 Unemployment Records, 1978–82

from the point of view of job opportunities. Former retail employees are relatively less restricted in their choice of future work (other things being equal) although, of course, this implies that ex-employees from similarly skilled industries may be competing for those same retailing opportunities.

REGIONAL VARIATIONS

The study of aggregate employment shifts serves, of course, to conceal very significant local variations in rates of change which are detectable at both regional and county levels.

For food retailing, perhaps the most significant change at the regional level is the decline reported for Greater London between 1971–81 of some 22 per cent, much of which occurred during 1978–81 (see Figure 4). (The Northern region, by comparison, declined by some four per cent during the same period.) It is tempting to associate London's decline with a concomitant growth of 22 per cent in such employment in the rest of the South East. This in itself is a reflection of proportional population trends over the same period. Indeed, a positive relationship between population change and that in food retailing employment has been suggested by a number of authors [Fothergill and Gudgin, 1978; Scottish Office, 1982] and would be expected because of the relative inelasticity of household expenditure on food. The most important component of the South East's increase and the least of London's decrease was that of part-time female employment, whereas for both London and the South

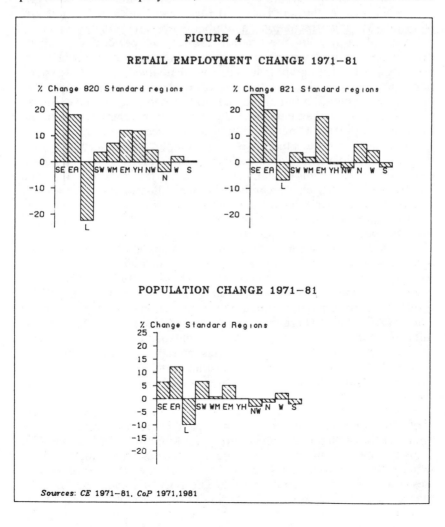

FIGURE 4

RETAIL EMPLOYMENT CHANGE 1971–81

POPULATION CHANGE 1971–81

Sources: *CE* 1971–81. *CoP* 1971,1981

East, the greatest loss occurred in both male and female full-time employment.

Apart from three cases, aggregate regional trends in population change elsewhere also appear to exhibit a pattern which is not dissimilar to that of employment change in Minimum List Heading 820. Figure 5 shows the pattern of change on a county basis (regions for Scotland) between 1971 and 1978. Unfortunately, detailed CE figures for 1981 were not available at the time of writing. Nevertheless, the figure reinforces the impression that the movement of population from the major conurbations and into outer 'rings' is associated with similar movements in food retailing employment, and particularly of part-time female employment.

The three anomalies are the South West, Scotland and the North West, and, whilst clearly the gross scale of the analysis does not permit any wholly convincing explanations, a number of observations may be made. For example, the South West had in 1981 at 20.8 per cent the highest proportion of retired persons of any standard region. One of the characteristics of such a demographic structure is the relatively lower food spend per capita. Hence net population growth of this type within the region, largely by in-migration rather than natural growth, may not be expected to have as beneficial an impact on the structure and employment of the food retailing sector as might otherwise have been expected.

As for Scotland, the situation is more complex in that a considerable decline in employment in food trades may be connected with the significantly different organisational structure of the trade there. A Nielsen Survey in 1978 [Neilsen Researcher, 1978] highlighted the much greater role of the Co-operative Societies and independents in Scottish food retailing: precisely those types of organisation which have experienced the most decline in percentage and absolute employment.

However, in the North West, a decline in population has not worked against an increase in Minimum List Heading 820 employment of over four per cent. This was an increase marked between 1977–81 when GDP per capita in the region was falling and, more importantly, when GDP growth in distribution performed below the national average at current prices [CSO, 1983]. There may be a partial explanation for this in that a fall in the number of self-employed in the independent sector was countered by a growth in employment amongst multiples (only the latter being reported by the Census). This would reflect a delay in the 'shake-out' of small firms in the North West which occurred earlier elsewhere in the country, with the possible exception of Scotland.

The non-food sector, being more diverse, is more difficult to account for on a regional basis. Superficially at least, there appears to be as similar a relationship with population growth as for Minimum List Heading 820. Equally, however, there are anomalies; perhaps the most outstanding of which is the East Midlands, where an 18 per cent increase in employment was recorded over the study period. The East Midlands possesses the highest regional per household expenditure on durable goods in the

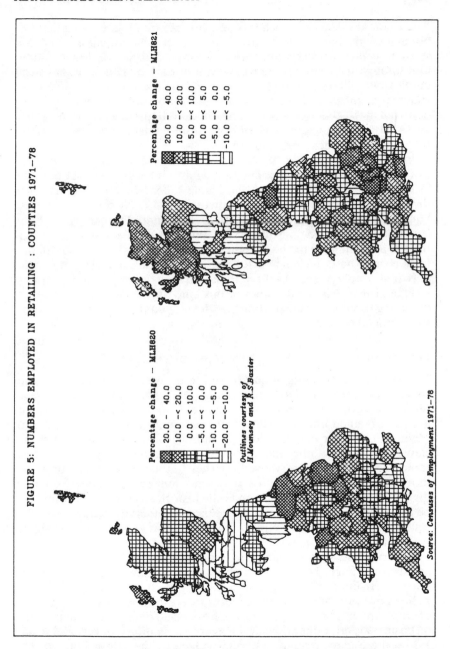

FIGURE 5: NUMBERS EMPLOYED IN RETAILING : COUNTIES 1971–78

Percentage change — MLH821

20.0 — 40.0
10.0 —< 20.0
5.0 —< 10.0
0.0 —< 5.0
−5.0 —< 0.0
−10.0 —< −5.0

Percentage change — MLH820

20.0 — 40.0
10.0 —< 20.0
0.0 —< 10.0
−5.0 —< 0.0
−10.0 —< −5.0
−20.0 —<−10.0

Outlines courtesy of
H.Mounsey and R.S.Baxter

Source: Censuses of Employment 1971–78

country (including the South East), itself mirroring certain other significantly prosperous economic indicators: presently the best industrial performance of all the regions, with the third highest level of personal
disposable incomes.

London has declined much less in terms of non-food retailing than its population decline would lead one to expect. The unique role of the strategic central area as a comparison goods centre and its 'export function' through the tourist trade will no doubt have helped to sustain such employment, despite losses from inner suburban locations. Figure 5 shows that much of the growth in the South East up until 1978 has occurred in the counties surrounding the capital, particularly to the north and west. However, almost all of the registered decline appears to have taken place between 1978 and 1981.

In the Northern region, an increase in non-food retailing employment has countered a decline in population against a background of declining GDP per capita and personal disposable income. Reference again to Figure 5 shows that much of this growth up to 1978 occurred in County Durham and in Northumberland. Indeed, County Durham is the only English county outside the South East and East Anglia to show a greater than 20 per cent increase in such employment over this period, admittedly from a small base, including a 102 per cent increase in male and female part-time employment. Again, population shifts must play a part in this kind of growth, but in all studies of this kind, particularly at this level of disaggregation, other means must be developed to supplement analysis from official sources.

THE VALUE OF ALTERNATIVE RESEARCH STRATEGIES

The merits and demerits of questionnaire or interview survey work are well documented. In relation to retailing, the elements are clear: surveys offer a potentially comprehensive data-set from which a detailed insight may be obtained into the relationships apparent between the data and other specified factors. In addition, more qualitative opinions may be canvassed. On the other hand, there is often a limit to the number of retailers who can be interviewed – either because of poor response or, more importantly, because of time and money constraints; opinion questions raise the issue of bias and little historical information is likely to be available for individual retailers. Hence, such surveys tend to be of the 'snapshot' variety, necessitating follow-up work if a consistent time-series is required.

Nevertheless, such a strategy may provide a detailed insight into the causes for change. For example, governmental statistical sources are of particularly limited use in the area relating to the internal employment policies of firms, and some of the most interesting and revealing aspects of employment change are those which are occurring at the establishment or business level, rather than at the aggregate national or regional scale. Whilst these may be significantly influenced by the external factors discussed above, there are likely to be considerable differences between organisations classed in terms of kind-of-business for all scales of operation.

A number of such surveys have been carried out [IGD, 1979: Sparks,

1982; Scottish Office, 1982], and the author's own work in North East England also falls into this category. Much more detailed analysis is possible as a result. Table 4 shows that, for example, there can be as much variation in employment characteristics between stores of a similar size as there is between the averages of stores in different size groups.

TABLE 4

RANGE IN STAFF NUMBER EMPLOYED FOR VARIOUS SIZES OF GROCERY STORES

	Ranges		
	FT	PT	TOT
−2,000 ft²	2–10	1–14	3–24
2–3,999 ft²	3–29	0–20	5–49
4–9,999 ft²	6–62	3–94	16–116
10–24,999 ft²	7–76	20–96	32–159
25–49,999 ft²	30–135	55–179	90–306

Source: IGD, 1979, Physical Characteristics of Grocery Stores in 1978, Watford.

The variation here, of course, can be ascribed to the different marketing policies and images of individual store groups, as well as through differences in firms' employment policies and employment opportunities. For example, recent changes in a number of the larger food retailers' images is resulting in the development of produce 'islands', staffed by relatively skilled (both socially and occupationally) mature female sales assistants at the expense of the ubiquitous part-time teenager.

However, recent work concludes that there is no consistent pattern characterising innovations in working practices or recruitment policies [Scottish Office, 1982]. Certainly, for many of the larger companies, in whatever field of trade, the recruitment of part-time labour appears to hold considerably less attraction than it formerly did (although the role of casual labour in this is unclear). The perception is that it tends to be less productive, reliable and attentive than the full-time equivalent, and there may be adverse consequences in terms of loyalty to the firm as well as of the image of the firm to the consumer. For a number of firms, the issue of overall labour costs is the one which chiefly determines recruitment policies, although again there is no readily predictable pattern amongst companies so organised. Part of the difficulty lies in the overall problem of analysing change which is on a day-to-day basis, although a stabilising role may be played by the levelling out of wage differentials between firms and the overall reduction of alternative employment opportunities in the present economic difficulties. (Figures for Scottish stores, at least, appear to show a reduction in the annual turnover of store leavers – as a percentage of total employment – from 7.5 per cent in 1976 to 4.3 per cent in 1981 [Scottish Office, 1982: 25].)

But the most useful potential attribute of individually designed retailer surveys lies perhaps in their ability to assess the health of a local labour market. The author's own work deals with changes in employment structures in two distinct kinds-of-business in the North East of England. Whilst context may be provided through national data sources, only a targeted survey of this kind may assess the characteristics of the retail labour force in any one catchment area and relate this information to the overall employment needs of the local economy, particularly amongst school-leavers and economically active adult females. It is hoped that such analysis will prove especially useful to local authorities, for example in assessing applications for new retail development. Knowledge of the employment characteristics and policies of applicants for planning permission, gained through business-based research, can be an important consideration in the overall assessment of a potential development's impact. For company rationalisation programmes, new employment practices (initiated from both within and outside the firm), changes in merchandising and management policies, and peculiarities in the local marketing environment may all have an effect on local employment levels and composition among existing stores.

CONCLUSIONS

The evidence would seem to suggest that a period of consolidation has set in nationally, in that radical restructuring of the labour force has been replaced by trends in levels of employment which apparently reflect more the relative health of particular markets for goods and changes in sales [Economist Intelligence Unit, 1983: 15]. How long this period will last will certainly depend upon issues such as the continued buoyancy of demand. But commentators have predicted a number of future influences on levels of employment: a medium-term shake-out as result of the changing competitive environment, and the longer-term, much less tangible, impact deriving from the introduction of new technologies [NEDO, 1981; Marti and Zeilinger, 1982].

The avenues for potential research are numerous, but several particularly significant and important gaps in our knowledge exist. There is a need to:

- develop a fuller analysis of the structure of employment within so-called 'part-time' working (in the change in casual labour's role since 1976, for example);
- obtain a better understanding of the changing age and occupational structure of the trade;
- understand the qualitative factors affecting the nature of recruitment of labour in the trade (by assessing employment policies in more detail); and
- examine the possibility of constructing an inter-trade classification of employment characteristics which will reflect these and other issues.

In the end, the ability to foresee to what degree and within what timescale the influences discussed above will make themselves manifest will be dependent on our capacity for ingenuity in the use of what government statistical series remain available to us, as well as to the judicious use of selectively targeted retailer surveys in these, and other, directions.

REFERENCES

Bluestone, B. and Huff Stephenson, M., 1981, 'Industrial Transformation and the Evolution of Dual Labour Markets: the Case of the Retail Trade in the United States', in Wilkinson, F. (ed.), *The Dynamics of Labour Market Segmentation*, Chicago: Academic Press.

Bucklin, L.P., 1978, *Productivity in Marketing*, Chicago: AMA.

Central Statistical Office, 1983, *Regional Trends 18*, London: HMSO

Davies, R.L., 1976, *Marketing Geography*, London: HMSO.

Davies, R.L., 1976, *Marketing Geography*, Corbridge: Retailing and Planning Associates.

Department of Employment, 1982, *Gazette*, December.

Distributive Industries Training Board, 1981, *Report and Statement of Accounts 1981/82*, Manchester: DITB.

Economist Intelligence Unit, 1983, 'Prospects for Consumer Spending to 1986', *Retail Business*, 300, February.

George K.D., 1966, 'Productivity in Distribution', *University of Cambridge Department of Applied Economics Paper* 8, Cambridge.

Guy, C.M., 1979, *Retail Planning and Retail Location in Britain*, London: Gower.

HMSO, 1981, *Government Statistical Services*, Cmnd. 8236.

Institute of Grocery Distribution, 1979, *Physical Characteristics of Grocery Stores in 1978*, Watford: IGD.

Livesey, F. and Hall, R.J., 1981, *Retailing: Development and Prospects to 1985*, London: Staniland Hall Associates.

Marti, J. and Zeilinger, A., 1982, *Micros and Money: New Technology in Banking and Shopping*, London: Policy Studies Institute.

Moir, C.B., 1982, *The Use of Employment Statistics*, Paper given at the Statistics Users Conference, National Economic Development Office, November 1982, London: NEDO.

NEDO, 1974, *Manpower and Pay in Retail Distribution*, London: Distributive Trades EDC.

NEDO, 1976, *The Measurement of Labour Efficiency in Retail Stores*, London: Distributive Trades EDC.

NEDO, 1981, *Technology. The Issues for the Distributive Trades*, London: Distributive Trades EDC.

Robinson, O. and Wallace, J., 1976, *Pay and Employment in Retailing*, London: Saxon House.

Scottish Office, 1982, *Retail Employment Change in Scotland with Special Reference to Superstores*, Report by Retail Planning Consultancy Services, Edinburgh: Scottish Office.

Sparks, L., 1982, 'Employment in Hypermarkets and Superstores', *URPI Information Brief* 82/7, Reading: URPI.

Tucker, K.A., 1978, *Concentration and Costs in Retailing*, London: Saxon House.

URPI, 1978, *Trading Features of Hypermarkets and Superstores*, Reading: URPI.

Ward, T.S., 1973, 'The Distribution of Consumer Goods: Structure and Performance', *University of Cambridge, Department of Applied Economics Paper* 38, Cambridge.

This study first appeared in *The Service Industries Journal*, Vol.3, No.3 (1983).

3

Employment Characteristics of Superstore Retailing

by

Leigh Sparks

Retail superstores in Great Britain have been the subject of much research and discussion. This article examines a neglected facet of superstores, namely employment, and considers some characteristics of superstore employment and their relationship to the size of superstore development. On the basis of the regression analyses undertaken, a predictive model of superstore employment and the scale of store is presented.

INTRODUCTION

The need for extensive use of part-time employees reflects a changing demand upon the retail industry. The extension of opening hours against the background of shorter 'normal' working weeks created new employment opportunities. The need for employers to maintain overheads at low levels caused both rationalisation and specialisation in the distribution of employment. The objective of cost efficiency in its turn created a demand for a flexible part-time labour force [Mallier and Rosser, 1979: 60].

Retailing has undergone major structural alterations in recent years. The last few decades have seen an enormous rise in the power of the multiples, concomitant with increasing average store size and the widespread adoption of new techniques, such as self-service. Self-service retailing has reduced the specialisation required previously in a shop assistant's job and has reduced the bulk of the tasks within larger stores to shelf-filling or till operation. Shopworkers have been transformed and de-skilled from assistants, who were expected to give customers personal service and have a detailed knowledge of the goods, into checkout operators. Robinson and Wallace [1976: 129-130] have summed up these changes in techniques:

> The de-skilling of the bulk of the retailing labour force has undoubtedly eased the problems of varying labour inputs to match the fluctuating daily and weekly trading levels in all retail outlets, greater flexibility being attained by the deployment of increasing proportions of part-timers.

This rationalisation and specialisation within the retail structure has led to the polarisation of the labour force, with a numerically small band of specialised managers on the one hand, and the larger 'army of day labourers' on the other [Alexander and Dawson, 1979]. The major focus for these changes has been the larger store. The trend towards larger outlets, tending to require less specialised and skilled staff, due to innovation adoption, allowed the easier substitution of part-time labour.

The logical extension of the drive for economies of scale by retailers is the superstore. The development and spread of superstore retailing in Britain has often been frustrated by the land-use planning system. Despite the many obstacles, however, there are presently over 300 such stores operational in this country. Their large scale, use of self-service retailing, and relatively high level of investment in equipment make them the focal point for changes in retail employment. The importance of superstores in providing work is undeniable, and superstore operators have lost little time in reminding planners and government of their continuing job creation capacity. This function of job creation was emphasized by Mr Firmston-Williams, Chairman of Asda, who commented that the opening of five Asda superstores in the autumn of 1980 created 1,800 jobs. In the same period, Tesco opened five new units producing a net gain of 1,200 jobs [McFadyen, 1980: 5]. These jobs are highly valued in the present economic climate, both by retailers and by those people seeking employment. The Asda superstore in Trallwn, Swansea, for example, had 8,000 written applications for 300 jobs when it opened in 1980 [*Western Mail*, 14 January 1981]. Whysall [1981: 46] has concluded: 'In job creation terms, such stores can compare favourably with more traditional industrial firms.'

A caveat on 'job creation' must be made however. Do superstores actually create jobs in an area, or is employment merely relocated through the trading effects of the new superstore? A comprehensive analysis of this topic is still awaited, and only tentative suggestions have been made to date [see NEDO, 1981; Whysall, 1980; Sparks, 1982a]. Initial results suggest that superstores do provide a net benefit in employment terms. The data presented here do not allow examination of this subject, and thus this discussion concentrates on the employment characteristics within superstores. The question of their overall impact in employment terms remains for substantive analysis again.

Much of the discussion concerning employment and superstores has used generalised or approximate data. Exceptions to this have been studies by Jones [1978] and the recent Distributive Trades Economic Development Committee (EDC) Report [NEDO, 1981]. In order that detailed data be made available, a survey was mounted into superstore employment during the summer and autumn of 1980. All the superstores then trading were contacted and requested to provide limited information on employee levels by reference to sex, hours worked and job type. Seven levels of employment were delineated and limited guidance given to stores on job types and employment categories. Seventy-one useful responses covering most of the superstore operators were generated by the survey. Full details of the survey and the responses have been presented elsewhere [Sparks, 1981, 1982a, 1982b]. Initial analysis of the data has examined the mean responses of the stores and commented on the level of part-time and female employment within the respondent superstores [Sparks, 1981, 1982a]. The question of the importance of store operator and a general discussion of the effect of store size on employment is presented in Sparks [1982b]. This article focuses in detail on the relationship between the size of superstores and their employment levels and characteristics.

SURVEY RESULTS

Table 1 provides the mean responses from the superstores. The layout and framework of the table is identical to that completed by the superstores in the survey. A mean total employment level of approximately 230 is revealed, 71.4 per cent of which are female employees. If this is converted to Full-Time Equivalent (FTE) Employees, by rating part-timers and casual workers at 0.5 and 0.2 of a full-time employee respectively, then a FTE employment level of 173 is obtained. This is comparable with the FTE level of 170 reported by Jones [1978]: see Table 2. An examination of Table 1 underlines the overwhelming importance of sales workers within superstore employment. Female sales workers are numerically the largest category within the stores, with the majority of sales workers being employed on a part-time basis. In percentage terms, female part-time sales workers are the largest grouping of employees in the store: 32.5 per cent of the total workforce. It can also be seen from the Table that female employees are concentrated in the clerical and, to a lesser extent, the supervisory categories, in addition to the sales category. Male employees on the other hand dominate the managerial and the numerically small, trainee categories. Additionally, more men than women are employed under the 'other' category, reflecting perhaps the balance between warehousing and catering elements.

The question of labour force levels and the size of superstores has been examined by Jones [1978] and NEDO [1981]. Table 2 compares results from Jones [1978] (reprinted in NEDO [1981]) with results from the present survey. To facilitate comparisons, the present survey data have been categorised by net floorspace of the stores, using the categories designed by Jones [1978]. The figures for the net floorspace of the stores have been drawn from the Unit for Retail Planning Information (URPI) list of hypermarkets and superstores [1980]. The mean results from the two surveys show similarities in overall employment levels. There are differences, however, when the data are considered in relation to size category. Within the lower size categories, the recent data suggest a smaller part-time workforce, although the levels of FTE employment are broadly comparable. The major differences arise within the higher size categories, where the present survey has produced a greater employment

TABLE 1

STAFFING LEVELS IN SUPERSTORES - MEAN SURVEY RESPONSE

	Male				Female				Grand Total
	Full Time	Part Time	Casual	Total Male	Full Time	Part Time	Casual	Total Female	
Managers	8.68 (3.78)	-	-	8.68 (3.78)	1.35 (0.59)	-	-	1.35 (0.59)	10.03 (4.37)
Supervisors	4.66 (2.03)	0.03 (0.01)	-	4.69 (2.04)	7.72 (3.36)	1.10 (0.48)	0.01 (0.01)	8.83 (3.85)	13.52 (5.89)
Prcf & Tech	0.58 (0.25)	0.04 (0.02)	-	0.62 (0.27)	0.90 (0.39)	0.07 (0.03)	-	0.97 (0.42)	1.59 (0.69)
Sales	17.65 (7.69)	13.72 (5.98)	2.65 (1.15)	34.02 (14.82)	53.17 (23.16)	74.59 (32.49)	4.89 (2.13)	132.65 (57.78)	166.67 (72.60)
Clerical	0.25 (0.11)	0.03 (0.01)	0.03 (0.01)	0.31 (0.13)	6.90 (3.01)	2.58 (1.12)	0.14 (0.06)	9.62 (4.19)	9.93 (4.32)
Trainees	2.65 (1.15)	0.01 (0.01)	-	2.66 (1.16)	0.72 (0.31)	-	-	0.72 (0.31)	3.38 (1.47)
Others	10.70 (4.66)	3.56 (1.55)	0.52 (0.23)	14.78 (6.44)	5.38 (2.34)	3.92 (1.71)	0.38 (0.17)	9.68 (4.22)	24.46 (10.66)
Totals	45.17 (19.67)	17.39 (7.58)	3.20 (1.39)	65.76 (28.64)	76.14 (33.16)	82.26 (35.83)	5.42 (2.37)	163.82 (71.36)	229.58 (100)

TABLE 2
STAFFING LEVELS OF HYPERMARKETS AND SUPERSTORES

Net Floorspace (m²)	Number of Stores in Group	Mean Staff per Store			Floorspace per FTE (m²)
		Full Time	Part Time	FTE	
(a) Jones (1978)					
2300-2799	11	91	100	140	19
2800-3299	19	109	88	153	21
3300-4649	12	126	97	175	23
over 4650	11	174	100	224	35
All	53	122	95	170	24
(b) Sparks (1982)					
2300-2799	20	85	84	125	20.0
2800-3299	21	106	91	148	20.2
3300-4649	16	147	116	205	19.8
over 4650	14	166	159	242	25.4
All	71	121	108	173	21.4

Note   The figures for the Jones survey have been reprodu ?ed from
NEDO (1981 : 36).   For the Sparks survey the part-time total
includes casual employees.   In calculating Full Time Equivalent
(FTE) employees, casual workers have been rated as 0.2 of a full
time worker, and part time workers as 0.5.

KEY TO TABLE 1

Figures refer to mean responses in numbers of workers. Figures in brackets refer to workers
in each category as a percentage of the total store workers.

Occupational level	*Example of specific occupation covered*
Managers	Working directors
Supervisors	Sales supervisors, foremen
Prof & Tech	Personnel officers, buyers, accountants
Sales	Sales assistants, cashiers, shelf fillers, display staff
Clerical	Typists, secretaries, telephonists, payroll clerks
Trainees	Apprentices
Others	Craftsmen, drivers, warehouse staff, catering et al

Full time employee	– 30 + hours per week
Part time employee	– 8 to 30 hours per week
Casual employee	– less than 8 hours per week

level, due chiefly to a higher level of use of part-time labour. This may be due to the composition of the two samples or the increasing use of part-time labour within the stores.

Differences between the results of the two surveys also occur when the net floorspace per FTE employee is considered. The results from Jones [1978] exhibit a trend of increasing floorspace per FTE employee as store size increases. The present study exhibits this trend overall, although the values are substantially lower, and there is a decline in the third size category. In their recent study on Inner City Retailing, the Distributive Trades EDC [NEDO 1981: 35-36] found that their two major survey stores were anomalous to the results of Jones [1978]; this was particularly the case for a CRS superstore in Liverpool, which had only 80 employees with a net floorspace of 2,650 sq. ms. The figures presented in Table 2 are thus not set levels of employment, but represent guidelines for possible superstore employment. The Distributive Trades EDC [NEDO 1981: 36] commented on the relationship between scale and employment:

> Information collected (by URPI) ... suggested that the store size was not the sole determinant of staffing levels ... analysis revealed a very strong relationship between total turnover and total numbers of staff. ... In addition, the type of goods sold could influence the level of staffing, with some of the larger hypermarkets stocking a wide range of non-food as well as food goods and possibly, there-fore, requiring proportionately more staff ... more specialist sales staff being required to sell certain types of merchandise.

Data on turnover are unavailable for the 71 stores in the present study. Data on the percentage floorspace devoted to non-food goods are available, however, for some of the stores through the Institute of Grocery Distribution's (IGD) publication on superstores [IGD, 1981]. Figures for 48 stores were obtained from this source and their employ-ment levels analysed according to the percentage of net floorspace devoted to non-food goods. The results suggest that, as this percentage increases, the level of total employment increases $(R = .238)$. This relationship is not, however, statistically significant at the 99 per cent level. The results are affected both by the small sample size and by the influence of store size. Stores with the highest proportion of non-food (for example, the Woolco stores) tend to be those in the largest size categories, and are so different in merchandise floorspace allocation and product mix to other superstores, that they produce a level of non-food percentage floorspace quite unique within the sample. The correlation between size and percentage non-food floorspace is strong (.734) and statistically significant. The use of a partial correlation technique for total workers and percentage non-food floorspace, whilst controlling for size, does not produce a significant result. More generally, and using the 71 stores in the survey, a Spearman's rank correlation coefficient was calculated between total workers and store operator; the result being not significant at the 99 per cent level.

THE EFFECT OF STORE SIZE

The superstore employment data can be disaggregated by hours worked and sex, and analysed according to store size. With 71 responses in the data set, classification into size categories is unnecessary, except where direct comparisons with previous work are required [Sparks, 1982b]. Instead, simple regressions can be used to explore relationships. Linear regression has been used for the remainder of the analysis. Other, curvilinear relationships were explored, but the 'best results', that is, the highest correlations generally occurred using linear regression. There is little point in reproducing the scattergrams for these regressions, and in their place, the regression equation, coefficient (R) and a significance test (the t-test) will be given in various tables. Throughout the discussion, a significance level of 99 per cent has been adopted.

The overall relationship between store size and numbers employed is given in Table 3(a). A positive relationship, significant at the 99 per cent level is found. The remainder of Table 3 disaggregates this overall relationship in terms of employment by sex and hours worked, and gives the results of regressions with store size. In section (a) of Table 3 only one of the elements proves to be not significant. Casual employees are found to be unrelated to the size of the store, in terms of numbers employed. Each of the other categories (sex or full-time and part-time) has a positive, statistically significant relationship with store size. The slope coefficients in section (a) of Table 3 can be treated as an approximate 'employment generation index'. They provide the numbers of additional store workers employed for a set level of floorspace (1 sq. m.). For example, a store that expands by 1,000 sq. ms. would be expected to employ 40 extra workers. Of these, 33 would be female and seven male. These extra workers would be approximately balanced between full-time and part-time employment with additionally, a small transfer of workers from the casual labour 'pool' within the store.

Table 3(a) demonstrates that full-time and part-time employees are almost identically related to the size of store (similar slope coefficients), but that full-time workers are more numerous (larger intercept value). Female workers are numerically more important than male workers. The equations suggest that this numerical superiority increases as store size increases. This can be explored through the regressions between size of store and the percentage of total store workers in each subdivision. Female employees dominate in percentage terms ($Y = 62.058 + 0.0022X$), and indeed, this percentage increases as store size increases, that is, the larger the floorspace of the store, the greater the proportion of female employees. This relationship is statistically significant. When hours worked are considered, however, no relationship is significant. This analysis is extended by disaggregating the data further and the results are displayed in Table 3(b).

Table 3(b) demonstrates three statistically significant relationships. As store size increases, both male and female full-time workers and

TABLE 3

REGRESSIONS OF EMPLOYMENT BY SEX AND

HOURS WORKED BY SIZE OF SUPERSTORE

Y Variable	Equation	Correlation	Significance
(a) Numbers of Employees			
Total Workers	$Y = 80.745 + 0.0401X$	.497	*
Female	$Y = 40.353 + 0.0333X$	.526	*
Male	$Y = 40.393 + 0.0068X$	.293	*
Full time	$Y = 48.495 + 0.0196X$	.422	*
Part time	$Y = 20.595 + 0.0213X$	.499	*
Casual	$Y = 11.655 - 0.0008X$	-.083	n/s
(b) Numbers of Employees			
Female Full time	$Y = 26.689 + 0.0133X$	.395	*
Female Part time	$Y = 8.292 + 0.0199X$	.478	*
Female Casual	$Y = 5.372 + 0.00001X$	.002	n/s
Male Full time	$Y = 21.806 + 0.0063X$	.353	*
Male Part time	$Y = 12.304 + 0.0014X$	.128	n/s
Male Casual	$Y = 6.283 - 0.0008X$	-.162	n/s

Note In this and subsequent tables, significance has been denoted with an asterisk (*), non-significance by n/s.

female part-time workers increase in numbers, to a significant level. The predominance of full-time employees is again apparent, although female part-time workers increase in numbers most rapidly (the largest slope coefficient) as store size increases. When this is converted into percentage terms no relationship is statistically significant, however, although that for female part-time workers is almost accepted under the test. At a sufficiently large size of store, female part-time workers could be expected to be the largest grouping of workers.

Further disaggregation can be made by employment category, and the regressions of workers by employment category with size of superstore

TABLE 4

REGRESSIONS OF EMPLOYMENT BY

CATEGORY WITH STORE SIZE

Y Variable	Equation	Correlation	Significance
(a) By Numbers of Employees			
Managers	Y = 3.832 + 0.0017X	.318	*
Supervisors	Y = 2.219 + 0.0031X	.47	*
Prof & Tech	Y = 0.347 + 0.0003X	.226	n/s
Sales	Y = 79.06 + 0.0236X	.388	*
Clerical	Y = -8.054 + 0.0049X	.695	*
Trainees	Y = 3.966 + 0.0002X	-.056	n/s
Others	Y = -0.626 + 0.0068X	.34	*
(b) By Sex, By Numbers of Employees			
Male			
Managers	Y = 3.39 + 0.00143X	.306	*
Supervisors	Y = 0.279 + 0.00092X	.281	*
Others	Y = -0.376 + 0.0041X	.378	*
Female			
Supervisors	Y = 0.94 + 0.00213X	.432	*
Sales	Y = 45.515 + 0.0235X	.441	*
Clerical	Y = -7.844 + 0.0047X	.699	*

are given in Table 4. Table 4(a) reinforces the earlier results, by highlighting the dominance of the Sales worker category. Five employment categories produce significant results, the exceptions being Professional and Technical and Trainees. Of the five categories that have a significant relationship, the Sales category has the most rapid increase in numbers with increasing store size, although the Clerical and Other categories also increase numbers quite rapidly (regression slope gradients of 0.0049 and 0.0067 respectively). Translating the numbers into percentages of total workers radically alters the relationships. Only two categories are now statistically significant: the Sales ($Y = 80.645 - 0.002X$) and the Clerical

(Y = 0.099 + 0.0012X), and of these, the Sales category has a negative relationship with the store size; that is, as store size increases, so the percentage of workers employed in the Sales category declines. On the other hand, the Clerical functions become proportionately more important in employment terms.

The sex of the employees in each category can also form the basis of a regression. Those regressions that are statistically significant are given in Table 4(b). Male employment is statistically significant in the Managerial, Supervisory and Other categories, whereas female employment is significantly related to store size in the Supervisory, Sales and Clerical groupings. This corresponds to the results of section (a) but shows clearly the sex bias of employment between the categories. Male employees tend to be found in the Managerial, Trainee and Other categories, with female workers overwhelmingly present in the Sales and Clerical groups. The regression equations suggest that, as store size increases, the additional labour takes the form of male Managers and 'Others' and female Sales, Clerical and Supervisory workers. These relationships can be further explored using the percentage of workers in each grouping by sex. Only two groupings are statistically significant at this stage. The two statistically significant results are for Sales workers and Clerical workers, and are differentiated not only by direction of the relationship, as seen above, but by the sex. It is the male element of Sales workers that is significant, in that a statistically significant negative regression is obtained (Y = 24.949 − 0.0024X). With the Clerical workers on the other hand, it is the female side that has the significant relationship, and in this case a positive one (Y = 0.00119X + 0.16289).

It is possible to go beyond the differentiation by sex, and to analyse each of the results in Table 4 with respect to hours worked (that is, at the level of each 'cell' of Table 1). The results of this process are given in Table 5, which reports whether a relationship is significant or not. Most of the regression equations have been given in the previous Tables, and there is no need to repeat them here. In general, Table 5 reinforces the analysis that has been outlined previously. The significant relationships on the male side involve full-time workers, whereas on the female side they chiefly concern part-time employment. This is especially of interest in the 'Other' category, where it can be suggested that male full-time workers are used to operate the warehousing facility, and the female part-time workers to staff the catering aspect of the stores. If percentages of employees are considered, the importance of the Sales and Clerical categories is again apparent. The negative significant relationship between store size and male Sales workers, however, demonstrates no significance in terms of the hours worked. This suggests that the relationship derives from considerably increasing numbers of female Sales workers, and in particular female, part-time Sales workers, as opposed to any decline in the numbers of male Sales workers. Within the Clerical category, the significant increases are on the female side and involve both full-time and part-time workers. This suggests a wholesale

TABLE 5

THE RELATIONSHIP BETWEEN SIZE AND NUMBERS

EMPLOYED BY SEX, HOURS WORKED AND JOB TYPE

| | Male | | | | Female | | | | |
	Full Time	Part Time	Cas-ual	Total Male	Full Time	Part Time	Cas-ual	Total Female	Grand Total
Managers	*	-	-	*	n/s	-	-	n/s	*
Supervisors	*	n/s	-	*	*	*	n/s	*	*
Prof & Tech	n/s	n/s	-	n/s	n/s	n/s	-	n/s	n/s
Sales	n/s	n/s	n/s	n/s	n/s	*	n/s	*	*
Clerical	n/s	n/s	n/s	n/s	*	*	n/s	*	*
Trainees	n/s	n/s	-	n/s	n/s	-	-	n/s	n/s
Others	*	n/s	n/s	*	n/s	*	n/s	n/s	*
Totals	*	n/s	n/s	*	*	*	n/s	*	*

Note *denotes significance at the 99 per cent level

expansion of clerical facilities at a certain stage, rather than incremental additions to the existing clerical base.

In addition to an analysis by store size, the way in which additional labour is employed by store operators as the need for extra labour arises, can be examined. As the total number of workers in the store increases, so the relationships within the labour force, in terms of hours worked and sex, change. The regression equations for these relationships are given in Table 6. The number of workers in the store is, of course, related to the store size, but the regressions in Table 6, despite their inter-relationships, do provide a useful framework for discussion. The majority of the results are as would be expected from the earlier discussion, in that male, female, full-time and part-time employment increase in numerical terms as total employment increases. When percentages of total employment are examined, however, only casual labour $(Y = 9.747 - 0.0212X)$ is statistically significant. The relationship is in fact a negative one, that is, as total employment increases, casual employment as a percentage of total employment falls.

TABLE 6

REGRESSIONS OF EMPLOYMENT BY SEX AND HOURS

WORKED BY TOTAL STORE EMPLOYMENT

Y Variable	Equation	Correl-ation	Signif-icance
(a) By Numbers of Employees			
Female Workers	Y = -11.958 + 0.7656X	.976	*
Male Workers	Y = 11.958 + 0.2344X	.81	*
Full time Workers	Y = 5.062 + 0.5064X	.878	*
Part time Workers	Y = -17.981 + 0.5124X	.871	*
Casual Workers	Y = 12.918 - 0.0187X	-.152	n/s
(b) By Sex, By Numbers of Employees			
Male			
Full time	Y = 2.228 + 0.1871X	.846	*
Part time	Y = 4.023 + 0.0582X	.439	*
Female			
Full time	Y = 2.834 + 0.3193X	.762	*
Part time	Y = -22.004 + 0.4541X	.877	*

Table 6(b) demonstrates again the importance of female part-time labour. Full-time and part-time employment for both sexes is statistically significant, but the relative sizes of the equation coefficients point to the major use of female part-time labour as employment levels rise (a slope gradient of 0.454). This is further reinforced when percentage of total employment is used, as female, part-time employment is the only statistically significant relationship (Y = 25.522 + 0.0365X). These relationships can also be examined in terms of the category of employment and by sex. For male employment, the categories of Managers, Supervisors, Sales, Trainees and Others produce statistically significant relationships in numerical terms. For female employees, the results are identical, except that Clerical replaces Trainees. Using percentage

TABLE 7

NUMBER OF EMPLOYEES BY STORE

SIZE : A MODEL

| | Hypothetical Store Sizes (Net Floorspace, Sq M) | | | |
	2500	3000	5000	7000
Total	181	201	281	362
Male	57	61	74	88
Female	124	140	207	274
Full time	98	107	147	186
Part time	74	85	127	170
Casual	10	9	8	6
Managers	8	9	12	16
Supervisors	10	12	18	24
Prof & Tech	1	1	2	3
Sales	138	150	197	244
Clerical	4	7	17	26
Trainees	5	5	5	5
Others	16	20	33	47

values, however, no significant relationship is revealed. Subdividing further, that is, by sex, hours worked and employment category, produces only one statistically significant relationship in percentage terms. This is for female part-time Sales workers ($Y = 0.033X + 23.169$).

A PREDICTIVE MODEL

The regression equations obtained during this analysis can be used to estimate employment levels for various hypothetical stores, on the basis of the store size. Table 7 gives the results for four such hypothetical stores. In sex terms, female employment dominates. The growing importance of part-time employment is well-marked, although full-time employment still comprises over 50 per cent of total employment at the largest size of store chosen. Whilst sales workers are the dominant category numerically, their importance in percentage terms declines as store size increases. Major changes in numerical strength occur in the Clerical and Other categories, with the former being especially important. The composition by categories of the stores employment is thus changing markedly as store size increases. An increase in employment in the Clerical, Other and to a lesser extent Supervisory categories suggests that at the larger store sizes, a different style of retailing is occurring. More functions external to the shop floor are being introduced and expanded, for example, offices and warehousing, possibly suggesting the growth of a more autonomous unit with functions additional to, or vastly more extensive than, the 'standard' superstore. Similarly, it is possible that these changes represent an increased allocation of space to non-food goods and the consequent need to support this operation in different ways.

The results presented by the regression analysis aid understanding of the employment potential of superstores. The 'model' outlined here could be of considerable application to planners, in providing a broad guideline to the types of employment generated by superstores, and the way in which this alters according to store size. Whilst it is accepted that other factors in addition to the size of store influence the employment level, the model does at least provide an introduction and initial analysis of the subject, and a degree of quantification previously unavailable.

CONCLUSIONS

> Only by employing just enough full-time staff for minimum basic requirements and by supplementing them with part-timers can the necessary adjustments be made to meet the inevitable – and predictable – variations in consumer flow. [Forrester, 1976: 20].

The results presented here have analysed in depth the employment distribution within superstores. The impact of these stores on British retailing is undeniable. What has often been underestimated is their importance for employment. The larger stores are major employers, for example, the joint British Home Stores/Sainsbury Savacentres employ over 650 people each; Tesco at Weston Favell reputedly employs over 1,000 workers. This article has attempted to go beyond such general figures and comparisons, and to analyse more closely the employment generated within superstores.

The overall result produced by the survey was for a mean store employment of 230 (173 FTE) of which 71.4 per cent were female and 43.4 per cent were part-time employees (additionally, 3.7 per cent were casual workers). The distribution of these employees, within the various employment categories, exemplified the notion of a polarised labour force. Workers are heavily concentrated into the Sales category, that is, shelf-fillers, checkout operators: the point-of-sale end of the store. This category also contained a very high proportion of part-time employees, reflecting the retailers' use of the labour force to meet the peak consumer demands. The majority of these jobs were female, demonstrating both the ability of employers to use 'marginal' elements of the labour force in routine jobs, and the desire of many women for employment that combines paid work with their traditional role as housewife. In addition, arguments can be raised that male workers simply do not want part-time employment, and that in any case, stores prefer female staff ('a happy smile on the checkout'?).

The effect of the size (net floorspace) of superstores on employment has been discussed in detail. The relationships between size of superstore and the various categories of employment, disaggregated by sex, hours worked and job type, have been examined through regression analysis. The importance of female labour, and particularly part-time female labour, to the stores' operation is apparent. As the stores increase in size, Sales workers as a group decline in percentage terms, and other functions such as Clerical and warehousing became more important. As Sales workers increase in number, however, so part-time female Sales workers increase, reflecting the need to have a flexible workforce to cover the peaks of consumer demand. A sex bias in the various categories is also apparent from the results. Male workers tend to be concentrated in the Managerial, Trainees and Other categories, with females in the Sales and Clerical groupings.

The scale of superstore is not the only variable influencing employment levels. Turnover, operator characteristics, floorspace allocation could all be of importance in producing the total employment figure for a store. Data for these variables are very difficult to obtain, although obviously the operator for each of the 71 stores considered, is known (see Sparks [1982b] for disaggregation by store operator). It is far more relevant to consider the sample as a whole, rather than to disaggregate by operator, as disaggregation by operator in this way would not enable the scale of the stores to be considered. Initial work on this data (see Sparks [1982a]) has in any case suggested that store size is a stronger influence on total store employment than the operator, although differences within employment category by operator could be expected [Sparks, 1982b].

This article has provided a more detailed introduction on superstore employment than existed before, but there are other major areas still to be examined. The discussion here has concentrated on sex and hours worked in terms of other factors such as age, journey to work and perceptions/conditions of store employment. Another major consideration, as introduced previously, must be the overall effect of superstore employment on existing labour markets. The Distributive Trades EDC [NEDO, 1981] has begun this in broad terms. Research is required on whether jobs created by superstores are 'new' jobs or whether merely relocations in the retail labour market. The problem is to isolate out these factors from 'natural' trends in retailing. As Whysall [1981: 46] suggested, however, if there is no substantial case for superstores to answer over trading levels, then it seems difficult to mount a case over impact on employment levels. This discussion has demonstrated that many of the jobs created by superstores are for female and/or part-time positions. That should not detract from their importance: jobs are vital in the present economic climate and retailing has an important part to play, through its development of superstores, in producing employment opportunities.

REFERENCES

Alexander. I. and Dawson, J. A., 'Employment in Retailing: A Case Study of Employment in Suburban Shopping Centres,' *Geoforum*, Vol. 10.

Forrester, R. A., 1976, 'Matching Staff Levels to Customer Flow', *Retail and Distribution Management*, Vol. 4, No. 6.

Institute of Grocery Distribution, 1981, *Superstores 1981*, Watford: Authors.

Jones, P., 1978, *Trading Features of Hypermarkets and Superstores*, Reading: URPI U7.

Mallier, T. and Rosser, M., 1979, 'The Changing Role of Women in the British Economy', *National Westminster Bank Quarterly Review*, November.

McFayden, E., 1980, 'Forward into the 1850s', *Retail and Distribution Management*, Vol. 8, No. 6.

National Economic Development Office, 1981, *Retailing in Inner Cities*, London: NEDO.

Robinson O. and Wallace, J., 1976, *Pay and Employment in Retailing*, Farnborough: Saxon House.

Sparks, L., 1981, 'A Note upon Retail Employment and Superstore Development', *Service Industries Review*, Vol. 1, No. 3.

Sparks, L., 1982a, 'Female and Part-time Employment within Superstore Retailing', *European Journal of Marketing*, Vol. 16, No. 7.

Sparks, L., 1982b, 'Employment in Hypermarkets and Superstores', *URPI Information Brief 82/7*.

Unit for Retail Planning Information (URPI), 1980, *List of Hypermarkets and Superstores*, 6th edition, Reading: Authors.

Western Mail, 1981, 14 January, p. 1.

Whysall, P., 1981, 'Retail Competition and the Planner – Some Reflections', *Retail and Distribution Management*, Vol. 9, No. 3.

This study first appeared in *The Service Industries Journal*, Vol.3, No.1 (1983).

4
The Importance of Store Operator on Superstore Employment Levels

by

John A. Dawson, Anne M. Findlay and Leigh Sparks*

Information from 175 superstores, operated by three companies, is used to investigate the importance of store operator in setting superstore employment levels and types of employment. Store operator is shown to be a significant factor determining employment numbers and types in British superstores.

Employment within British superstores increasingly has come under close scrutiny. This has been due to many factors: the growing awareness of the magnitude of retail employment in Britain; a realisation that changes in retail structures have implications for retail employment; wider changes in overall employment structure; and the continuing debate over the impact of superstores on job creation or job transfer in retailing. Despite studies explicitly attempting to quantify the impact of superstores on local employment [Scottish Office, 1982], the debate continues [e.g., *Grocer* 1985, *Supermarketing*, 1985]. The difficulty experienced in superstore employment impact assessment stems from the enormous problems not only in disentangling national and local trends at local levels, but also from the fact that employment structures within superstores themselves are as yet imperfectly understood.

The work of Jones [1978] has been developed by Sparks [1981, 1982a, 1982b, 1983a, 1983b] to illustrate the employment characteristics of superstores using results from a sample survey. This work concentrated on deriving general relationships between store floorspace and employment numbers and types, as well as providing information on the composition of the superstore work-force in terms of gender, hours worked and job type of the employees. The limitations of a sample survey covering approximately 33 per cent of all superstores then open, with responses drawn from a wide range of companies, meant that only superficial and tentative data disaggregation by store operator was possible [Sparks, 1982b].

As part of a wider project on the characteristics of 'Employment in British Superstores', three major superstore operators provided information on

*This work has been undertaken as part of a project on 'Employment in British Superstores', financed by the Economic and Social Research Council under grant F00 23 2052. The authors wish to thank the three superstore operators involved in this project for access to the data.

store employment. Information has been obtained for 35 Fine Fare superstores, 65 Tesco superstores and 75 Asda superstores. This provides data for 175 superstores or approximately 60 per cent of all superstores trading in Britain at the time of the data collection (Autumn 1984). For all three companies, the information was derived from the company's central administration, and so has the benefit of consistency of categorisation at least within each company. While the main part of this article concerns different superstore employment levels associated with operator, results are also presented on store floorspace and various employment relationships. The floorspace figures have been taken from the Unit for Retail Planning Information (URPI) [1984] list, supplemented where appropriate by information from the Institute of Grocery Distribution (IGD) [1984]. The various definitions used in the discussion, and a store employment table of the type used to supply data for each superstore, have been given in Sparks [1983b].

EMPLOYMENT STRUCTURES IN SUPERSTORES

The employment composition of superstores is related to several variables. At a general level these include decisions on labour policy made by corporate planners and by individual store managers. These decisions are themselves influenced by the local labour market conditions and the type, quantity and mix of labour available. More specifically, superstore employment is related to the sales turnover, the size of the store, the store operator, the store opening hours, and the type of goods retailed by the store. Data on sales turnover are not readily accessible, and so the surrogate measure of floorspace has been used to predict employment levels. Previous studies showed that floorspace was related to employment at the total sample level [Sparks, 1983a], but the relationships have been less clear when disaggregated by store operator [Sparks, 1982b]. It is hypothesised here that store operator is a significant factor in determining both the size and the composition of the superstore work-force.

Table 1 presents both the aggregate results from the survey, allowing comparison with the previous sample survey [Sparks, 1982b] and the disaggregated results by store operator. Sparks [1982b] previously suggested in preliminary analysis that Tesco was atypical of other superstore operators in having a high percentage (64 per cent) of full-time (over 30 hours per week) employment in a large work-force (mean 280, full-time equivalent (FTE) 228). This contrasted with the earlier results for Fine Fare which showed a much lower store employment level (mean 191, FTE 138) and a predominance of part-time (8–30 hours per week) employees (53 per cent). Both companies had a majority of female (71 per cent) employees, concentrates in the Sales worker category (74–76 per cent).

The results from the present survey show a mean employment level considerably higher than the earlier survey. The difference is probably due to the removal of co-operative and independent superstores from the analysis. This larger work-force results in a lower sq.m./FTE ratio. This

TABLE 1

EMPLOYMENT IN BRITISH SUPERSTORES; MEAN NUMBER OF EMPLOYEES
PER STORE

	Sparks (1982)	Present Survey			
		Aggregate	Asda	Fine Fare	Tesco
Number of Stores	71	175	75	35	65
Average Floorspace (sq.m)	3707	3650	3731	4017	3360
Standard deviation	1371.5	847.9	712.4	1001.0	817.7
Total Employees	230	285	326	202	281
F.T.E.	173	195	210	140	205
Sq.m/F.T.E.	21.4	18.7	17.8	28.7	16.4
Full-time	121(53)	108(38)	100(31)	79(39)	132(47)
Part-time	100(43)	170(60)	215(66)	120(59)	144(51)
Casual	9(4)	7(2)	11(3)	3(2)	5(2)
Male	66(29)	80(28)	77(24)	59(29)	96(34)
Female	164(71)	204(72)	249(76)	143(71)	185(66)
Male					
Full-time	45(20)	52(18)	51(16)	38(19)	60(21)
Part-time	17(7)	27(9)	23(7)	21(10)	34(12)
Casual	3(1)	2(1)	3(1)	-	2(1)
Female					
Full-time	76(33)	56(20)	49(15)	41(21)	72(26)
Part-time	82(36)	143(50)	192(59)	99(49)	110(39)
Casual	5(2)	5(2)	8(2)	3(1)	3(1)

Note: Figures in brackets are the percentage of total store employment within each category. Figures may not sum due to rounding.

ratio is considered later in this article. The gender composition of the work-force is overwhelmingly female (72 per cent) with the percentage of female labour within the superstore work-force remaining constant between the surveys. In terms of hours worked, however, differences between the surveys are marked. Results of the previous survey showed that the majority (53 per cent) of workers were full-time employees. The present survey reveals that only 38 per cent of the superstore work-force are full-time employees. This 'switch' can be traced to a markedly higher level of female, part-time labour. This sub-category in the present survey accounts for approximately 50 per cent of the total superstore work-force.

While the aggregate figures allow comparison with earlier work they do not illuminate the central theme of the article: namely, the relationship of superstore operator to superstore employment. Disaggregation of the data into the three component superstore operators reveals several interesting points. The level of employment between the operators varies considerably from Asda (mean 326, FTE 210) to Fine Fare (mean 202, FTE 140). This wide difference is reflected in the sq.m./FTE figures where Fine Fare is very much higher than the other two operators (and also previously published figures). This suggests either that the Fine Fare stores are comparatively understaffed or that other variables such as ancillary activities and the range of products sold are of major importance. Differences in gender composition of the work-force between the operator show Asda with the lowest percentage of males (24 per cent) and Tesco with the highest (34 per cent). A similar pattern of differences appears in examining the hours worked of the employees. Asda have only 31 per cent of their work-force in full-time employment, whereas Tesco have 47 per cent. It is important to note that in the Sparks [1982] survey, 64 per cent of the Tesco work-force were in full-time employment. While the earlier survey was a sample survey, comparison of results confirms the widely held, but until now unproven, view that part-time employment generally is increasing in superstores. Female workers fill the majority of the part-time jobs; for example in Asda female part-time workers comprised almost 60 per cent of the total work-force, with female workers being 89 per cent of the part-time category. In Fine Fare and Tesco, the female proportion of the part-time category is 83 per cent and 76 per cent respectively.

TABLE 2

ANALYSIS OF VARIANCE TEST FOR EMPLOYMENT DIFFERENCES BETWEEN
SUPERSTORE OPERATORS

Variable	F Ratio	Significance (99% level)
Floorspace	8.02	*
Total Employees	32.66	*
Part-time Employees	49.60	*
F.T.E. Employees	24.09	*
Sq.m/F.T.E.	62.43	*
Female Employees	50.66	*

Note: *denotes relationship statistically significant at the 99 per cent confidence level

In order to assess the extent to which these different types of employment profiles are associated with specific operators, two series of statistical tests have been undertaken. The first involved tests for the analysis of variance for a series of key variables. The results of these tests are shown in Table 2. It can be seen from the table that where a significant F ratio was found, between group differences were more important than within group differences, i.e., the differences between the operators were significantly more important than the differences within a superstore operator's stores. The table therefore indicates, via significant F ratios at the 99 per cent confidence level, that store operator has a significant influence on the size and composition of the work-force. Examination of the results showed that in each significant case, Fine Fare had a mean value much lower than those for the other store operators. In terms of FTE and sq.m./FTE, Asda and Tesco had mean values, which were close together and the 95 per cent confidence levels based on the pooled standard deviation showed a high degree of overlap. These differences and similarities can be investigated further in terms of the relationship between store size and employment size and composition.

STORE FLOORSPACE AND EMPLOYMENT

Sparks [1983a] has shown a statistically significant relationship between store size (floorspace) and total store employment, as well as with employment disaggregated into various categories. Initially, in the present study, an analysis of the aggregate data was undertaken to investigate such relationships. This was subsequently expanded by disaggregating the data by store operator. Table 3 shows the significance or otherwise of the regression equation for each relationship; for space reasons, the regression equations themselves are not presented here, but are available from the authors. Throughout this section a significance level of 99 per cent has been adopted.

TABLE 3
REGRESSION ANALYSIS BETWEEN FLOORSPACE AND EMPLOYMENT

	Sparks (1982)	Present Survey			
		Aggregate	Asda	Fine Fare	Tesco
Total Employees	*	n/s	n/s	n/s	*
F.T.E.	*	*	*	n/s	*
Full-time	*	n/s	*	*	*
Part-time	*	n/s	n/s	n/s	n/s
Male	*	n/s	*	n/s	*
Female	*	n/s	n/s	n/s	n/s
Male					
Full-time	*	*	*	*	*
Part-time	n/s	n/s	n/s	n/s	n/s
Female					
Full-time	*	n/s	n/s	n/s	*
Part-time	*	n/s	n/s	n/s	n/s

Note: *denotes relationship statistically significant at the 99 per cent confidence level

Table 3 shows that for the aggregate data from the present study, only two relationships proved to be significant at the 99 per cent level. First, a significant relationship was shown to exist between store floorspace (X) and FTE (Y) employment (Y=145+0.014X). This is perhaps the relationship most expected. The only other significant relationship was between store floorspace (X) and male full-time (Y) employment (Y=35.5+ 0.004X). The finding of only two significant relationships with store floorspace is contrary to those found by Sparks [1983b], who, for the ten categories under review, found only one non-significant relationship (male part-time employment with store size). The reasons for this perhaps lie in the nature of the two surveys. The earlier survey was a sample survey, drawing data from many superstore operators, and including several very small Co-operative superstores and two very large, in both floorspace and employment terms, Savacentre stores. The earlier survey thus included stores from the whole range of superstore sizes open in Britain. On the other hand, the present survey, while more comprehensive than the sample survey, is restricted to only three companies, which might be categorised as being 'middle of the road' superstores in floorspace terms, as shown by the standard deviation scores in Table 1. The earlier survey is thus a valid predictor of employment by store size when store operator is not known; but when the superstore operator is limited to certain operators, this relationship breaks down, although it is still present for FTE employment. The presence of a statistically significant relationship with FTE employment leads to a hypothesis that store operator policies differ significantly for different categories of employee, i.e., the composition of the work-force, but that overall labour quantity is related directly to store size in a similar way irrespective of operation. This finding was masked by the sample nature of the data used by Sparks [1983b].

Table 3 presents the significance or otherwise of the relationships with store size, disaggregated by store operator. The results for store operator are consistent with the findings of the analysis of variance tests reported above, with Fine Fare having the fewest statistically significant relationships. Within Fine Fare, the only statistically significant relationships which were found were between, first, store size and total full-time employment and, secondly, store size and male full-time employment. Indeed these relationships were also statistically significant for the other operators, and in the case of male full-time employment at the aggregate level. This suggests the presence of a 'base' male full-time employment component in the superstore work-force, and as additional departments are included in the stores (associated with larger floorspace) so numbers of male full-time employees increase.

At Asda, several other significant relationships were found, notably male employment and FTE employment. Both these relationships were statistically significant also at Tesco. In addition, Tesco exhibited statistically significant relationships with total employees, male part-time and female full-time employees. The Tesco stores therefore have significant relationships in all categories including a full-time element, as well as total and FTE employment. These latter two cases are possibly significant because of the higher level of full-time employment in Tesco superstores. It might be suggested, therefore, that the increasing use of part-time employment, which closely matches customer-flow and therefore sales turnover, has eroded the previously found relationships between store size and employment. This in turn suggests that as retailers have become more sophisticated in their use of labour, and in tailoring the in-store retail mix to local conditions and requirements, the size of the store has become less deterministic in decisions on labour levels.

THE SIZE OF THE WORK-FORCE AND EMPLOYMENT COMPOSITION

The analysis can be extended by examining the ways in which the employment composition changes, in terms of gender and hours worked, as the employment level increases. Table 4 presents the results of regression analyses between employment level and various employment types, at both the aggregated and disaggregated levels. As might perhaps have been expected, the relationships are statistically significant in the majority of cases. From an examination of the constant and coefficient values (not shown, but available from the authors) for the aggregated data, three groups are suggested as being of particular significance in total employment (Y): part-time (Y=23.9+0.68X) female (Y=−6.68+0.741X) and female part-time (Y=22.1+0.579X) employees. These were the groups less well predicted in the earlier analysis.

TABLE 4

REGRESSION ANALYSIS BETWEEN SEX AND HOURS WORKED OF EMPLOYEES
AND NUMBERS EMPLOYED

	Aggregate	Asda	Fine Fare	Tesco
Full-time	*	*	*	*
Part-time	*	*	*	*
Casual	*	*	*	n/s
Male	*	*	*	*
Female	*	*	*	*
Male				
Full-time	*	*	*	*
Part-time	*	*	*	*
Female				
Full-time	*	*	*	*
Part-time	*	*	*	*

Note: *denotes relationship statistically significant at the 99 per cent confidence level

Again, analysis of variance can be used to study differentials in the relationships between operators. These results are summarised in Table 5. The results indicate that significant differences exist between the operators on all the variables considered, with between group differences outweighing within group differences thus giving high F ratio values. In particular it is worth noting that the pattern of part-time employment in Tesco was shown to be very different from that of Asda and Fine Fare.

TABLE 5

ANALYSIS OF VARIANCE TEST OF DIFFERENTIAL EMPLOYMENT
CHARACTERISTICS BETWEEN STORE OPERATORS

Variable		F Ratio	Significance (99% level)
% female	]	45.4	*
% male	]		
% full-time		77.7	*
% part-time		69.0	*
% male full-time		30.3	*
% male part-time		22.8	*
% female full-time		63.8	*
% female part-time		101.4	*

Note: *denotes relationship statistically significant at the 99 per cent confidence level

Examination of the constant and coefficient values by store operator provides further information on the differences between operator. The overall pattern of the gradient coefficients remains largely consistent between the individual operators and the aggregated data, with female employment (Y) increasing at the fastest rate (Y=−6.68+0.741 X for aggregate data) with size of work-force (X). The values of the constants in the regression models for a particular labour type vary considerably by operator, e.g., for part-time employment (Y) with size of work-force (X) the regression equations are Y=−14.0+0.662X for Fine Fare, Y=−19.8+0.718X for Asda, and Y=23.3+0.597X for Tesco. These results suggest that the nature of the distribution of store operators is that each occupies a different part of the overall distribution while displaying the same trend characteristics, thus when aggregated producing the consistent trend.

JOB CATEGORIES IN THE SUPERSTORE WORK-FORCE

The data base established from store employment tables also permits disaggregation by company and by job category. Table 6 lists the job categories and shows the profiles found in this survey with both aggregate and disaggregate data. The table compares current results with those of the earlier sample survey [Sparks, 1983b]. A comparison between the two aggregate data analyses shows a marked similarity between the profiles, with little change between the two surveys.

TABLE 6

EMPLOYMENT IN BRITISH SUPERSTORES BY JOB CATEGORY – MEAN TOTALS AND PERCENTAGES

	Sparks (1982)	Present Survey			
		Aggregate	Asda	Fine Fare	Tesco
Mean No. of Employees per Store	230	285	326	202	282
Managers	10(4)	19(7)	22(7)	12(6)	19(7)
Supervisors	14(6)	19(7)	19(6)	14(7)	21(7)
Prof & Tech	2(1)	1(0)	1(0)	1(1)	1(1)
Sales	167(73)	206(72)	233(72)	151(74)	205(73)
Clerical	10(4)	8(3)	13(4)	7(3)	5(2)
Trainees	3(2)	2(1)	-	2(1)	3(1)
Others	25(11)	30(10)	38(12)	16(8)	29(10)
Male					
Managers	9(4)	16(6)	18(6)	10(5)	16(7)
Supervisors	5(2)	4(1)	2(1)	6(3)	7(2)
Prof & Tech	1(0)	-	-	-	-
Sales	34(15)	38(13)	28(9)	34(17)	52(18)
Clerical	-	-	-	-	-
Trainees	3(1)	1(0)	-	2(1)	3(1)
Others	15(6)	21(7)	29(9)	8(4)	19(7)
Female					
Managers	1(1)	3(1)	4(1)	2(1)	3(1)
Supervisors	9(4)	14(5)	17(5)	8(4)	14(5)
Prof & Tech	1(0)	1(1)	1(0)	1(0)	-
Sales	133(58)	168(59)	205(63)	117(58)	153(54)
Clerical	10(4)	8(3)	13(4)	7(3)	4(1)
Trainees	1(0)	-	-	-	-
Others	10(4)	9(3)	9(3)	8(4)	10(4)

Note: Figures in brackets are the percentage of total store employment within each category.

Disaggregating the results by store operator produces some differences, but again the profiles found are broadly similar. In terms of mix and shares of job category the profiles are highly similar. It is only when job category is further disaggregated by gender that differences between store operators emerge, as might be expected from the results presented earlier on the different male/female ratios by store operator. The main differences lie in the Sales category where Asda have proportionately fewer men and more women than the other operators, within a broadly similar overall proportion of Sales workers in total store employment.

The composition of the work-force by job category (Y) also can be investigated with respect to store size (X), again using regression analysis. Table 7 summarises the results of such analyses. The categories of Professional & Technical, and Trainees were omitted from the analyses because of the highly skewed nature of the data. Only the most significant categories have been chosen for inclusion in Table 7.

TABLE 7

REGRESSION ANALYSIS BETWEEN JOB CATEGORY AND STORE SIZE

	Aggregate	Asda	Fine Fare	Tesco
Managers	n/s	*	n/s	*
Supervisors	n/s	n/s	n/s	*
Sales	n/s	n/s	n/s	n/s
Clerical	*	n/s	*	n/s
Others	n/s	*	n/s	*
Male				
Managers	n/s	n/s	n/s	*
Supervisors	*	n/s	*	n/s
Others	n/s	*	n/s	*
Female				
Sales	n/s	n/s	n/s	n/s
Clerical	*	n/s	*	n/s

Note: *denotes relationship statistically significant at the 99 per cent confidence level

The aggregate data reveal statistically significant relationships with the Clerical group (Y=2.83+0.002X), male Supervisors (Y=1.01+0.001X), and female Clerical (Y=2.95+0.002X) workers. This can be contrasted with Sparks [1983a] who found significant relationships with all five categories given in the first part of Table 7. Again this may be due to the different nature of the two surveys. Disaggregation by store operator reveals few statistically significant relationships. Most are present in Tesco. The importance of male workers in the Managerial and Others categories for both Asda and Tesco can be noted. This is reinforced by the analysis of variance test which suggests that Fine Fare is significantly (F ratios) different from the other two operators.

This analysis by job category must be qualified by considering how numbers in the various job categories increase or decrease as the size of the work-force increases. The results are summarised in Table 8. A significant relationship is found for all the categories detailed in Table 8, at the aggregate level. Disaggregated by store operator, however, the number of significant relationships falls, especially in the case of Fine Fare. Nevertheless the number of significant relationships should be noted.

TABLE 8

REGRESSION ANALYSIS BETWEEN JOB CATEGORY AND SIZE OF WORKFORCE

Managers	*	*	n/s	*
Supervisors	*	*	n/s	*
Sales	*	*	*	*
Clerical	*	*	*	*
Others	*	*	n/s	*
Male				
Managers	*	*	n/s	*
Supervisors	*	n/s	n/s	*
Others	*	*	*	*
Female				
Supervisors	*	*	n/s	n/s
Sales	*	*	*	*
Clerical	*	*	*	*

Note: *denotes relationship statistically significant at the 99 per cent confidence level

TABLE 9

ANALYSIS OF VARIANCE TEST FOR EMPLOYMENT BY JOB CATEGORY
DIFFERENCES BETWEEN SUPERSTORE OPERATORS

Variable	F Ratio	Significance (99% level)
% Managers	3.75	n/s
% Supervisors	17.27	*
% Sales	4.37	n/s
% Clerical	108.79	*
% Others	19.18	*

Note: *denotes relationship statistically significant at the 99 per cent confidence level

Table 9, however, shows that the F ratio test by job category was far less conclusive than in earlier cases. The two categories of Sales and Managers had non-significant F ratio values. In view of the consistency of the composition of job types, relative to the size of the work-force, it may be concluded that it is possible to predict the types of jobs which will expand with a given increase in the size of the work-force. This would appear to apply almost regardless of the operator involved, while the distribution of the jobs between male and female employment and part-time and full-time employment remains dependent upon the store operator.

CONCLUSIONS

This article has examined the importance of store operator on superstore employment levels and characteristics. This has been possible through analyses of data on employment for 175 superstores operated by three companies. A major finding of the analyses is that there are significant differences between employment levels and employment types in superstores operated by different companies. These differences are greater than the variation in employment levels and types within the superstores operated by any one company. The data have allowed statistical testing of Sparks' [1982b] tentative results, proving that differences by store operator are present and significant but disproving the strength of his model of superstore employment [Sparks, 1983a] based on superstore floorspace. The divergence in results compared with the earlier work can be explained by differences in data collection and to changes in the employment composition within superstores since the time of the earlier survey.

The differences in employment level and type by store operator show themselves in various ways. For example Tesco is noted as having the highest proportion of full-time and male employees, relative to the other companies. It is very important to note, however, that the level of part-time employment within Tesco superstores has risen since the earlier survey. This process of employing more part-timers, probably associated with renewed deskilling of certain tasks, is a major corporate policy associated with the search for increased operating efficiency.

Other differences are found by store operator in terms of employee characteristics. The main conclusion of this article is that these differences, i.e. the balance between part-time and full-time, and male and female employment within superstores, are dependent upon store operator. The next stage is to consider why these differences exist and to explain why store operators pursue different corporate employment policies for their often seemingly similar superstores.

REFERENCES

Grocer, 1985, 'Planner hits out at retail jobs claim'. Grocer, 6 July 1985.
Institute of Grocery Distribution, 1984, Superstores Directory. Watford: Authors.
Jones, P.M., 1978, Trading Features of Hypermarkets and Superstores. U.R.P.I.: Reading.
Scottish Office, 1982, Retail Employment Change in Scotland. Edinburgh: H.M.S.O.
Sparks, L., 1981, 'A note upon retail employment and superstore development'. Service Industries Review, Vol. 1, No. 3.

Sparks, L., 1982a, 'Female and part-time employment within superstore retailing'. *European Journal of Marketing*, Vol. 16, No. 7.

Sparks, L., 1982b, 'Employment in hypermarkets and superstores'. *U.R.P.I. Information Brief 82/7*.

Sparks, L., 1983a, 'Employment and superstores'. *Planner*, Vol. 69, No. 1.

Sparks, L., 1983b, 'Employment characteristics of superstore retailing'. *Service Industries Journal*, Vol. 3, No. 1.

Supermarketing, 1985, 'Superstores defend their new jobs record'. *Supermarketing*, 12 July 1985.

U.R.P.I., 1984, *List of U.K. Hypermarkets and Superstores*. Reading: Authors.

This study first appeared in *The Service Industries Journal*, Vol.6, No.3 (1986).

5

Employment Policies in the Service Sector: Training in Retail Distribution

by

O. Robinson

This article presents in summary the results of the recent study by the Distributive Trades EDC's Part-Time Employment Group, which focussed attention on the training practices and career opportunities for this major and increasing component of the labour force of retail firms. There is no great certainty or unanimity about the training needs of retail staff, and differences in skill requirements are evident across the various retail trades and diverse organisational structures. Retailing is a dynamic and rapidly changing industry and employers are not unaware of the training needs associated with labour intense operations yet the training implications of the industry's considerable dependence on part-time workers do not appear to be fully appreciated. In discussing the Report's findings in the context of the ongoing training debate in Britain, it is argued that the corporate strategies of retailers must comprehend the centrality of the training function, if effective use is to be made of all their employees.

Retailing is being increasingly recognised as 'one of the more dynamic and rapidly changing sectors of the British economy', attracting growing attention to its changing organisational structures, levels of business concentration, size of outlets, marketing methods and general competitive strategies. Although employment in retailing 'has historically been one of the least considered aspects of the distributive trades', the present decade has witnessed a burgeoning of interest in the industry's labour utilisation for a number of reasons [Sparks, 1987]. Distribution accounts for the employment of some 3 million people, about 14 per cent of the work-force in Britain, and is a major source of job provision. The industry's labour force structure exhibits distinctive features: a large proportion of young workers (about one fifth of all employees), a high female (54 per cent) and a large and growing part-time component (some 35 per cent, rising to almost 50 per cent of the 2 million employees in the retail trades). Retailing is a labour intense industry despite the moves towards larger more capital intensive operations widely apparent in food retailing through the development of superstores, but also evident in other sectors, particularly larger mixed businesses and many specialist non-food retailers, which are achieving greater capital intensity by investing in the refurbishment of existing stores. Labour costs represent up to 50 per cent of gross margin, making the industry's use of the labour force of vital importance to overall operating efficiency [NEDO, 1985, 1987, 1988; Brodie, 1986; Johnson, 1987; Alexander, 1988; Bamfield, 1988]

The report on employment perspectives and the distributive trades [NEDO, 1985] in concluding that the labour intensity of retailing operations and the high levels of customer contact 'mean that a less than competent workforce could have a major effect on industry performance', highlighted the role of training in the industry. It was observed that while 'required degrees of competence vary considerably across different jobs in the industry, for most they are a direct result of some form of training'. An 'unevenness' was found in the provision of training, 'particularly in the generation of the basic retailing skills – social skills, numeracy and literacy', 'the impression' being of 'a minority of companies incurring the cost of training for the benefit of the majority'. The concern of the Distributive Trades Economic Development Committee about labour performance, coupled with awareness of the growing significance of part-time work in retailing led to the commissioning of a further study of employment, to be focused on 'the training implications of growth in part-time working in the distributive trades and the practical problems and opportunities raised at establishment level for employer and employee alike'.

It is the purpose of this article to summarise and consider the results of the latter study, carried out in 1987/88 under the direction of the EDC's Part-Time Employment Group of which the writer was a member and responsible for the in-depth case study investigation of employers' utilisation of part-time labour [NEDO, 1988]. Section I of the article looks at the evidence pertaining to part-time work in retailing as reflected in employment structure, labour force composition and working hours patterns prevalent in the 15 organisations which participated in the study, including evidence regarding employers' reasons for hiring workers on a part-time basis. In Section II training in retailing is reviewed on the basis of the case-studies of employers' policies and practices relating to training and the results of the associated employee attitude survey of 859 part-time workers employed in small, medium and large retail establishments located throughout Britain. In conclusion the report's findings are discussed in the context of the contemporary training debate in Britain and elsewhere.

SECTION I: PART-TIME EMPLOYMENT IN RETAILING

1. Employment structure, labour force composition and work schedules

(i) *Industry profile.* The increasing significance of the part-time labour component in the employment structure of the distributive trades is evident from aggregate industrial statistics. In the retail and distributive trades 1.03 million employees worked part-time in 1987, one in three in the distributive trades in total, rising to one in two in retailing. Although the employment of men in distribution has increased in absolute and relative terms, the bulk of the 47 per cent increase in part-time employees since 1971 is accounted for by females. There are, of course, considerable variations in the proportions of part-timers employed by different types of business. The 1984 Census of Employment showed the highest representation in tobacconists and newsagents (62.1 per cent), in footwear and leather businesses (58 per cent) and in food retailing (49 per cent), with household goods outlets employing only 28 per cent and motor vehicle retailers and filling stations under 17 per cent of their employees on a part-time basis. In absolute terms, the retail food sector employed the greatest number of part-time workers, some 280,000 or one third of all part-time staff in retailing. Growth in the numbers of part-time employees in Retail Distribution has been accompanied by significant changes in the hours worked by (female) part-time staff. New Earnings Survey data on hours, for example, show that the proportion of sales assistants working fewer than 16 hours per week rose from 26.2 to 45.6 per cent between 1982 and 1987; over the shorter period 1977 to 1987 the proportion of check-out operators working for fewer than 16 hours more than doubled from 21.3 to 46.8 per cent [NEDO, 1988].

(ii) *Company profiles and policies*. The employment structures of the 15 retail organisations participating in the 1987/88 EDC study constituted a non-random sample, the majority having in excess of 10,000 part-time employees; together the firms employed approximately 300,000 people. Particular attention was paid to large companies 'in the expectation that they would be able to demonstrate good and interesting examples of best practice'. The employment structures of these companies indicated that part-time employment ratios were greatest in mixed and in grocery retailing and lowest in specialist and in department stores. In all examples part-timers were predominantly women, employed throughout the working week; male part-timers were generally employed on Saturday and during late trading hours. Variations in the composition of the weekend and evening labour forces reflected neighbourhood labour market conditions such as the availability of a local student population. Working patterns varied between organisations in accordance with opening hours, trading patterns and the hours and schedules worked by full-time employees. Weekly opening hours with six-day trading as the norm could reach 59 hours; in the case of seven-day trading found in the DIY business and in mixed retailing companies (Scotland only), branches were open for 75 hours per week.

Shift and hours patterns were related to the size of the organisation. In large firms with small outlets, and in small firms, the arrangement of part-timers' schedules was left to the discretion of branch managers. In the case of a footwear retailer with just under 1000 employees and almost 200 branches, varying in employment size from two to 17 staff, uniformity in working schedules was found only in 9 per cent of the branches with wholly full-time staff. Across the company 34 per cent of branches employed part-time staff to cover fluctuating requirements throughout the week, 9 per cent relied on full-time and Saturday only staff and the remainder utilised all three categories. Over half of the Saturday-only workers were employed for six or fewer hours, and a similar proportion of the part-timers employed throughout the week worked from 10 to not more than 16 hours. The part-time working week was constituted in several ways – whole days, whole day and part day work. In isolated instances a working week of 30-33½ hours was spread over five or six days (the part-timers were defined as employees working fewer than 34 hours per week), but only 15 per cent of those contracted to work on whole days worked for more than three days per week. Approximately 60 per cent of those employed during the week also worked for the whole or part of Saturday to provide a more mature element for a staff which would otherwise have consisted mainly of sales assistants aged under 18. Among companies employing at least 15,000 to 20,000 full-time and part-time workers, there was evidence of much more central control over levels of part-time employment and working hours schedules. Full-time equivalent employment levels were set centrally in respect of each branch or store, leaving local managers to determine the mix of employment within the constraints of wage budgets related to annual sales targets. Staff requirements were expressed variously in terms of whole-time equivalent numbers or total hours to be worked in each establishment. Part-time workers' shift and hours schedules were also determined centrally, using computerised data which identified fluctuations in hourly, daily and weekly trading. Part-time hours were generally uniform in specialist retailers, with typical morning, lunch and afternoon shifts of 3½ or 4 hours per day, giving a 17½ to 20 hour week, or alternatively two full day shifts (Friday and Saturday) producing 15–16½ hours work. Nevertheless, within these shifts there could be numerous schedules. In the men's clothing department of a department store, of the 37 selling staff 15 worked on a part-time basis on 12 separate schedules for 15 to 16 hours, and seven on Saturday only for 8.3 hours. Seven of the 10 employed for 15 or 15.6 hours and one of the four employed for 16 hours a week worked on either one or two whole days; the part-time hours on other days were staggered to cover the lunch period for full-time staff, and peak trading hours from 10.00 am to 4.30 pm and until 7.30 pm on Wednesdays. In grocery and mixed retailing hours were varied to match a greater variety of tasks such as deliveries of merchandise, preparing food and meeting trading levels which were usually higher in the second half of the week. In the specialist retailers a three-shift system was typically the practice; in self-service food stores there might be almost as many schedules as part-time employees, most of whom worked on two, three or four days per week.

The numbers of part-time staff employed exclusively for weekend or late evening trading on one night each week also varied across the different sectors and ranges of establishments. The smallest proportion, engaged for Saturday-only and evening work, was 10 per cent in a company operating 22 department stores, with full-time staff working on Saturdays and on one evening per week on a rota basis. Elsewhere, the need for Saturday-only staff was eliminated through the employment of full-time staff working on a rota system to incorporate Saturday as part of their normal working week. The actual hours worked by Saturday-only staff were also subject to wide variation. While full-day working on Saturday is still widespread, in a branch of one high street chain where 55 per cent of the branch's total staff was composed of Saturday-only and late-evening staff, Saturday part-timers worked on 11 different schedules giving working weeks of four to six hours, with Saturday staffing covered by three overlapping four-hour shifts. Sunday staffing was organised similarly in the stores of a DIY group, which dispensed with any need for lunch-time relief staff by operating two 4½ hour Sunday shifts for part-timers.

The complexity and diversity of the working hours patterns which result from the employment of part-time labour in retail organisations is amply illustrated in an example taken from four stores of a company trading in a wide range of merchandise, with above 70 per cent of its labour force working part-time in some 200 stores. Part-time sales assistants in one store open for 51 hours per week were employed on five days in two shifts of 3½ hours to give a 17½ hour week. Most of the part-time staff in a second store trading for 58 hours each week worked on similar shifts but with earlier starting and later finishing times for a 20-hour week, supplemented by a smaller 'lunch relief' shift employed for three hours each day. In the smallest of the companies' stores with a 51-hour trading week and with fewer full-time sales assistants, the part-time hours covered the whole of the working day. Those employed between 10.00 am and 3.00 pm worked on two or three days; two worked on Saturday as supervisors, as did one of the full-time sales assistants. The closest accommodation of working schedules to a store's trading hours in this group was seen in a store recently opened in a relatively new and innovative shopping complex in an area of relatively high unemployment. Virtually all of the 95 sales staff were engaged for three whole days in separate groups covering Monday to Wednesday and Thursday to Saturday. Within each group approximately 60 per cent worked for the whole of three days giving a 27-hour week; the remainder worked from 12.30 to 5.00 pm for a 13½ week to cover business peaks and meal breaks, or for 18 hours to include Saturday working. The store employed only three full-time staff, who worked alternate Saturdays; the use of a predominantly part-time staff allowed managers to avoid recruitment of Saturday-only staff and reduced the provision of time-off in lieu for Saturday working by full-timers.

The working hours schedules of the part-time employees of all the retail companies reported above confirm the downward trend in the part-timers' weekly hours suggested by the New Earnings Surveys. At least three-quarters of all part-time staff normally worked for not more than 21 hours in each organisation. Employment for not more than eight hours a week (chiefly for weekend and evening-only work) varied more widely and accounted for at least 20 per cent of part-time staff in each company, rising to 54 per cent in the DIY organisation; in one of the large multiples, 72 per cent of part-timers worked from four to 12 hours per week to cover Saturday and late evening trading. Contracted hours of employment were frequently exceeded by the actual hours worked by Monday to Friday part-time staff and by students normally employed only on Saturdays and evenings. This flexibility was essential, particularly where the numbers employed in small outlets allowed no margin for transferring staff from other duties within the same branch.

2. Hiring choices – why part-time employment?

(i) *Employers' reasons for engaging part-time labour.* The reasons put forward for the employment of part-time staff by the managers interviewed at head offices of all the retail organisations investigated not only varied little except in emphasis, but differed little from those recorded in earlier studies [Robinson and Wallace, 1984; Robinson 1985, 1986, 1988; Blanchflower and Corry, 1986; NEDO, 1986; Beechey, 1987; Rubery, 1988]. These reasons related to maximum flexibility of working arrangements, combined with a reduction of direct wage costs. The use of part-time labour allows managers greater freedom in matching labour demands with changing patterns in operational or customer requirements, simplifying the implementation of a five-day working week for full-time employees when weekly business hours commonly extend to six and in some cases seven days. Managers seek flexibility which enables them to adjust labour inputs to trading levels which vary in fairly predictable patterns throughout the day and week. In this way direct savings in wage costs are achieved, most pronounced where companies cover the working day by three or more 'shifts' of part-time workers and avoid statutory requirements for meal breaks after a continuous work period of six hours.

While the employment of part-timers stems primarily from internal pressure to minimise direct labour costs in an increasingly competitive industry, the prevalence of short working weeks means that substantial proportions of companies' labour forces have earnings under the weekly national insurance contribution thresholds, generating savings on indirect wage costs. Such indirect savings may not be dismissed as insignificant, since 'any earnings-related NIC enables employers to reduce indirect wage costs, provided their operational requirements and labour force composition allow adjustments to hours worked' [Robinson, 1986]. The evidence, however, does not suggest that part-time working patterns were the result of any general aim to ensure that weekly hours and pay fell within thresholds that determine national insurance contributions and employment protection rights (dependent on thresholds of at least 16 hours per week for employees with two years' continuous service in the same employment, or at least eight hours a week for those with at least five years' continuous service).

(ii) *Terms and conditions of part-time employment.* Full-time and part-time staff were commonly engaged on the same basic hourly rate and terms of employment, but a minimum length of working week was usually required to qualify for sick pay, unsocial hours payments for weekend work and for membership of company superannuation schemes. In two organisations, lower hourly rates were paid in respect of work performed only at weekends or for fewer than a specified number of weekly hours. Seasonal fluctuations and unforeseen labour requirements were met partly by extending the working hours of part-time employees which would not incur premium rates unless they exceeded the length of the normal full-time week. Similar considerations applied in respect of regular late evening and weekend work.

As noted in the preceding section, employers stand to make indirect labour cost savings through non-payment of NIC in respect of employees with weekly hours which keep their earnings below the prevailing NIC threshold, in 1987/88 of £39 per week. In the organisations studied, this threshold was generally reached with a working week of 17 to 18 hours for an adult sales assistant employed in the provinces, or 13¾ hours in central London. Although the range of part-time staff with earnings below the prevailing NIC threshold varied widely, the levels reflected the high proportions of part-time staff working for not more than 21 hours per week, already seen. In one store with virtually all its selling staff employed on a part-time basis, only 28 per cent had earnings below the threshold, but the proportions in other retail organisations or branches ranged from 57 to 96 per cent; the highest ratios occurred in food supermarkets and department stores.

SECTION II: TRAINING IN RETAILING

1. Employers' policies and practices

(i) *Training objectives and implementation.* In all retailing sectors the large companies characteristically had formal training policies setting out their training objectives and implementation arrangements. The policies of these organisations were specifically explicit, detailing objectives, standards of training provision and delivery arrangements. Company training programmes were mainly devised centrally at head office levels together with systems for ensuring their implementation through diffuse organisational structures.

Provision of training was normally related to immediate business needs, and largely, if not wholly in most companies, internally provided (cf. *The*

Study of Funding of Vocational Education and Training, 1988: 6, 8). In practice employers sought to provide newly recruited employees with induction training, to train all employees to work to agreed standards of performance and to ensure that they were given appropriate training before or immediately following promotion or transfer. Exceptionally, however, there were companies which saw training as a long-term issue. In one case training was regarded as fundamental to a corporate strategy designed to raise profitability by changing radically management and staff attitudes and behaviour. In another example it was board policy to pursue the longer-term development of the vocational skills (professional, technical and manual) of all employees as an essential prerequisite of operating efficiency.

Formal training arrangements were variable, but the training function, as distinct from design and planning was typically devolved from head office on a regional, area or district basis to the individual retail store or branch. Training of sales assistants (the majority of retailers' employees) was the responsibility of a chain of people. Those involved included head office policy staff, area personnel and training staff, in-store staff/personnel managers and training officers, store managers, instructors, supervisors and in some instances, experienced sales assistants.

Companies relied on either specialists (training officers) or line managers for the implementation of training policy. In large organisations training officers were employed in-store to train staff in basic skills. Generally these trainers worked under the general control of district training managers, having been selected as trainers for their personal qualities and practical experience rather than the possession of any formal training qualifications; they were given both in-house and external training in appropriate skills – institutional and interpersonal skills, behavioural training techniques and training needs analyses. In some organisations personnel and training functions were combined, with branch personnel managers (frequently professionally qualified) formally responsible for all training, and for creating and overseeing the execution of company training programmes; in practice their training duties were often restricted mainly to induction, staff appraisal and maintenance of training records. Training by line managers on the other hand, although in many instances the only option for smaller retailers, was adopted by large companies as a more cost-effective approach to training, simplifying training organisation and placing on line management (with centrally provided expert advice) the main responsibility for identification of training needs, introduction of training plans/programmes and monitoring of in-store training practices.

(ii) *Training content.* Induction training was regarded as the vital introductory stage of the total training process for sales staff. The objectives ranged from the setting of broad guidelines, the provision of comprehensive checklists under as many as 40 headings, to detailed guidelines for the first day of induction training to allow employees to identify with the company as employer rather than the management of a single retail store. Induction training covered store and stock layout and presentation, health and safety, hygiene, fire procedures, security of cash and stock, ticketing and pricing, till operation and credit payments, and some aspects of retail law. New employees were informed on matters relating to their terms and conditions of employment, including standards of appearance, with job descriptions and in some companies with details of basic training programmes. The training for the initial day was normally done off-the-job, and could be spread over a period of up to three days. For part-time staff, induction training was provided on their working days; in the case of those with short weekly hours (particularly Saturday workers), the induction process often extended into the second or third week of employment and merged into basic skills training.

For all retail staff basic skills training is of necessity a continuous process, with the common goal of enabling staff to reach and sustain within periods varying from six to 12 weeks, uniform company proficiency levels in the duties specified in job descriptions. The identified skill requirements of sales/general assistants in various retail trades are summarised in Table 1.

The skill requirements expected of sales/general assistants in specialist and general retailers are broadly similar, except that in the former, merchandise knowledge and goods handling procedures and customer assistance skills are to an extent more exacting than those required by general retailers. Among the small independent retailers, skill requirements are less specific and call for little or no further training, for example in cleaning duties or product care and presentation. Installation of electronic point of sales (EPOS) facilities in progress in larger stores, entailed additional training for checkout operators and general assistants. On the whole the adoption of EPOS was not expected to lead to significantly greater training requirements for checkout operators, though the system could generate delays at checkout points and more frequent customer queries [Jarvis and Prais 1989: 22: 'the impact of new technology in retailing is not as great as sometimes suggested; retraining of checkout operators to use EPOS seems to require little more than 1–4 hours'].

(iii) *Continuing/Further training*. The greatest pressure on retail companies' training provision derives from a requirement to maintain and update staff skills, arising from the pervasive operational changes associated with organisational restructuring, extension of product lines and technical developments. These changes, often occurring rapidly with changes in company ownership and control, combined with the employment of large numbers of young workers and endemically high labour turnover, confront many companies with the need to provide annually both basic and continuous skills training for several thousand employees. In such circumstances the employment of high proportions of part-time workers may serve to exacerbate the difficulties of training

TABLE 1
SKILL REQUIREMENTS OF SALES AND GENERAL ASSISTANTS IN VARIOUS RETAIL
TRADES

Food supermarkets

Checkout/till operation
Customer service
Preparation, display and
replenishment of stock
Appreciation/product knowledge
of at least one specialist dept (meat,
bakery, fish, delicatessen)

**Department stores and specialist
retailers**

Cash and credit handling
Product and merchandise
knowledge, including awareness
of the product's technical
specification
Customer care skills
Security/shrinkage
Special promotions
Consumer law

Multiple stores

Customer care
Assisting customers to select
stock; secondary selling
Use of measuring equipment and
fitting room facilities
Customer queries
Correct till procedures
Maintenance of stock – quality
control, rotation, withdrawal,
display
Stocktaking
Housekeeping – personal
appearance and cleanliness of
fitting rooms, shop and checkout areas
Security, including avoidance
of shrinkage

Small Retailers
Cash and stock security
Ticketing systems
Cash and credit handling
Product care
Presentation/display
Care and appearance of shop
counters and stock

Source: NEDO, 1988.

implementation and delivery, particularly evident at store level. The
employment of greater numbers of part-timers for short hours at
peak periods of demand makes conventional training arrangements
increasingly inappropriate. Multiple and department stores may use
late opening on one morning per week to allow for half-hour training
sessions, but this practice leads to the exclusion of part-time staff
whose working hours start later in the day. In companies deploying
training officers, one-off training sessions must be repeated for part-
time staff during their working hours, a procedure which becomes
expensive with complex working hours patterns permitting only small
training group sessions for part-timers. Moreover, the normally high
levels of trading activity characteristic of part-timers' working hours
complicate the arrangement and consequent cost of associated on-
the-job and off-the-job training for part-time staff. Where companies

had introduced new or specially focused training programmes on store layout or customer care for example, part-time staff were required to attend for one- or two-hour training sessions outside business hours, for which they were paid their hourly rate, but this was a sparingly used option. In consequence the period allowed to part-time staff for the achievement of full proficiency was inevitably lengthened. For Saturday staff induction and basic training, particularly checkout and sales service training, were of necessity combined and extended over longer periods than for full-timers. The types of course conducted largely away from the job, included refresher training sessions, specific product training relevant to some types of retail business, training videos and courses of varying kinds and length. The latter were often intended to broaden the individual's knowledge of the business and not confined to developing an employee's technical skills. Training delivered by video and training films, while more cost-effective than traditional labour-intensive forms of delivery, was not infrequently rendered less effective by absence of supervisory monitoring and follow-up.

Some of the problems of training large numbers of part-timers were diminished in companies which placed responsibility for training unequivocally with line managers and employees themselves, through the use of open learning as the principal means of delivery of induction and continuing training. With this approach determination of the training period was left to store or departmental managers and supervisors, sometimes helped by experienced general sales assistants and check-out operators. Certified open learning packages characterised by friendly, light writing styles, study aid symbols, self-assessed questions and overall high quality presentation, were easy to use by part-timers and allowed job training to be conducted as activity fluctuated during trading hours of up to 75 per week. There are of course limitations to the use of open learning programmes as a training device for part-time employees. Because of high labour turnover, the 12-month period allowed for part-time staff to attain full proficiency meant that large numbers never reach targeted levels of efficiency. The extent to which domestic commitments restricted part-time workers from studying in their own time could also be overlooked by central personnel divisions, although payment for successful completion of open learning programmes by individuals in their own time was seen as a way of overcoming the problem. At the same time it was often not appreciated by senior management and training providers that all-embracing open learning packages may be of less use to some sections of the part-time work-force than others, especially Saturday-only staff whose general educational levels tend to be higher than those assumed by the programmes.

(iv) *Development of part-time employees and promotion prospects.* For staff recruited as sales assistants (normally over 80 per cent of a retailer's labour force), supervisory positions offer the main promotion prospect. The supervisor is regarded as a sales assistant with additional duties of assisting department or section managers to achieve operational targets. The extra duties involve general oversight of all the tasks performed by sales assistants in the supervisor's section to ensure that they are carried out according to company procedures and standards; to provide assistance to personnel/department managers with the induction, basic training and appraisal of sales staff; and to alert section or store managers to any problems requiring managerial attention. Training provision for supervisors was largely the responsibility of their immediate supervisors (section or department managers), aided as necessary by store managers, store personnel training managers and regional training managers. Sales staff were selected for promotion on grounds of experience and above-average competence/performance in all the specified duties of a sales assistant including experience in assisting in the induction/training of new staff; the training required for supervisory functions was largely covered by continuing training designed to maintain and build on the sales assistants' basic skills. Specific supervisor training tended to be off the job, concerned mainly with topics such as staff control (interviewing and communication techniques, appraisal methods) and the introduction of new company operational procedures.

The proportions of part-time staff employed as supervisors ranged at best from eight per cent in DIY retailing to less than one per cent in food retailing and in department stores. While part-time employees were free to apply for supervisory or other positions, with few exceptions the vast bulk of supervisory posts during normal trading hours on Monday to Friday were filled by internal promotion of full-timers. Indeed, there was widespread evidence that retailers had little difficulty in filling vacant supervisory posts by promoting full-time sales assistants, recruiting experienced full-timers from other retailers or promoting part-timers who were willing to become full-time. There were in practice very few promotions actually required by the businesses, since the numbers of supervisory positions were low relative to the total of non-managerial sales staff employed: about two per cent in food retailing and 17 or 18 per cent in mixed retailing and department stores.

Part-time supervisors were concentrated within a narrow range of tasks associated with a single occupation, while full-timers were involved in wider aspects of branch operations and thus more favourably placed for promotion to managerial positions. The infrequent employment of part-time supervisors on Monday to Friday schedules (as opposed to Saturday-only supervisors) was also restricted to part-time staff working for up to 30 hours per week and allocated to departments with above-average checkout provision. Generally therefore, despite board level employment policy statements asserting the need to develop the potential of every employee, part-time staff were widely seen by store managers as a 'pair of hands', employed to sell at periods of peak trading activity; a need to promote part-timers to supervisory positions (usually checkout supervision) arose only when the working hours schedules of full-time supervisory staff did not provide adequate cover for Saturday or late evening opening. Apart from the claim by some store managers that full-timers would refuse to accept the authority of part-time supervisors, most personnel and store managers believed that part-time sales staff were not anxious to take on supervisory jobs, and that those interested would accept full-time employment; this is a belief which was not borne out by the evidence from the employee attitude survey.

2. Retail employees and training perspectives

(i) *Part-time employee profiles.* The vast majority of the 859 part-time respondents to the employee attitude survey were women, most of them married. In the four sizes of retail establishment separately identified as places of employment (with 1–4, 5–10, 11–50 and over 50 part-time workers), about half the respondents were aged 25–44 in all except the 11–50 group, where there were high proportions of younger, Saturday-only staff. Part-timers were mainly employed as sales assistants on checkout or shelf-filling functions. In smaller-sized establishments (fewer than 11 part-timers) they were more often involved in a variety of duties than was the case in largest where they tended to work on a specific task. About half of the part-time workers had previously done jobs similar to their current work, either for another employer or for their current employer on an earlier occasion. In the smallest and largest retailers part-timers appeared to have longer service records, approximately one third working for the same employer for over five years; nevertheless, there was a considerable range in the periods worked, with between 21 and 36 per cent having worked for less than one year for their present employer.

Part-timers' working hours were longer in the smaller retail businesses: 47 and 37 per cent of part-timers in the two smallest retail establishment sizes (up to 10 part-time employees), respectively worked fewer than 16 hours per week, while 64 and 49 per cent in establishments with 11–50 and 51+ part-time employees worked these weekly hours. The great majority of part-timers both in large and small retail establishments worked set weekly hours, although some 25 per cent in the smallest and 20 per cent in the largest outlets reported varying weekly hours. The majority worked part-days only, ranging from 51 per cent in the largest retail establishment category to 69 per cent in the smallest. About one third of respondents in the larger establishments worked whole days only, compared with 15 per cent in the smaller outlets, a reflection of the greater number of Saturday-only staff working in the 11–50 group.

Part-timers reported the same basic hourly rates of pay as their full-time counterparts, confirming the evidence provided by employers. A relatively low proportion received higher rates for working weekends, evenings or nights. Those working in large multiples were most likely to receive a higher rate of pay if working outside normal hours (62 per cent), while those in the small firms were least likely (14 per cent). Part-timers also enjoyed at least some of the additional benefits associated with full-time employment in their firms. For example, 88 per cent of part-timers in the larger firms received holiday pay and 54 per cent bonuses, compared with 65 and 16 per cent respectively in the smaller establishments. Bonus payments were most prevalent in the electrical, mixed retail and other non-food outlets – the specialist retailers. About one-third of part-timers in the largest category had pension rights, but in all other sizes of establishment (particularly in food stores and for shop floor work) this benefit was available to significantly fewer than one in ten. Again, sickness benefit was received by over two-thirds in the largest category, but by less than half in the middle two categories, dropping to 22 per cent in the smallest. Commission payments were not a major factor in the rewards of part-timers, being paid to only a small proportion in any group of retailers.

Of all respondents, between 77 and 95 per cent gave financial reasons as the main reason for working at all [Rubery, 1988: 124]. Choice between full-time and part-time work, however, was strongly influenced by 'family reasons' which represented the most important reason for working part-time rather than full-time: about half of all interviewees said that their personal circumstances meant that they could only work part-time and that they were happy with this situation [1988 Labour Force Survey, preliminary results]. Non-availability of full-time employment was cited as the reason for working part-time by 11 to 14 per cent of part-timers, a proportion which rose significantly to between 20 and 59 per cent among young people aged 16–24. While the prime motivations for working part-time were the financial benefits and the personal contacts available through work, aspects of personal convenience notably proximity to home and suitability of hours packages offered by employers to those the individual was able to work, represented the chief reasons for choosing a particular part-time job. In the main, part-time workers surveyed were satisfied with their current job, and well over 80 per cent were either 'fairly satisfied' or 'very satisfied' and did not aspire to any other type of work within their store; younger part-time sales assistants (up to age 24), with some kind of formal qualification, thought that office and supervisory roles would offer more job satisfaction.

(ii) *Employees' experience and attitudes to training.* The main skills which interviewees considered they used in their jobs included those related to retail trade customer activities and within this group, customer relationships were seen as the most important. Handling money and till and checkout skills ranked a poor second and third. Next in importance to the general area of retail trade customer skills were personal attributes: good personality, politeness, friendliness, ability to use common sense and intelligence [Jarvis and Prais, 1989]. About half the respondents had earlier experience of their current job whether for another or the same employer on another occasion. While they were thus familiar with relevant basic skills, the vast majority had introductory training in their present task on entry to current employment. Formal induction training, though not well established in smaller shops, appeared to be treated with progressively more care and attention and over a more prolonged period, as the employment size of the establishment increased. For example, over half of the respondents working in the smaller retail establishments claimed that on employment they were 'just-shown what to do and left to get on with it'; in the largest stores this proportion fell to 26 per cent. In the smaller establishments some 20 per cent had received either formal training for the first few days or regular training over the first few weeks, with a comparable proportion of 78 per cent in the largest stores. Almost half the part-timers in the larger establishments (over 11 part-time employees) felt that their present job did not make full use of their work experience, abilities and qualifications, and even in smaller establishments over one third said that their qualifications were not fully used. The skills most underused, particularly in the smaller businesses, were office skills from shorthand typing and book-keeping through to telephonist, accounting, computing and cashier skills. In all sizes of establishment about 50 per cent of part-time workers were trained by supervisors or managers. However, in retail establishments with over 50 part-time employees 29 per cent of part-timers who had training received it from training officers and 41 per cent from a manager or supervisor. 'Another person in the same job' was reported as the source of training by just a third of all respondents in respect of all store sizes.

Employees' experience of further training, stated by employers to be an important element in their training programmes, varied widely with size of establishment, type and location of outlets, and hours worked. There was little or no continuing training in smaller shops, but in larger establishments it was provided for up to 80 per cent of staff. Training videos were used in all but the smallest shops; regular refresher training sessions were given only in the large multiple outlets, decreasing as a training device with the size of establishment; they were not provided in the independent sector. Occasional training of one to two days' duration was by contrast much more widely available, although its incidence also declined with size of outlet. Very little product training was provided to part-timers in any size or type of outlet (seven per cent of all the retail part-timers received such training and only 10 per cent of those in specialist electrical retailers), but training facilities were more generally available the more specialised the retail firm. There were more facilities, for instance, in department stores and in clothing, footwear and electrical stores than in grocery retailing. Locational variations in the provision of further training as in staff induction, showed outlets in Scotland in the lowest position (only 47 per cent were offered any) compared with London and the South East region where the comparable proportion was 61 per cent. The take-up of continuing training (Table 2) was, as emphasised by employers, strongly dependent on the total hours worked: the longer a

TABLE 2
INCIDENCE OF CONTINUING TRAINING FACILITIES BY HOURS WORKED

	Size of retail establishment by number of part-time employees								
	5-10			11-50			51+		
	All	<8hrs	21+ hrs	All	<8hrs	21+ hrs	All	<8hrs	21+ hrs
	%	%	%	%	%	%	%	%	%
Any training	44	50	46	67	58	74	80	54	87
Regular refresher training sessions	12	0	11	15	20	13	21	4	27
Occasional training sessions	20	0	22	24	15	35	44	23	49
Regular showings of training videos	5	50	0	9	8	3	17	4	23
Occasional showing of training videos	12	0	14	31	15	52	44	35	50
One-day training courses	5	25	5	6	8	16	9	0	19
Product training	9	0	14	9	3	13	7	15	6
Number interviewed	100	4	37	171	40	31	389	26	122

Source: NEDO, 1988.

part-timer worked the greater the opportunities for additional training. In the largest retail establishments, for example, 54 per cent of part-timers working fewer than eight hours received some kind of further training, compared with 87 per cent of those working over 21 hours per week; in the latter group 49 per cent received occasional further training compared with 23 per cent of those working fewer than eight hours.

(iii) *Promotion and careers*. Employees' views on career opportunities and promotion reflect their perceptions of what was available to them. As Table 3 indicates, a very high proportion reported that the specific job they were doing currently was the only job they had done with their present employer. This proportion was highest in the smaller retail establishments and generally declined with the size of the business: 95 per cent of part-timers in the 1–4 size establishments said that this was their only task for this employer, compared with 64 per cent in the 51+ size establishment. In firms with 5–10 part-time employees, promotion for part-timers was more commonly found within the mixed retail, food, grocery and CTN trades, and was more often available to those employed in office administration than shop-floor positions. In the largest retail establishments, only about one-third of part-timers had opportunities for advancement, and this proportion fell on average to well under 20 per cent in the smallest outlets.

The predominance of low-graded work for part-timers clearly affects their expectations of promotion or career advancement. Between 78 and 95 per cent of part-time employees interviewed in the survey felt that there would be no promotion in their present part-time job. In the three

TABLE 3

PROMOTION RECEIVED BY PART-TIMERS

	Size of retail establishment by number of part-time employees			
	1–4	5–10	11–50	51+
	%	%	%	%
Have been promoted or given higher grade[a]	8	21	16	36
Have never been given any advancement[a]	92	79	84	64
Have never had any other job with their employer	95	89	74	64
Number interviewed (100%)	199	100	191	389

[a]Either in current job or in another job with the employer

Source: NEDO, 1988.

largest sizes of retail establishments, between 52 and 66 per cent felt that there might be promotion if they were to become full-timers, compared with between 14 and 22 per cent if they were to remain part-time workers; in outlets with fewer than five part-time employees, it was believed that there were no significant promotion opportunities either on a full-time or part-time basis. Despite the virtual absence of part-time promotion opportunities, a significant proportion welcomed the prospect, including younger female employees with children. On average just over half (53 per cent) of those interviewed wanted to be considered for promotion within their part-time job. Those within the larger multiple outlets were more open to change and more ambitious than those working in smaller stores, although almost half (46 per cent) in the smallest stores wanted to be considered for promotion. Where men were employed in significant numbers on a part-time basis as in the larger multiple sector, they were more ambitious than the women employees and less likely to turn down promotion prospects. Rejection of promotion opportunities by women was concentrated among older women doing the more mundane jobs.

Overall, promotion opportunities were seen by part-time employees to be severely limited. The survey of part-time workers employed in a range of firm and outlet sizes across the various retail sectors supported the findings from the investigation of employer practices that the majority of managers and supervisors were full-time. Only in the largest establishments was there evidence of part-time promotion: 21 per cent of the employee respondents saying that there were some part-time supervisors in their stores, reflecting the greater degree of flexibility found in the larger establishments than in smaller outlets. In the large- and medium-size multiples, part-time workers were more likely to be employed in the same type of work as full-time staff and less likely to be confined to particular job designated to part-time staff.

CONCLUSION

As stated in the introduction, the prime purpose of the study of part-time working in the Distributive Trades was to direct attention to the training implications of the continuing growth in part-time employment in retailing. It is abundantly clear from the examples of company employment profiles and the policies and practices which shaped them that the deployment of part-time labour is integral to the industry's labour process. While there may be questions surrounding possible constraints on the extension of part-time working in some companies [Sparks, 1987], at operational levels part-time employees now constitute the bulk of labour input, producing considerable and increasing diversity in the labour packages which make up an organisation's human resources. It was the view of the Distributive Trades EDC expressed in 1985, that 'a major element of the workforce might lack effective training and career development opportunities, to the detriment of employee, employer and the customer'. The findings of the ensuing investigation of employer practices and employee attitudes commissioned by the Committee in 1987 suggest that this expectation was not ill-founded; training provision is extending rather than reducing differential treatment of part-time employees in retailing in Britain, and if unimproved may deprive the industry of some of the longer term advantages to be expected from the deployment of part-time labour, the more so in the changed demographic circumstances of the coming decade [cf. *Employment for the 1990s*, 1988; T. Walsh, 1989; NEDO/ Training Agency, 1989].

That retailers as employers recognise the need for training is reflected in the inclusion of a formal training function within organisational structures. Nevertheless, the evidence revealed sharp differences between the formal policies and objectives of companies' training arrangements and their practical application. Particularly in the larger firms, training policies were detailed, covering not only objectives but the mainly internal training delivery arrangements, the content and standards of training provision. Training was largely devised centrally to apply to all company stores along with implementation instructions to guide local staff. The needs of part-timers were not mentioned explicitly in companies' formal policy statements, and in practice the extent of formal training beyond induction procedures and instruction in basic job skills was limited, most notably for part-timers employed for a few hours per week. Among the smaller organisations, the evidence revealed that both induction and further training for part-timers could be rudimentary. It is markedly evident that operational and organisational restructuring, together with changes in ownership and store design, developments in technology and in cash and credit control, create a need for more extensive updating of training for staff, whether working full-time or part-time. While large employers had a firm sense of the standards expected, often defined in terms of competences, they had less certainty about how to arrange the training for part-timers. Organising further staff training and retraining for part-timers was difficult, not least in getting sufficiently large numbers together to make the provision of courses cost-effective. In stores where occasional further training courses were available, less than half of the part-time workers in the largest stores had attended them, since courses or training sessions frequently occurred outside the part-timers' normal work hours. The problem was overcome in some instances, where employers paid part-timers to attend for training at hours not in their contracted work schedules, an approach infeasible when part-timers' domestic and other commitments were rigid. The use of text-based open learning packages undoubtedly facilitated the provision of training to part-timers and put training on a systematic footing which allowed a uniform standard to be achieved across company branches. Yet only in companies which had introduced open learning as the principal means of training delivery was successful completion of training accompanied by some form of certification for full and part-time staff. Part-timers seemed to be largely excluded from product training whether employed in large or small stores, with 7 per cent of all retail part-timers included in the attitude survey reporting the availability of product training; even among specialist electrical retailers this proportion reached just 10 per cent. Actual evaluation of training for part-timers was seldom attempted. Few employers appeared certain about how to evaluate or monitor the results of training for part-timers; indeed, evidence that firms undertook specific quantification of training investment expenditure and associated cost benefit analyses was generally sparse [*The Study of Funding of Vocational Education and Training*, 1988: 7: 'one in five training employers evaluated the benefits of training, despite the fact that the criteria adopted were sometimes basic and easy to measure (e.g., qualification pass rates). Only 3% measured costs against benefits'].

Not surprisingly, the comparative disregard for the training needs of part-time employees was mirrored in their lack of career development and promotion prospects. While opportunities for promotion for sales assistants to supervisory grades in retail business tend to be low relative to the total of non-managerial sales staff employed, there was very little advancement for part-time workers, irrespective of individual merit or potential. Very few supervisors and even fewer junior managers worked part-time, and part-timers accepted that their chances of promotion were likely to be tied to changing to full-time work. Employers were inclined to emphasise perceived difficulties in promoting part-timers, stressing logistical and operational complications, particularly where part-timers would be involved in supervision of full-time staff. Moreover, they were generally able to fill vacancies for supervisory posts by full-time staff or part-timers prepared to switch to full-time hours, a policy little queried because of the widespread belief that part-timers were uninterested in assuming responsibilities linked with promotion; employee response to questions about promotion indicated, however, that a substantial proportion were interested in advancement, and many in the younger age groups felt that their capabilities were not being fully utilised.

In an analysis of the Failure of Training in Britain, it is claimed that training has been affected adversely by the long-term shift in British employment from manufacturing to low skill, low quality services: 'the largest growth in employment is in the part-time service sector where jobs typically require and offer little or no training'. None the less, it is acknowledged that while the type of goods or services which a company produces sets limits on the skills required, it does not determine the necessary level of training; it is noted for example that in the retail trade, 75 per cent of German employees have at least an apprenticeship qualification compared with just 2 per cent in the United Kingdom [Finegold and Soskice, 1988: 27–8]. Jarvis and Prais in their comparative study of training for retailing in Britain and France observe that questions have to be asked about how much training is really essential for most employees in the retail trades, 'which may require much common sense, but few technical skills'. Although in France as in Britain the majority of shop employees are without formal qualifications (one in 30 in Britain and one in four in France have acquired examined vocational qualifications), they suggest that the higher proportion in France sets the standard which helps the shop to be run in a more 'professional way' [NIESR, 1989]. More emphatically perhaps, in an inter-country OECD/CERI review of education and training implications of labour market developments associated with the application of advanced technologies in the service sector, it is concluded that as new technologies are rapidly penetrating into most activities in both service and manufacturing sectors, these imply on the whole an upskilling of the workers. At the same time, the need for training in the service sector is intensified by the emergence of 'a general concern to develop more client-oriented skills' [Bengtsson, 1988]. In similar vein the 1988 Training for Employment White Paper argues: 'even where jobs do not demand of workers a high level of technical skills, they will certainly require greater flexibility in approach, greater breadth of experience, and greater capacity to take responsibility' [Cm. 316].

The results of the examination of training practices with respect to part-time working in the distributive trades in Britain discussed in this article reinforce specifically such conclusions. They echo further the observations made in 1985 with respect to all industries that 'few employers think training sufficiently central to their business for it to be a main component in their corporate strategy' [Hillier, 1989], and confirm the need for 'new approaches to staff training and development as an important element in retailer development strategy' [Dawson in Johnson, 1987:237]. There are inevitably manifest differences in the ways enterprises develop their human resource strategies, but if retailers are to sustain the levels of labour productivity on which survival in a highly competitive environment so patently depends, decisive engagement in the 'national resurgence of training effort', and development of a training culture (involving also the industry's trade unions), are strategically imperative (Banham, 1988; Willis, 1988; Varlaam, 1989; European Agreement on Training in Retail, 1988).

REFERENCES

Alexander, N., 1988, 'Contemporary Perspectives in Retail Development', *The Service Industries Journal*, Volume 8, No 1.
Bamfield, J., 1988, 'Competition and Change in British Retailing', *National Westminster Bank Quarterly Review*, February.
Banham, J., 1989, 'Vocational Training in British Business', *National Westminster Bank Quarterly Review*, February.
Beechey, V. and T. Perkins, 1987, *A Matter of Hours: Women, Part-time Work and the Labour Market*, Cambridge: Polity.
Bengtsson, J., 1988, 'Human Resource Development in the Service Sector: The Need for More Research', *The Service Industries Journal*, Volume 8, No 2.

Blanchflower, D.G. and B.A. Corry, 1987, 'Part-time Employment in Great Britain: An Analysis using Establishment Data', *Research Paper No. 57, Dept of Employment*, London.
Brodie, I., 1986, 'Distributive Trades', in A.D. Smith (ed.), *Technological Trends and Employment, 5, Commercial Service Industries*, SPRU, Aldershot: Gower.
Changing Work Patterns, How Companies Achieve Flexibility to Meet New Needs, 1986, London: NEDO.
Davis, N., 1986, 'Training for Change', in P.E. Hart (ed.), *Unemployment and Labour Market Policies*, NIESR, Aldershot: Gower.
Employment for the 1990s, 1988, Cm 540, London.
Defusing the Demographic Time Bomb, 1989, NEDO/Training Agency, London.
Employment Perspectives and the Distributive Trades, 1985, London: NEDO.
European Agreement on Training in Retail, 1988, *EIRR* 1989, 181, February.
Finegold, D. and D. Soskice, 1988, 'The Failure of Training in Britain: Analysis and Prescription, *Oxford Review of Economic Policy*, Volume 4, No 3.
Hillier, R., 1989, Making Training a Key Factor in Business Performance, *Employment Gazette*, Volume 97, No 5.
Jarvis, V.J. and S.J. Prais, 1989, 'Two Nations of Shopkeepers: Training for Retailing in France and Britain', *National Institute Economic Review*, No. 128, 2/89, London: NIESR.
Labour Force Survey 1988, Preliminary Results, 1989, *Employment Gazette*, Volume 97, No. 4.
Martin J. and C. Roberts, 1984a, *Women and Employment: a Lifetime Perspective*, London: HMSO.
Part-time Working in the Distributive Trades, Training Practices and Career Opportunities, 1988, Volumes 1 and 2, London: NEDO.
Robinson, O., 1985, 'The Changing Labour Market: the Phenomenon of Part-time Employment', *National Westminster Bank Quarterly Review*, November.
Robinson, O., 1986, Employment Protection, National Insurance, Income Tax and Youth Unemployment, (P.E. Hart and C. Trinder), *Comment*, in P.E. Hart (ed.), *Unemployment and Labour Market Policies*, NIESR, Aldershot: Gower.
Robinson, O., 1988, 'The Changing Labour Market: Growth of part-time Employment and Labour Market Segmentation in Britain', in S. Walby (ed.), *Gender Segregation at Work*, Milton Keynes and Philadelphia: Open University Press.
Rubery, J., 1988, *Women and Recession*, London: Routledge & Kegan Paul
Sparks, L., 1987, 'Employment in Retailing: Trends and Issues', in G. Johnson (ed.), *Business Strategy and Retailing*, Chichester: Wiley.
The Study of Funding for Vocational Education and Training, Some Early Research Findings, 1988, Background Note No. 2, Sheffield: Training Commission.
Technology and Training in the Distributive Trades, 1987, London: NEDO.
Training for Employment, 1988, Cm 316, London: HMSO.
Varlaam, C., 1989, Training Needs of Trainers, *Employment Gazette*, Volume 97, No. 3.
Walsh, T., 1989, 'Part-Time Employment and Labour Market Policies', *National Westminster Bank Quarterly Review*, May.
Willis, N., 1989, 'A Worker's Right to Train', *National Westminster Bank Quarterly Review*, February.

This study first appeared in *The Service Industries Journal*, Vol.10, No.2 (1984).

6
Employment Patterns in Contemporary Retailing: Gender and Work in Five Supermarkets

ROGER PENN and BETTY WIRTH

This article examines trends in patterns of employment within contemporary retailing. It focuses upon five supermarkets in the Lancaster area. In each store the proportion of part-timers had increased during the 1980s and in four cases it stood at over 70 per cent in 1990. However, there were marked differences in the proportions of female full-time and part-time employees who were married. Management reported similar perceptions of the relative advantages and disadvantages of employing married women within their stores. These belief systems coexisted with radically divergent recruitment strategies by these managements. These variations were embedded within typical recruitment strategies in each of the firms examined.

INTRODUCTION

The purpose of this paper is to examine working patterns in contemporary retailing. Five supermarkets located in the Lancaster area form the basis of the analysis. All five supermarkets sell food, although four of them also sell other merchandise such as clothes and household articles. The data were collected by means of interviews at each of the stores. In addition, a questionnaire which dealt with issues of employment change was filled out by management at each supermarket.

Retailing has increasingly been seen as the archetypical 'flexible' sector of employment in Britain in the 1980s [Atkinson and Meager, 1985; Walsh, 1991]. Retailing itself employed over two million people in Britain throughout the period between 1981 and 1987, which represented almost 10 percent of the entire workforce.[1] In food retailing there has been an increasing concentration of ownership and an increasing proportion of sales through the five largest supermarket chains.[2] Retailing is also the most visible sector of contemporary employment. Everyone has a plethora of anecdotes, both favourable and unfavourable, about such retailers as Marks and Spencer, Tesco and Sainsbury's. Our research should be seen as contributing to an empirical assessment of such widespread imagery within the present conjuncture.

THE DEBATE ABOUT CHANGING PATTERNS OF WORK

There has been considerable debate about changing patterns of work over recent years. In particular, Atkinson and Meager [1985] have suggested that there is a generic trend towards increased flexibility of employment within contemporary organisations. Atkinson and Meager suggest that such flexibility takes a variety of forms. The first involves *numerical flexibility*, which signifies the capacity to adjust the number of workers or the level of hours worked in line with variations in the level of demand. This can include the employment of part-time, temporary and casual employees or the organisation of flexible shift patterns during the working day. This is complemented by *distancing*, which involves the use of contract labour to undertake what are seen as peripheral activities to the organisation. These include such features as contract cleaning and catering. The third form of flexibility involves *functional flexibility*, which signifies the ability to deploy workers over a broader range of tasks. Functional flexibility is often synonymous with 'dual-' or 'multi-skilling'. The final form of flexibility is *pay flexibility*, which includes both moves towards more individualised payment schemes and the realisation that functional flexibility often requires parallel modifications to salary structures.

Atkinson and Meager examined four sectors of employment in their research, one of which was retailing. The other three were engineering, financial services and the manufacture of food and drinks. In their report Atkinson and Meager found that almost all retailing firms had increased their use of part-time workers between 1980 and 1984. A major reason for this was the lengthening opening times of such firms. Rather than paying overtime to their existing full-time staff in order to cope with such longer hours, retailing organisations had increased their use of part-time employees. Such economies could be made relatively easily since, according to Atkinson and Meager, most jobs in retailing required very little training. Indeed, some retailing firms used nearly 80 per cent part-timers within their stores. Most part-time employees in retailing were female. The growth of part-time employment in retailing has been a major factor in the general growth of female part-time employment over the last 20 years [Elias, 1989]. In particular, retailing is a sector where married women have been traditionally employed in very large numbers [Joshi, 1989].

Atkinson and Meager provided the following detailed explanation for the growth of part-time employment in retailing. They argued that 'intensive competition and squeezed margins, particularly in the retail food multiples, have meant that there is a strong need to match manning levels during the day and during the week to fluctuations in customer demand' (p.25). Retailers also mentioned the lower costs of part-timers, both in terms of lower hourly rates of pay and reduced employer contributions to national insurance. Two supermarket chains were cited as examples by Atkinson and Meager of how working patterns had become more flexible during the 1980s. 'ABC Foodstuffs' had increased the numbers of part-timers to match the peaks and troughs of customer demand. 'Everopen Ltd' had increased the proportion of part-time staff to 70 per cent since 1980.

Curson [1986] has also emphasized the growth of part-time and temporary employment during the 1980s. He revealed that in 1951 only 2.7 per cent of the workforce were employed for 30 hours or less per week. By 1986 this had climbed to over 20 per cent of the workforce. Indeed, 46.5 per cent of all female workers were part-timers by the mid-1980s. Curson argued that part-timers had replaced full-timers to a larger degree in retailing than within any other sector of employment because staffing constituted such a very high proportion of overall costs. The hourly cost of a part-time employee within retailing stood at around 12 per cent less than the equivalent for a full-timer. Such views have received additional support from Meager's report on Temporary Work [1985], from Hakim's [1987] research at the Department of Employment and from Elger's [1987] article which suggested that numerical flexibility, and particularly the increasing use of part-time labour, were general features of retailing in Britain, whereas functional flexibility was more typical in manufacturing industry.

There is widespread agreement, therefore, amongst researchers that part-time employment is increasing in Britain. This growth is seen to be concentrated within specific sub-sectors of service industries. Retailing is seen as the major, and often the archetypical, example of these developments [National Economic Development Office, 1988a and 1988b]. Most of the increase in such part-time employment affects women, many of whom are married with dependent children [Beechey and Perkins, 1987; Robinson, 1988]. Such a strategy of employment is a 'rational' response by retailers to increasing competition, longer opening hours, fluctuations in demand, high overall staffing costs and the relative cheapness of part-time employees. Women, and particularly married women with children, are seen as the main source of such a flexible workforce in retailing [Martin and Roberts, 1984]. This image of employment patterns in retailing is very powerful and is reinforced every time social scientists go shopping. There is certainly strong *prima facie* evidence for the view that food supermarkets employ a high proportion of female, married, part-time employees.

Pollert [1988], however, has argued a counter case. She cites evidence from Casey [1987] which showed that there had been an 'absence of significant change' in the use of temporary work between 1983 and 1985. Pollert also cautioned against exaggerating the growth of part-time employment in the 1980s. She reported that within the service sector, as a whole, the rise in part-time employment between 1979 and 1984 had only been from 40 per cent to 42 per cent. Likewise, the rise in part-time employment in retailing had only been from 34 per cent to 36 per cent over the same period. She criticised Atkinson and Meager for over-generalising from their own small sample of retailing firms. However, as is clear from Table 1, part-time employment *had* increased significantly in retailing during the 1980s, particularly amongst women.[3] Interestingly, from this longer time perspective than the one adopted by Pollert, the growth of female part-time employment has been accompanied by a parallel growth of full-time female employment in retailing.

TABLE 1

EMPLOYMENT IN RETAILING IN GREAT BRITAIN, 1981–1990
(THOUSANDS)

	1981	1984	1987	1990	% Change 1981–90
Male Full-time	637	641	642	676	+ 6.1
Male Part-time	131	117	135	140	+ 6.9
Female Full-time	582	544	546	640	+10.0
Female Part-time	698	722	745	800	+14.6
Total	**2049**	**2024**	**2068**	**2256**	+10.1

Source: Census of Employment

THE SAMPLE

The sample included five supermarkets that retail food in the Lancaster area. The firms selected were Asda, J. Sainsbury, Marks and Spencer, Littlewoods and E. H. Booth. The latter is a locally-based food supermarket chain, whilst the other four are well-known national organisations. These stores are the five largest outlets for food retailing in the Lancaster area. Whilst the sample is relatively small and is based in one locality, it does have the advantage that the central features of the labour market and the basic contours of labour supply can all be held constant.[4] The other advantage of such a research design is that we can situate each of the stores contextually within our analysis. We therefore provide a discussion of each supermarket separately prior to our general discussion of the results.

THE QUESTIONNAIRE

Our questionnaire was designed to examine various aspects of changing working patterns in the retail sector between 1980 and 1990. We sought data on the numbers of male and female full-time and part-time employees in 1980 and 1990. We also inquired about the use of sub-contractors within the store and the use of casual workers. We inquired about the proportion of married women within the workforce and the relative advantages or disadvantages of employing such staff. We asked for details of full-time and part-time hours of work and the relative advantages or disadvantages of utilising full-time and part-time employees. The data were collected by means of interviews at each of the stores with personnel managers.

Sainsbury's

This firm had come to Lancaster in 1985 as part of its national strategy of 'moving north' from its historic roots in the southern half of England. The store employed 80 full-time staff (40 men and 40 women) and 90 part-time staff (15 men and 75 women) when it opened initially. A small number of its early staff had been brought to Lancaster temporarily from other localities in the North West. By the time of our survey the store had increased its full-time staff to 50 men and 50 women. However, there had been a greater increase in the number of part-time employees to 22 men and 118 women.

Flexibility in the workforce was well-organised and streamlined. Managers worked three different weekly rotas (6.00 a.m. to 2.00 p.m., 8.00 a.m. to 5.00 p.m. and 1.00 p.m. to 9.00 p.m.) and were required to work on three Saturdays out of four. Full-time staff worked 39 hours per week and were employed on an alternating weekly rota of Monday to Friday followed by Tuesday to Saturday.

The part-time staff worked various shift patterns and their hours varied considerably. The 'day' part-timers were on four rotas (8.15 a.m. to 6.15 p.m., 8.15 a.m. to 1.30 p.m., 12.30 p.m. to 6.15 p.m. and 12.30 p.m. to 8.30 p.m.). The staff who worked the 8.15 a.m. to 6.15 p.m. and

12.30 p.m. to 8.30 p.m. shifts only worked odd days, usually two or three a week, which were organised to suit staff and store. Another set of part-timers were employed for three nights per week from 5.30 p.m. to 8.30 p.m. Students were also employed on such a 'late' shift for one night a week and also on Saturdays from either 8.45 a.m. to 6.45 p.m. or 12 noon to 8.00 p.m. There was also an evening shift from 7.00 p.m. to 11.00 p.m. which also employed part-timers for a maximum of three days a week.

Clearly, Sainsbury's in Lancaster had a very complex set of hours for both their full-time and part-time employees. Sainsbury's found that part-timers were often available at short notice for extra overtime working. However, they were also subject to relatively high turnover. Full-time employees, on the other hand, were more stable and had a lower turnover but they were often unavailable for overtime (or if they were, it was far more costly than the overtime rates paid to part-timers).

Forty-six per cent of the female workforce were married. However, 75 per cent of the part-time female employees were married. There was no explicit policy connecting marital status and hours of work. The Personnel Manager reported that married men were allowed to take time off for family problems on an equal basis with married women. Sainsbury's also utilised what they termed 'multi-skilling'. This meant in practice that all staff were expected not just to be cashiers or shelf-fillers but to take a hand with other tasks where necessary. Indeed, it is a relatively common sight to see managers at the store filling shelves during peak periods of demand. Sainsbury's also employed sub-contractors for cleaning the store.

There had been two significant changes in working patterns during the five years since the store had opened. Firstly, there had been a change in management structure, termed 'Management for the 90s'. This occurred in 1988 and involved the introduction of the three-week rota system for this group. Also at that time higher supervisory staff were promoted to junior management positions. The second important change (in 1987) was the introduction of late-night working for full-time staff: the 12.30 p.m. to 8.30 p.m. shift. This occurred because Sainsbury's extended late-night opening hours to include Monday, Tuesday and Saturday. Previously there were only three late nights (Wednesday, Thursday and Friday).

Marks and Spencer

Marks and Spencer opened in Lancaster in 1935. No records of employment in 1980 were available. At the time of the survey they employed 36 full-timers (seven males and 29 females) and 71 part-timers (eight males and 63 females). Casual workers were hired on Saturdays. These numbered 17 and were overwhelmingly female. The store employed around six temporary staff over the Christmas and Easter periods. Ninety per cent of full-time female staff were married as were 83 per cent of part-time female employees. The Personnel Officer reported that married women were more settled in their home-life and gave a greater commitment to their jobs. However, in the main, they were not seen as career-minded since they tended to view their husbands' jobs as more important. The main disadvantage of hiring married women was the effect on work commitment of having children.

Patterns of hours varied considerably within the store. Full-time staff worked between 8.50 a.m. and 5.40 p.m. Part-timers were employed on four different shifts (7.30 a.m. to 9.30 a.m., 12 noon to 2.00 p.m., 12 noon to 5.30 p.m. and 8.00 a.m. to 5.30 p.m.). The latter shift was only worked for one or two days per week. The main change in hours at Marks and Spencer during the 1980s had been the introduction of late nights over the Christmas period and Bank Holiday working. Marks and Spencer employed no sub-contractors.

E. H. Booth

This firm has been a local retailer of food for some time. The Lancaster store was opened in 1982. At that time the workforce numbered 18 male and 20 female full-time staff and 12 male and 30 female part-time workers. All the male part-timers were students as were 10 of the females. This partly reflected the proximity of the store to the University.[5]

This pattern of employment had changed significantly during the 1980s. Part-timers were a far larger percentage of the workforce by 1990. The store only employed 10 male and 10 female full-timers. There had also been a reduction of male part-time employees to 10. All of these were students. However, the number of female part-timers had increased to 55 (15 of whom were students). Booths also utilised subcontractors extensively. They used a firm of cleaning contractors, two waste disposal contractors and a number of electrical/freezer contractors. The firm reported that it employed casual workers. All the part-time student employees were employed on a casual basis.

Married women occupied a high proportion of the female staff. Forty per cent of full-timers and 80 per cent of part-timers were married. These proportions of married women had increased during the 1980s. The main factor in this growth was the firm's increasing reliance on part-time workers. Management reported that young, unmarried females were 'not interested in part-time jobs'. A number of advantages were mentioned regarding the employment of married women. Management stressed the greater reliability, stability and loyalty of this group. On the other hand, the stated disadvantages were that a greater proportion of such women would leave employment to have babies and that there was a greater likelihood of them being absent as a result of illness amongst their children.

Many advantages were put forward for employing part-time workers. These included savings on wages and a lower likelihood of lethargy, particularly towards the end of the week. The disadvantages included the perception that they were less loyal to the firm. E. H. Booth denied that they had any strict pattern of hours of work. They informed us that it was 'more a mosaic of hours that had been fitted in over a number of years'. They did not operate a flexi-system of hours and admitted that they coped with peaks of shoppers 'with difficulty'. At such times they would attempt to call in part-time staff on an *ad hoc* basis. If they were under extreme pressure they would call back full-timers for evening hours and even for Sunday work. Many of the staff were reported as willing to work extra hours during periods of pressure and to be called in at short notice. The most significant change in working patterns during the 1980s was the increased use of part-time employees, particularly involving the employment of younger workers. Overall, however, there seemed little consideration at this firm of strategic planning of labour inputs. Management relied on *ad hoc* arrangements at peak times that were set up at very short notice. Whilst employment patterns at E. H. Booth looked similar in form to those at Asda and Sainsbury, they were not based upon any coherent managerial strategy of *planned* labour flexibility. Rather, management was engaged in a poorly coordinated series of reactive decisions.

Asda

The Asda supermarket is the largest in the Lancaster area and opened on a green-field site in 1982. Asda employed 428 in that year, of whom 60 were full-time female and 290 part-time female employees. They also employed 48 full-time males and 30 part-time males in 1982. By 1990 employment had fallen overall to 390. Asda employed 41 males and 45 females full-time and 24 males and 280 females part-time. A contract cleaning firm was also used to clean the windows, walls and offices. Forty per cent of the full-time and 80 per cent of part-time female staff were married. The proportion of married female labour had not changed during the 1980s. They did not utilize casual labour.

Asda had a very complex set of shift systems in operation. These included three-hour rotas throughout the day, three-hour evening shifts, six-hour rotas over five days, four-hour rotas and one-day rotas for part-time employees. Full-timers were on five-day rotas for eight-hour shifts. The days themselves varied from week to week.

This supermarket practised considerable functional flexibility. At peaks of shopping, staff are moved from one area to another fairly rapidly to deal with queues and bottlenecks. The main change in working practices had been the advent of longer opening hours. The store was now open between 8.30 a.m. and 8.00 p.m. for six days a week.

Management reported that flexibility of hours was the main advantage of employing married women and that absence due to children's illnesses was the main disadvantage. The saving on National Insurance contributions and fewer meal or tea-breaks were the main advantageous reasons given for utilising part-time staff. However, part-timers were seen as low on commitment to their job. Full-timers were seen as giving more loyalty and continuity but as costing more in National Insurance contributions.

Littlewoods

Littlewoods first came to Lancaster in 1957. In 1980 the workforce consisted of 6 full-time males and 18 full-time females. There were 50 part-timers, all of whom were female and 27 of whom only worked on Saturdays. There had been a general pruning of staff during the 1980s. The store employed three males and 15 females full-time and three males and 43 females part-time (two male and 25 female part-timers worked only on Saturdays). In addition the store hired two sub-contractors as cleaners for six days a week between 6.00 a.m. and 9.00 a.m. Littlewoods reported that 'the store is run by Saturday (i.e. part-time) staff on Saturdays'.

The proportion of female full-time staff who were married was 17.1 per cent and the proportion of married female part-timers was 15.6 per cent. This was due to a clear managerial policy of employing younger women, most of whom were single. Management reported that the main advantage of employing married women was their availability to work part-time hours that could cover full-timers' lunch breaks. The main disadvantage was perceived to be the priority given by such women to their families and children. Clearly, Littlewoods and Marks and Spencer had radically different recruitment policies in relation to married women.

There were complex patterns of hours worked in the store. Part-time staff worked on five different rotas between 6.00 a.m. and 5.30 p.m. They included 6.00 a.m. to 1.30 p.m., 7.30 a.m. to 12.30 p.m., 9.30 a.m. to 1.30 p.m., 11.30 a.m. to 2.30 p.m. and 1.30 p.m. to 5.30 p.m. Full-time staff worked standard opening hours between Monday and Friday (8.45

TABLE 2

CHANGING PATTERNS OF EMPLOYMENT IN FIVE SUPERMARKETS

	Sainsbury's	E. H. Booth	Asda	Littlewoods	Marks & Spencer
Size of Workforce, 1980–90	Increased +41.2% (170–240: 1985–90)	Increased +6.3% (80–85: 1982–90)	Decreased −8.9% (428–390: 1982–90)	Decreased −13.5% (74–64: 1980–90)	Not known (124 in 1990)
Proportion of Part-Timers, 1980–90	Increased (52.9% – 58.3%: 1985–90)	Increased (52.5% – 75.5%: 1982–90)	Increased (74.8% – 77.9%: 1982–90)	Increased (67.6% – 71.9%: 1980–90)	Not known (71.0% in 1990)
Proportion of Women 1980–90	Increased (67.6% – 70.0%: 1985–90)	Increased (62.5% – 76.5%: 1982–90)	Increased (81.8% – 83.3%: 1982–90)	Decreased (91.9% – 90.6%: 1980–90)	Not known (86.0% in 1990)
% of Married Female Full-time 1990	46%	40%	40%	17.1%	90%
% of Married Female Part-time 1990	75%	80%	80%	15.6%	83%
Proportion of Married Women 1980–90	Constant	Increased	Constant	Constant	Constant
Sub-Contractors	✓		✓	✓	✗
Casual Workers	✓	✓	✗	✓	✓

a.m. to 5.45 p.m.). Peaks in shopping, particularly at lunch-times, were dealt with by the use of part-timers, particularly those employed on the 11.30 a.m. to 2.30 p.m. shift.

Since 1988, all new staff employed at Littlewoods had been given a 'flexible' contract. This meant that the store could change hours of work to suit the needs of the business. The firm was required to give 2 weeks prior notification of such changes.

FINDINGS

As is clear from Table 2, which summarises our results, employment in the five supermarkets had increased overall during the 1980s. Sainsbury's, Asda and E. H. Booth had all opened new supermarkets in the Lancaster area during this period. However, these new stores have to be balanced against the closure of the Coop and Fine Fare stores in Lancaster in the early 1980s. Nevertheless, employment at Littlewoods and at Asda had fallen during the 1980s. Such a downward pressure on employment was consistent with both firms' difficulties in the latter part of the 1980s.

The proportion of part-timers had increased in the four stores where information was supplied. In these four cases the employment of part-timers stood at over 70 per cent by 1990. Most employees in these stores, therefore, were indeed part-timers. Such results confirmed the picture painted in general terms by Atkinson and Meager and refuted Pollert's notion that the 1980s had not witnessed a significant increase of part-time employment in retailing.

A very high proportion of employees were women. *In all five stores the proportion of female employees stood at over 70 per cent in 1990.* At Littlewoods and Marks and Spencer it stood at over 85 per cent. However, *there were marked differences in the proportions of female full-time and part-time employees who were married.* At four stores the percentage of female part-time staff who were married stood above 75 per cent. However, Littlewoods had a distinctive managerial policy of excluding married women and of selecting overwhelmingly single, predominantly younger women for employment. Marks and Spencer, on the other hand, clearly preferred married women. Their employees, *whether full-time or part-time*, were overwhelmingly married women. At Sainsbury's, Asda and E. H. Booth the pattern was one of high proportions of married, female part-timers but of far lower percentages of married female full-timers. Each of these stores had been opened during the 1980s and each had evolved broadly similar patterns of employment for both married and non-married women.

TABLE 3

REASONS GIVEN BY MANAGEMENT CONCERNING THE ADVANTAGES AND DISADVANTAGES OF EMPLOYING VARIOUS CATEGORIES OF WORKERS

	Sainsbury's	Marks and Spencer	E. H. Booth	Asda	Littlewoods
Employment of Married Women					
Advantages	Flexibility – cover for different schedules. Commitment.	Greater commitment.	Greater reliability. Greater loyalty.	Flexibility of work.	Available to work part-time. Give the store better coverage over lunch-time when full-timers must take breaks
Disadvantages	None.	Not Career-minded. Children inhibit flexibility.	Greater likelihood of being absent due to children. Greater proportion leaving to have children.	Absence due to children's illness.	Their children and families come first.
Employment of Part-Timers					
Advantages	Availability for overtime.	Greater flexibility of hours.	Costs. Effort. Flexibility	No National Insurance contributions.	Flexibility.
Disadvantages	Higher labour turnover	Higher labour turnover.	Less loyal.	Not enough continuity or commitment	They tend just to work for the money.
Employment of Full-Timers					
Advantages	More stable. Turnover lower.	Continuity of employment.	Greater loyalty.	Loyalty. Motivation. Continuity.	Pride in the jobs. They know all the work routines.
Disadvantages	Not available for overtime. Overtime expensive	Lack of flexibility.	Cost of wages.	National Insurance contributions. Absence causes more problems.	They need breaks for lunch, which necessitates extra coverage on the floor.

We conclude that *all supermarkets in Lancaster employ high propor-tions of female and part-time workers, but that this universal tendency co-exists with widely divergent managerial strategies in relation to the kinds of women recruited to fill these jobs.* We also conclude that such differences were relatively longstanding features of the management of these companies. In all cases, other than E. H. Booth, management re-ported that there had been no change in the proportions of married women employed by their firms in Lancaster during the 1980s. Whilst the formal structure of employment in retailing had indeed changed during the 1980s with the continued growth of female and part-time employment, the social bases of recruitment of women to these jobs had not changed significantly in each of the firms examined.

The picture of flexible employment suggested by Atkinson and Meager was also confirmed in relation to the employment of sub-contractors and casual workers. Most firms used sub-contractors for cleaning, although Marks and Spencer relied on their own domestic workforce for this. Casual workers were also employed at four stores, although in all cases this amounted to a small proportion of total employment. *Part-time rather than casual employment is the dominant form of flexible employment in these stores.* However, our data also re-veal that whilst part-time employment had indeed increased during the 1980s, *part-timers are by no means a new group within such firms.* There has been a longstanding tradition of such part-time employment in these firms dating well back into the 1960s and 1970s. The 1980s had witnessed a continued growth of part-time employment in such retailing estab-lishments rather than any dramatic structural transformation.

The reasons provided for the employment of married women and of part-timers were interesting (see Table 3). Four of the five stores emphasised the significance of children for married women's capacity to work continuously. Marks and Spencer and E. H. Booth stressed the greater commitment of married women, whereas Asda, Sainsbury's and Littlewoods emphasised their greater flexibility, particularly in relation to part-time, non-standard hours of employment. All firms saw the main disadvantages of employing part-timers as their lack of commitment and the ensuing problems of high labour turnover. On the other hand, four of the stores highlighted the flexibility of part-timers.

Clearly, there was a general managerial perception of the relative pros and cons of employing full-time and part-time employees in re-tailing. There was also a very similar image of married women. They were seen as far more reliable and flexible but as putting their families, particularly their children, first. Management also had a stereotypical view of married women as having young children and spouses in career-dominated forms of employment. Interestingly, *the same system of beliefs co-existed with the radically divergent managerial recruitment strategies at Marks and Spencer and Littlewoods*. Indeed, on the basis of these data we conclude that the precise social effects of the growth of female part-time employment in retailing during the 1980s were *more complex* than most commentators have suggested and that *managerial recruitment systems are far more company-specific than many had imagined*.

NOTES

1. Employment in retailing stood at 9.6 per cent in 1981, 9.7 per cent in 1984, 9.7 per cent in 1987 and 9.8 per cent in 1990: data from the triennial Censuses of Employment.
2. See G. Akehurst [1983], 'Concentration in Retail Distribution', and L. Sparks [1987], 'Employment in Retailing: Trends and Issues'. Also see L. Wood, 'Five Largest Supermarkets have 50% of Grocery Sales', *Financial Times*, 27 Oct. 1987; and the 'Financial Times Survery of UK Retailing', *Financial Times*, 19 Sept. 1988.
3. The 1988 NEDO Reports on *Part-time Working in the Distributive Trades* show that the proportion of check-out operators working less than 16 hours more than doubled between 1977 and 1987 [see O. Robinson, 1990].
4. For an illuminating analysis of the Lancaster labour market, see P. Bagguley *et al.* [1990].
5. V. Gayle [1990] has shown that retailing was the second most frequent form of paid part-time employment amongst Lancaster undergraduates after catering. Around 10 per cent of his sample had been employed in retailing part-time whilst studying.

REFERENCES

Akehurst, G. P., 1983, 'Concentration in Retail Distribution: Measurement and Significance', *Service Industries Journal*, Vol. 3, No. 2, pp. 161–79.
Atkinson, J. and N. Meager, 1986, *Changing Working Patterns: How Companies Achieve Flexibility to Meet New Needs*, London: National Economic Development Office.
Bagguley, P., J. Mark-Lawson, J. Shapiro, J. Urry, S. Walby and A. Warde, 1990, *Restructuring: Place, Class and Gender*, London: Sage.
Beechey, V. and T. Perkins, 1987, *A Matter of Hours: Women, Part-time Work and the Labour Market*, Cambridge: Polity.
Casey, B., 1987, 'The Extent and Nature of Temporary Employment in Great Britain', *Policy Studies*, Vol. 8, No. 1, July, pp. 64–75.
Curson, C., 1986, *Flexible Patterns of Work*, London: Institute for Personnel Management.
Elger, T., 1987, 'Flexible Futures? New Technology and the Contemporary Transformation of Work', *Work, Employment and Society*, Vol. 1, No. 4, pp. 528–40.
Elias, P., 1989, 'A Study of Trends in Part-time Employment, 1971–86', *Institute for Employment Research*, Warwick University, February.
Gayle, V., 1990, 'University Students' Participation in the Flexible Workforce', Department of Sociology, Lancaster University (mimeo), February.
Hakim, C., 1987, 'Trends in the Flexible Workforce', *Employment Gazette*, November, pp. 549–60.
Joshi, H. (ed.), 1989, *The Changing Population of Britain*, Oxford: Basil Blackwell.

Martin, J. and C. Roberts, 1984, *Women and Employment: A Lifetime Perspective*, London: HMSO.

Meager, N., 1985, *Temporary Work in Britain: Its Growth and Changing Rationales*, Brighton: Institute of Manpower Studies.

National Economic Development Office, 1988a, *Part-time Working in the Distributive Trades: Training Practices and Career Opportunities*, London.

Robinson, O., 1988, 'The Changing Labour Market: Growth of Part-time Employment and Labour Market Segmentation in Britain', in S. Walby (ed.), *Gender Segregation at Work*, Milton Keynes: Open University Press.

Robinson, O., 1990, 'Employment Policies in the Service Sector: Training in Retail Distribution', *Service Industries Journal*, Vol. 10, No. 2, pp. 284–305.

Sparks, L., 1987, 'Employment in Retailing: Trends and Issues', in G. Johnson (ed.), *Business Strategy and Retailing*, Chichester: John Wiley, pp. 239–55.

Pollert, A., 1988, 'The "Flexible Firm": Fixation or Fact?', *Work, Employment and Society*, Vol. 2, No. 3, pp. 281–316.

Walsh, T., 1991, '"Flexible" Employment in the Retail and Hotel Trades', in A. Pollert (ed.), *Farewell to Flexibility?*, Oxford: Basil Blackwell, pp. 104–15.

This study first appeared in *The Service Industries Journal*, Vol.13, No.4 (1993).

7

Developments in the Superstore Labour Market

PAUL FREATHY

This article applies labour segmentation theory to the labour market in superstores. Whilst there are limitations over the applicability of this theory, broad divisions between primary and secondary sector employment conditions may be recognised. Moreover, the labour supply reveals a distinct gender bias with women being used primarily as sales assistants and males occupying managerial positions.

The employment implications of superstore retailing has attracted considerable academic attention [Sparks 1982; 1985; 1991; Dawson *et al.*, 1986; 1988]. This article aims to contribute to this process by empirically examining the structure of superstore employment relations within a local labour market. In so doing, it aims to provide a theoretical framework through the application of labour segmentation theory to the retail sector. By taking one geographical labour market, the research represents a limited study of employment change within the superstore sector. The article is divided into five sections. The first section puts forward a theoretical framework within which superstore employment may be understood. The second provides the context for the empirical section through a broad overview of contemporary developments within the retail sector. This puts forward a framework in which to view employment change. The third section explains the methodology used, whilst the fourth provides the empirical investigation of the superstore labour market. The final section draws out a series of conclusions concerning the applicability of segmentation theory to an understanding of the superstore labour market.

UNDERSTANDING LABOUR MARKETS

Labour segmentation theory developed as a reaction to the neo-classical treatment of human capital theory. The relative merits and weaknesses of each approach have been presented elsewhere [Morrison, 1990; Peck, 1989; Hunter and Mulvey, 1981; Becker, 1964]. What is provided here is an overview of the major theoretical components of contemporary segmentation theory. This first section is not intended to break new boundaries, rather its objective, is to provide a basic understanding of the key concepts applicable to labour market segmentation which can then be applied to the superstore sector.

The starting point for a review of the literature is the concept of the internal labour market. Based upon the work of Slichter [1950], Lester [1952] and Kerr [1954], internal labour markets were seen as methods of sheltering specific groups of workers from the open market. Entry into the internal market is defined by the organisation and, once achieved, the pricing and allocation of labour is not affected by the market but is governed through a series of institutional rules and procedures. The internal market is distinguished from the external when labour is no longer controlled by economic variables.

Access into an internal labour market is through a 'port of entry'. Entry at a specific port provides access to higher positions through an internal promotion system. Piore [1975] argued that the existence of a defined career structure for individuals provide benefits for both employer and employee. Internal labour markets give employers greater flexibility. Employees acquire a range of specific company skills which makes it difficult for them to transfer to comparable positions elsewhere. Once a worker has begun to move up the career ladder, switching to another firm becomes less attractive as they may be relegated to a lower port of entry. The internal labour market therefore places a voluntary tie upon the individual by making it unattractive to leave the firm. The practice of restricting entry in this way also allows firms to use their internal markets as screening devices against opportunistic labour, those workers who were hired in error can either be dismissed or the firm can minimise its losses by halting the progression of an individual on the career ladder [Williamson, 1975; Wachter, 1974].

The notion that specific groups of workers were governed by institutional rather than economic rules was expanded upon by Doeringer and Piore [1971] who maintained that a duality existed within the labour market between different groups of workers. The most basic distinction was between the primary and secondary elements of the labour market. Individuals working under primary conditions received high wages, secure employment and related benefits. Turnover was consequently low. In contrast, the secondary sector was characterised as comprising low status, poorly paid jobs that experienced high employee turnover. Such conditions were not attached exclusively to any single industry or organisation, and it remained possible to identify both sectors and firms that operated a combination of both secondary and primary employment conditions.

This basic dichotomy was expanded upon by Piore [1975] who maintained that the primary sector itself could be segmented between upper and lower tiers of employment. The upper tier is typically composed of those in managerial work or qualified professions; it is distinguished from the lower tier by higher pay, status and promotion opportunities. Upper tier posts are also distinguished from the lower tier by the absence of elaborate sets of work rules and formal administrative procedures. Job demands for primary, lower tier workers place emphasis upon stability and routine. While the conditions of employment are relatively secure, the work itself is often repetitious, rule bound and lacking in interest. Unlike the upper sector, formal educational qualifications are not a fundamental prerequisite for lower tier employment, with performance and experience contributing to career opportunity.

As with the primary sector, the secondary sector is also structured into tiers. Employment is both hierarchical and segmented, with jobs differing in both quality and quantity. A degree of differentiation therefore exists within the secondary sector. The terms and conditions attached to the job will be dependent upon a variety of internal and external influences including the availability of labour, the strength of the overall economy and the nature of the organisation itself. What is of importance in this context is the dynamic nature in which labour markets operate. The terms and conditions that surround employment categories are not fixed and change as market conditions change. Thus in periods of labour shortage employers may increase the attractiveness of the package they offer to employees [Pyke, 1986; 1988].

Michon [1987] maintains that the existence of a secondary labour market provides employers with a series of material benefits. Its main advantage is in allowing managers to respond flexibly to changing economic circumstances. Employees in the secondary sector may be hired by the hour, day, week or month. A variety of different employment contracts exist to provide the employer with the maximum level of flexibility. For example, in the retail sector part-time employees have been successfully used to cover trading peaks. Paid by the hour, they undertake part-time shifts to cover periods of peak customer flow.

In addition to providing a degree of flexibility, secondary sector employment can provide significant savings on labour costs. In many instances secondary employment is part-time. Because of the lack of hours worked, part-time employees are often ineligible for sickness, maternity or holiday benefits. Their attractiveness as a low cost, flexible labour force is reinforced with their easy substitution. While economic conditions may regulate the overall demand for labour, the low level of skills typically required for secondary employment allows their easy replacement.

In addition to its hierarchical and segmented nature, the labour market displays a distinct social composition. Women workers are disproportionately represented in the secondary sector. A number of studies have attempted to identify the factors behind this allocation process [Labour Studies Group, 1985; Wilkinson, 1981]. Such research has revealed the enormous complexity behind labour market allocation. Traditional theoretical analysis viewed the allocation of labour as a wholly demand side process. Employers had control over both the quality and the type of labour they employed. Rubery [1978], however, maintained that while demand side factors played a prominent role in the allocation of labour, supply side influences are also integral to understanding labour market structure. This is not to argue that the relationship between the supply of, and demand for, labour is symmetrical. Typically, the demanders of labour have greater control over the market. The relationship is therefore best viewed as an asymmetrical one that is reliant upon a degree of interdependence for its operation [Peck, 1989]. For example, demand side issues, such as the operation of collective pay agreements and union negotiations, can play an important role in structuring the labour market. In addition, however, supply side influences, such as responsibility for social domestic arrangements, means that part-time employment often lends itself more favourably to female employment [Dex, 1988].

Whilst differentiation based on gender remains the most obvious social segregator, other divides within the labour market include both race and age. Forms of segmentation are therefore not mutually exclusive but mutually reinforcing. Furlong [1990], for example, notes how traits such as physical stamina or family responsibility may also be used to determine an individual's suitability for employment.

The labour market may therefore be viewed as being both hierarchical and segmented. However, its structure is not static and may be viewed as a dynamic operation. The conditions attached to particular jobs vary over time, as will the nature of the job itself. No single influence is responsible for such change, with both supply and demand side factors structuring the operation of the labour market [Rubery, 1978; Peck, 1988; Risley, 1989]. This can now be explored in the retail sector.

CONTEMPORARY DEVELOPMENTS IN THE RETAIL SECTOR

Prior to an empirical investigation of how employment relations are structured within Manchester superstores, it is helpful to review the major developments that have occurred within the retail sector. Changes in the labour process and in the labour composition have not happened in isolation from other retail developments. This section provides the context for understanding the process of labour market allocation.

The 1980s represented a period of growth for a number of retail sectors, such as food and DIY. This is in contrast to other sectors, manufacturing for instance, where the 1980s became a period of stagnation and decline [Fothergill *et al.*, 1986; Rowthorn, 1986].

Underlying this growth has been an increasing concentration of market power amongst a small number of multiple outlet retailers. The CIG [1991] estimate that the 10 largest retailers in the United Kingdom account for nearly 30 per cent of total retail turnover. The top 500 firms (0.2 per cent of total) account for between 60 and 65 per cent. Evidence indicates that this increasing concentration will continue to accelerate throughout the decade [Davies and Sparks, 1989]. The market domination of the large multiples has been most strongly evidenced in the grocery sector. Figure 1 illustrates how food retailing is dominated by six organisations. The retailers who have been most affected by this increasing domination have been the medium size retailers and supermarket chains. Sparks [1987] argues that the small independent trader has been relatively less affected by this market concentration. Customers continue to use such outlets for convenience and 'top up' shopping.

Accompanying the growth of the large multiple retailers has been a transformation in the retail shopping environment. Superstores have experienced incremental growth over the past 20 years, however their penetration into the United Kingdom has accelerated since the beginning of the 1980s [IRS, 1989; McGoldrick, 1990].[1] Retailing has therefore experienced a transformation in its competitive environment. A polarisation has developed within the sector between the large multiples and a proliferation of the small independent outlets.

EMPLOYMENT IN SUPERSTORES: RESEARCH TO DATE

The transformation that has occurred within the retail sector has brought about significant changes in the nature of retail employment. This is most clearly evidenced in the superstores sector. Of the 2.2

million persons employed within retailing over 380,000 are directly employed by superstores [CSO, 1990; IGD, 1990]. A food superstore may employ between 150 and 350 persons. Non-food superstores are less labour-intensive, employing on average 46 employees per store [Sparks, 1991]. The growth of superstores has therefore had a significant impact upon employment in the local economy. The growth of the superstore trading format has led to a restructuring of both the labour composition and the labour process within the retail sector.

Women have traditionally been employed within the retail sector with their participation in the labour market increasing since the First World War. Although the rise has not been steady, there has been a phase of female employment expansion since the early 1970s [Sparks, 1982]. In superstores this trend has been particularly marked. Currently it is estimated that over 70 per cent of total superstore employment is female [Dawson et al., 1987; Booz et al., 1990].

Accompanying the growth of female employment in superstores has been the increased use of part-time labour. The increased emphasis upon cost reduction and the extension of opening hours in superstore trading has rendered the traditional five-day employment contract increasingly redundant. The fluctuation of demand throughout the working day and week requires retailers to maintain a high degree of flexibility in order to manage the large variations in customer flow. A distinction exists between the labour composition of food and non-food superstores. Sparks [1991] provides an employment breakdown between food and DIY superstores (Table 1).

FIGURE 1

MARKET SHARE OF SIX LARGEST GROCERY MULTIPLES 1989

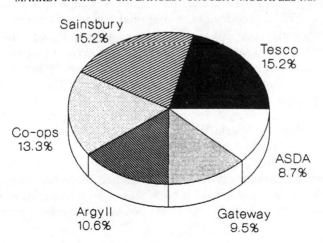

Sainsbury
15.2%

Tesco
15.2%

Co-ops
13.3%

ASDA
8.7%

Argyll
10.6%

Gateway
9.5%

SOURCE: CIG 1991

TABLE 1

EMPLOYMENT IN FOOD AND DIY SUPERSTORES: MEAN NUMBER OF EMPLOYEES
PER STORE BY GENDER AND HOURS WORKED

	Food Superstores	DIY Superstores
Average total employees	285	46
Average FTE	195	34
Full-time	108	23
Part-time	170	20
Casual	7	3
Male	80	21
Female	204	25
Male		
Full-time	52	14
Part-time	27	6
Casual	2	1
Female		
Full-time	56	9
Part-time	143	14
Casual	5	2

Source: Sparks 1991.

The overwhelming majority of part-time positions within food super-stores have been filled by women workers [Dawson *et al.*, 1987]. The use of a female, part-time workforce provides employers with a variety of benefits. In addition to the flexibility they provide, part-time employees are less costly than full-timers. A substantial proportion of part-time workers within the retail sector do not receive maternity benefit, holiday allowances or sick pay entitlement.

The high proportion of female part-time workers within food super-stores highlights an important occupational variation. Female workers have traditionally occupied the majority of unskilled and semi-skilled occupations working as sales assistants and check-out operators. In contrast, male employees have been disproportionately represented in the managerial function. Thus, store managers and their deputies are more likely to be male and to be employed full-time. In contrast to food retailing, non-food superstores have a more even split between male and female workers. Sparks [1991], for example, notes a more balanced gender division within the DIY labour market.

While employer-led conditions play an integral role in structuring employment relations, the interdependence between supply and demand means that the role of labour cannot be discounted in shaping labour market outcomes. Women have found that working part-time is acceptable to their other demands. Retailers have therefore experienced difficulties in the recruitment of female staff for specific shifts, most notably those in the early morning and late afternoon. Domestic responsibilities, such as children and the provision of family meals, often take precedence. Retailers have therefore considered utilising other forms of labour [Bowlby, 1988; Pyke, 1986, 1988; Walby and Bagguely, 1989].

Women working part-time however represent only one form of labour utilised by superstores. The employment of under-18s and the over-60s also play a significant role. The retail sector has traditionally been a major port of entry into the work environment for school leavers [Lennon, 1990]. Dawson et al. [1986] maintain that young workers have become an increasingly important element of the labour supply for superstores. However, the decline in the number of school leavers entering the labour market and the increased competition to find young people available for work has meant that superstores have been forced to compete for a shrinking pool of young labour.

In the search for alternative forms of labour market supply, retailers have begun to focus upon the more 'mature', retired adult workers who until recently have been seen as an under utilised group. Indications are that superstores who have focused upon the recruitment of older workers have found the strategy successful.

PRIMARY RESEARCH METHODOLOGY

The aim of the remainder of this article is to examine whether the theoretical provisions of the labour market put forward earlier can be applied to the example of superstore employment. The research itself involved a series of in-depth interviews with superstore managers in the Manchester area. Twenty-six superstores were initially approached. This represented the entire population of superstores within the Manchester city centre. Interviews were finally conducted with 17. Of the 17 six were food and the remainder were non-food. The research took place in the latter half of 1988. For the usual reasons of confidentiality no individual company will be named.

EMPLOYMENT RELATIONS WITHIN MANCHESTER
SUPERSTORES

The research revealed a highly segmented labour market which broadly reflected the primary/secondary divide identified by Doeringer and

Piore [1971]. Table 2 provides a breakdown of the major employment categories within superstores.

Managerial and supervisory staff were the groups who enjoyed terms and conditions that most closely corresponded to primary sector employment. The positions were relatively secure and turnover averaged just over five per cent. One limitation of the dualist approach is that it provides a distinction between only two tiers of primary workers. A division is drawn between those who are governed by a rigid set of work rules and those who have a degree of autonomy and responsibility over their employment. In practice the managerial tier could be further sub-divided between senior store management (the store manager, the deputy manager and the personnel officer) and the department heads. The first three positions represented the top tier of the superstore hierarchy, individuals at this level were considered to be on a structured career path. They were expected to be both mobile and able to relocate should it be considered necessary.

TABLE 2
TOTAL EMPLOYMENT NUMBERS WITHIN SUPERSTORES
DISAGGREGATED BY JOB CATEGORY

	Full-time	Part-time
Managerial	145	1
Supervisory	65	26
Shop/Sales assistants	193	764
Clerical	54	35

Source: Retail Survey 1988.

Senior managerial staff were not subjected to elaborate work rules and enjoyed a degree of autonomy and responsibility over their working environments. However, the relatively privileged position that managers held must be viewed within the context of an industry that experiences a high degree of centralised control over both strategic and operational functions [Dawson, 1988; McGoldrick, 1990]. Consequently, while managers may have responsibility for recruitment and selection, functions such as wage bargaining and personnel policy tended to be directly controlled by head office.

Reinforcing both Cockburn's contention [1987] and Sparks' findings [1982], the senior managerial structure revealed a distinct gender bias. Store managers in all but two of the stores were male and only four women held the position of deputy store manager. In the four stores large enough to warrant a personnel department, six of the seven officers were female.

One level below that of senior superstore management were the Department Managers. They came under the direct control of the Assistant or Deputy Manager. These positions were differentiated from the supervisory by the level of responsibility individuals had over their jobs. Department heads were typically empowered with responsibility for specific areas of the store, for example, fresh foods, hardware and bakery. However, the function of departmental heads differed from senior management in that their duties were highly defined and the positions were governed by a formal set of work procedures. Reflecting the developments that have occurred within retailing generally, department heads had little or no control over space allocation, product placement, merchandising or promotion.

The role of the supervisor closely mirrored Piore's [1975] conception of lower tier primary employment. Like managerial positions, the conditions of employment were relatively secure, with over two-thirds of superstore supervisors working full-time. Supervisors were primarily in charge of the sales floor and check-out areas. The work tended to be repetitious and concentrated upon ensuring work schedules were maintained, co-ordinating the check-out areas and acting as the first line of query from the customer.

The overwhelming majority of supervisory staff had previously worked on the sales floor. This progression was seen as the traditional promotional path for the sales force. It was estimated that less than 5 per cent of either food or non-food supervisors had transferred from another company. Primarily this was due to the potential loss of status and earnings that could occur by transferring to a different store.

Supervisory skills were not company-specific and in theory an individual could change jobs without too great a difficulty. However, this would limit their ability to progress on to lower managerial positions. Within superstores the notion that retailing was 'experience-led' still found favour. Performance on the job was felt to be as accurate an indicator of ability for middle management as formal qualifications. While movements from the lower- to the mid-primary tier were limited, transferring to another company was felt to exclude an individual altogether from promotion. A distinct gender bias was noted in the composition of the supervisory labour force. All supervisor positions in the food superstores were occupied by females. The research failed to identify a single male supervisor occupying this lower primary position. In contrast, non-food retailing has a higher proportion of male supervisors (28 per cent), reinforcing Sparks' [1991] findings of a gender breakdown in DIY superstores.

The job categories over which supervisory staff had immediate control could loosely be defined as attracting secondary sector employment conditions. Doeringer and Piore [1971] maintained that the secondary sector was segmented with different terms and conditions applying to different jobs. This contention was reaffirmed in the division between clerical and sales staff within superstores. Partly reinforcing Sparks' [1982] findings, clerical workers occupied a labour market position that provided higher levels of job security than sales assistant. Although a structured career progression did not exist within the clerical sector and remuneration was lower than supervisory and managerial staff, the majority of clerical workers were employed full-time and turnover was low.

In contrast, sales assistants experienced many of the conditions that Doeringer and Piore [1971] identified as characterising the secondary labour market. The skill level required to work as a sales assistant was low, only one (non-food) superstore required any formal qualifications as a pre-requisite to employment. Related to this was the low level of training that sales assistants were given. Reflecting an industry-wide characteristic [Craig, and Wilkinson, 1985] priority was placed upon ensuring that individuals reached the minimum level of competence required to undertake the work. Further training for sales assistants was not an integral part of employment and was provided only in relation to specific changes in operation (such as the introduction of EPOS or EFT-PoS).

The concept of a secondary labour market within retailing was further reinforced by the low level of demarcation that existed between jobs. Thirteen of the 17 superstores interviewed had no strict definition of job title. Individuals were expected to undertake a range of duties such as shelf filling, check-out operations and dealing with customer inquiries. The ability to deploy staff wherever necessary provided superstores with an opportunity to respond flexibly to changes in customer flow during the working day, week and year. The level of turnover amongst the secondary workforce varied by company. Six of the 17 superstores had no accurate record of staff turnover and could provide only rough estimates of change in the past 12 months. Gauging an accurate estimate of store turnover by gender was equally difficult – no store was able to provide this information.

The majority of stores had a turnover of sales staff of over 20 per cent per annum, a figure far in excess of the level amongst supervisory staff. Little agreement, however, existed between stores over what comprised an acceptable level of turnover for their sales assistants. One non-food retailer had a turnover level of 23 per cent and felt that further steps could be taken to reduce the number of leavers. Conversely, the largest food superstore interviewed had a turnover level of just under 40 per cent for the financial year 1987–1988, a figure that was seen as acceptable especially as it was lower than the groups average of 41 per cent.

One of the most significant features of the sales assistant positions were the number who were part-time, reaffirming this as a labour market trend within retailing [Sheffield Low Pay Campaign, 1988; Sparks, 1983; 1987; Dawson et al., 1986; 1988; DTEDC 1988, 1986]. As Table 1 illustrates, approximately 80 per cent of those employed as sales assistants worked part-time. While this figure remained slightly higher than evidenced in previous research, it reinforces the notion that the largest percentage of employees within retailing operate under secondary employment conditions. Employment shifts varied from between one to six days per week with the timing of work schedules revolving around the peaks and troughs of the working day. The traditional nine-to-five shift represented an outmoded form of employment contract which did not provide retailers with the necessary degree of flexibility. Part-timers were therefore recruited by the half-day, the day or the week. All were paid by the hour.

Reaffirming previous research, the overwhelming majority of positions on the sales floor were occupied by women. In food superstores especially, women formed the largest proportion of the secondary workforce. In the four food superstores that employed over 200 people, it was estimated that over 90 per cent of the sales staff were female. Males working on the shop floor were mainly (though not exclusively) confined to specialist areas such as the butchery, bakery or warehouse. Within non-food superstores women were less predominant on the sales floor. In the furniture and DIY superstores male participation comprised approximately 40 per cent of the total sales force.

CONCLUSIONS

This article has sought to examine the applicability of segmentation theory to the superstore labour market. The maintenance of a core workforce with relatively secure employment conditions provides the operational stability required within the sector. The maintenance of large numbers of part-time workers gives superstores flexibility in responding to the cyclicality of consumer demand. Unlike traditional approaches to segmentation theory, however, it was found that a degree of access did exist between both sectors. In a relatively few instances individuals were provided with the opportunity to transfer from the secondary to the primary labour market. Although such opportunities were limited, it remained possible for some sales assistants to progress within the store to the position of supervisor, thus crossing the primary/ secondary divide. Therefore, an examination of the superstore sector does not fully reinforce the theory that a segmented labour market places restrictions upon mobility. From the evidence presented in this paper it may be concluded that the structure of employment relations is the outcome of both supply and demand side determinants operating within the context of specific sectoral, time and place constraints.

NOTES

1. Superstores are defined by Dawson *et al.* [1987] as a 'self service store offering a wide range of food and/or non-food merchandise with at least 2323 square metres of net floorspace, competing primarily on the basis of price and support directly by associated car parking'.
2. I would like to thank Leigh Sparks for his comments on an earlier draft of this paper.

REFERENCES

Becker, G., 1964, *Human Capital*, New York: National Bureau of Economic Research.
Booz, T., J. Allen and R. Hamilton, 1989, 'Staffing Supermarkets in the 90's', *The Coca-Cola Research Group Europe*, Europe.
Bowlby, S., 1988, 'From Corner Shop to Hypermarket : Women and Food Retailing', in J. Little, L. Peake and P. Richardson (eds.), *Women in Cities : Gender and the Urban Environment*, London: Macmillan.
Cockburn, C., 1987, *Two Track Training: Sex Inequalities and the YTS*, London: Macmillan.
Craig, C. and F. Wilkinson, 1985, 'Pay and Employment in Four Retail Trades', *Research Paper No 51 Department of Employment*, London: HMSO.
CSO, 1990, Annual Abstract of Statistics, No. 126, London: HMSO.
Davies, K. L. and Sparks, 1989, 'Superstore Retailing in Great Britain 1960-1986', Results from a new database, *Transactions*, Vol. 14, No.1, pp. 74-89.
Dawson, J., 1988, 'Futures for the High Street', *The Geographical Journal*, Vol. 154, Part 1, pp. 1–12.
Dawson, J., A. Findlay and L. Sparks, 1986, 'Anatomy of Job Growth : Employment in British Superstores', *Working Paper 8601*, Institute for Retail Studies, University of Stirling.
Dawson, J., A. Findlay and L. Sparks, 1987, 'Employment in British Superstores : Summary of Project Findings', Working Paper 8701, Institute for Retail Studies, University of Stirling.
Dawson, J., A. Findlay, and L. Sparks, 1988 'The Employment Implications of Locational Decision Making: The Case of In-Town and Out-of-Town Superstores', *International Journal of Retailing*, Vol. 3, No. 2, pp. 35–47.
Dex, S., 1988, 'Gender and the Labour Market', in D. Gallie (ed.), *Employment in Britain*, Oxford: Blackwell.
Doeringer, P. and M. Piore, 1971, *Internal Labour Markets and Manpower Analysis*, Massachusetts: D.C. Heath.
DTEDC, 1986, *Young Peoples Employment in Retailing*, London: NEDO.
DTEDC, 1988; *Part-Time Working in the Distributive Trades: Training Practices and Career Opportunities*, London: NEDO.

Fothergill, S., G. Gudgin, M. Kitson, and S. Monk, 1986, 'The Deindustrialisation of the City', in R. Martin and B. Rowthorn (eds.), *The Geography of Deindustrialisation*, London: Macmillan.

Furlong, A., 1990, 'Labour Market Segmentation and the Age Structuring of Employment Opportunities for Young People', *Work Employment and Society*, Vol. 4, No. 2, pp. 253–70.

Hunter, L. and C. Mulvey, 1981, *Economics of Wages and Labour*, London: Macmillan.

IGD, 1990, 'Food Retailing '90', Institute for Grocery Distribution, Watford.

IRS, 1989, 'Distributive Trades Profile – A Statistical Digest', Institute for Retail Studies, University of Stirling

Kerr, C., 1954, 'The Balkanisation of Labour Markets' in E. Bakke (ed.), *Labour Mobility and Economic Opportunity*, New York: John Wiley & Sons.

Labour Studies Group, 1985, 'Economic, Social and Political Factors in the Operation of the Labour Market', in B. Roberts, R. Finnegan and D. Gallie (eds.), *New Approaches to Economic Life: Economic Restructuring and the Social Division of Labour*, Manchester: Manchester University Press.

Lennon, P., 1990, 'Facing the Demographic Challenge', *Employment Gazette*, January, pp. 41–4.

Lester, R., 1952, 'A Range Theory of Wage Differentials', *Industrial and Labour Relations Review*, Vol. 5, July.

McGoldrick, P., 1990, *Retail Marketing*, London: McGraw Hill.

Michon, F., 1987, 'Segmentation, Employment Structures and Production Structures', in R. Tarling (ed.), *Flexibility in Labour Markets*, London: Academic Press.

Morrison, P., 1990, Segmentation Theory Applied to Local Regional and Spatial Labour Markets. *Progress in Human Geography*. Vol. 14, No. 4, pp. 488–528.

Peck, J., 1988, 'The Structure and Segmentation of Local Labour Markets : Aspects of the Geographical Anatomy of Youth Unemployment in Great Britain. Unpublished doctoral thesis, University of Manchester.

Peck, J., 1989, Reconceptualising the Local Labour Market: Space Segmentation and the State. *Progress in Human Geography*, Vol. 13, No. 1, pp. 42–61.

Piore, M., 1975, 'Notes for a Theory of Labour Market Stratification', in R. Edwards, Reich and D. Gordon (eds.), *Labour Market Segmentation*, Massachusetts: Lexington Heath.

Pyke, F., 1986, 'Labour Flexibility and the Use of Time', CURID, Department of Geography, University of Manchester.

Pyke, F., 1988, 'Local Labour Markets and the Organisation of Time: Reflections on the Rise of Part-Time Working', CURID, Geography Department, University of Manchester.

Rowthorn, B., 1986, 'Deindustrialisation in Britain', in R. Martin and B. Rowthorn (eds.), *The Geography of Deindustrialisation*, London: Macmillan.

Rubery, J., 1978, *Structured Labour Markets, Worker Organisation and Low Pay*, Cambridge, *Journal of Economics*, Vol. 2, No. 1, pp. 17–36.

Sheffield Low Pay Campaign., 1988, *The Price is White: A Summary of Black Employment in Sheffield Retail Sector*, SLPC Sheffield.

Slichter, S., 1950, 'Note on the Structure of Wages', *Review of Economics and Statistics*, February.

Sparks, L., 1982,' Female and Part-time Employment Within Superstore Retailing', *European Journal of Marketing*, Vol. 16, No. 7, pp. 16–29.

Sparks, L., 1983, 'A Review of Employment Since 1959, with Specific Focus on Aspects of Superstore Employment', PTRC Summer Annual Meeting, Conference Proceedings, London: PTRC.

Sparks, L., 1987, 'Employment in Retailing: Trends and Issues', in G. Johnson (ed.), *Business Strategy and Retailing*, London: John Wiley & Sons.

Sparks, L., 1991, 'Employment in DIY Superstores', *Service Industries Journal*, Vol. 11, No. 3, pp. 304–23.

Wachter, M., 1974, 'Primary and Secondary Labour Markets: A Critique of the Trial
   Approach', Brookings Papers on Economic Activity No. 3, pp. 637–93.
Walby, S. and P. Baggely, 1989, 'Gender Restructuring : Five Labour Markets Com-
   pared', *Environment and Planning D, Society and Space*, Vol. 7, pp. 277–92.
Wilkinson, F., 1981, *The Dynamics of Labour Market Segmentation*, London: Academic
   Press.
Williamson, O., 1975, *Markets and Hierarchies, Analysis and Antitrust Implications*, New
   York: The Free Press.

This study first appeared in *The Service Industries Journal*, Vol.13, No.1 (1993).

8
Employment in DIY Superstores

LEIGH SPARKS

Employment patterns in food superstores have received much research attention in recent years. Employment in non-food superstores has, however, been inadequately researched. Anecdotal and visual evidence suggests that non-food superstores employ fewer staff, more males than females, and more full-time than part-time workers, in comparison with food superstores,. This article quantifies employment in DIY superstores as a basis for future research.

Employment aspects of retailing received considerable research and press attention during the 1980s. Research focused in particular on the general trends in retail employment [e.g., Distributive Trades EDC, 1985] and on aspects of employment in food superstores [e.g., Dawson, Findlay and Sparks, 1986; Sparks, 1983]. One of the concerns that links these two research strands is the desire to understand how structural changes in retailing are being translated into employment changes, whether in terms of the location of employment [e.g., Dawson, Findlay and Sparks, 1988] or the type of employment. Concern has therefore been focused on the number and types of jobs in new forms of retailing and the transfer of jobs from existing outlets to new outlets as competitive pressure is experienced consequent on new store openings. Such concern has concentrated particularly on the effects of food superstores [e.g., Scottish Office, 1982] and more recently on the likely employment effects of regional shopping centre proposals [e.g., Drivers Jonas, 1987]. While there are still debates over the magnitude of effects of new outlets and centres in employment terms, there is at least some understanding and common ground over the magnitude of the employment opportunities at these new developments.

Concern has also been raised over employment aspects of non-food superstores, although here there has been little resolution of this concern.

While research has focused on food superstores, and consultants' reports for inquiries into regional shopping centres have sections on their likely employment capacity/effects, figures for non-food superstores are few and far between. When such data are presented they tend to be couched in terms of gross floorspace per employee (FTE) or in comparison with industrial employment generation [see e.g., Whysall 1981; London Research Centre, 1986; GLC 1986]. Alternatively they may be associated with planning applications and may thus be at an insufficient level of detail or subject to wide error margins.

This lack of data or detailed studies would appear to be not for lack of interest in the topic, nor for the need for anlaysis, as there have been requests for such further research made in these studies. Instead, it probably stems from early assumptions that non-food superstores were not as dramatically competitive with existing stores as were food super-stores and that employment in such stores was a bonus on industrial sites and therefore to be welcomed. Certainly a number of authorities have commented on the lack of information on employment in non-food superstores and regretted this anomaly [e.g., Portsmouth City Council, 1987]. What is required is a better knowledge of the employment in non-food superstores. Ideally data at the individual store level disaggregated in various ways are needed. Such data would form the building blocks towards an understanding of non-food superstore employment, and would help researchers and specialists (e.g. planners) in their delibera-tions and begin the process of understanding the number and types of jobs 'created' in this form of retailing.

SURVEY METHODOLOGY AND DATA COLLECTION

The aim of this article is to present the results of a small-scale investi-gative survey into employment in non-food superstores. This survey aimed to collect data at the individual store level, disaggregated by gender, hours worked and job category. In the autumn of 1988 a survey of non-food superstore operators was undertaken requesting co-operation in identifying levels of employment in their stores. Personnel offices were contacted and permission was requested to mount a survey of their individual stores, utilising the methodology (a postal survey) previously used for food superstores [Dawson, Findlay and Sparks, 1986; Sparks, 1983]. In addition, if the data requested were available in a suitable format, for each individual store, from the central office, then this was requested in place of the postal survey. The form in which the data was meant to be supplied ensured comparability with earlier surveys.

Resistance to assisting was quite considerable and in the end only six companies were willing to participate in the survey. Of these, four were DIY superstore operators, one was a home furnishings superstore chain and the other was an electrical retailer. A number of other operators considered the request but reported that they felt unable to assist owing to a desire not to disrupt store operations and/or the lack of suitable data at either central or store level. This unwillingness to assist with such a simple study is somewhat disappointing given that a better understanding of employment in retailing is likely to be an important consideration in the difficult employment years ahead.

Because of the difficulty in generalising for all non-food superstores from the six companies the results in the main part of this article are reported for only the four DIY chains. Of these six participants, only one agreed to the main methodology proposed and allowed a postal survey of their individual stores. Two companies provided computer-based details from central records for all of their stores individually. Two other companies provided details via the store manager for a small sample of stores only, while the final company provided only partial results, albeit for every store. The range of types of response clearly poses limitations on the representativeness of the study, but it is believed that the general picture presented here is an accurate one of DIY superstores. Details of the disaggregation of the data collected, the definitional terms used, and the companies involved (in terms of their responses) are found in Appendix 1 at the end of this article. The survey yielded data on employment by gender and hours worked for 336 DIY superstores (employing in total more than 15,000 people) and more detailed data at the job-category level for 247 of these stores. In addition, data for a further 178 non-food superstores were also obtained. It is difficult to estimate accurately what percentage of all non-food superstores this data collection exercise covers, but 514 non-food superstores is probably over 25 per cent of the total. The percentage for DIY superstores is nearer 45 per cent according to figures in IGD [1988].

Within the general aims of this study there are a number of narrower aims and these provide the structure for presenting the survey results. First, a brief examination of the non-food superstores sector is undertaken. Second, a comparison of the overall survey results for DIY superstores with the earlier study for food superstores [Dawson, Findlay and Sparks 1986] is presented to allow contrasts between the two sectors to be drawn. Third, the results by each DIY superstore operator are presented to facilitate comparisons across retail chains. Fourth, brief comparisons are made between the DIY superstore operators and the other two non-food superstore chains in the survey. Fifth, an examination of employment levels against store floorspace is made to ascertain what, if any, relationship exists. Finally, some conclusions are drawn.

NON-FOOD SUPERSTORES

It is not the purpose here to review in detail the development of non-food superstores as this has been thoroughly explored by other authors [Jones, 1984a; 1984b; Gibbs, 1987]. It is necessary, however, to consider briefly the importance of this form of retailing and the types of employment questions that it raises. The first retail outlets to leave the town and city centres were the forerunners of the modern food superstore, particularly in the 1960s and early 1970s. In the late 1960s and early 1970s there was also a developing DIY retail presence in the off-centre locations. In many cases these non-food stores were termed 'retail warehouses' and were located on industrial estates or other non-prime retail land. Through the 1970s and 1980s, however, these non-food elements have grown apace and have moved away from their initial focus in a number of ways. For example, the locations have 'improved' and become more high profile; the range of operators and products sold has extended dramatically; retail warehouse 'parks' have emerged [Bernard Thorpe and Partners, 1985]; and their competitive effects on existing centres have been questioned. These are no longer 'retail warehouses' but fully developed non-food superstores.

The employment issues raised by such developments range from the very basic to the complex. At a very simple level there is a lack of knowledge of the numbers of people such stores employ and the types of employees by gender, hours worked and job category. When applications for development are made, a jobs-'created' figure is often given. Planning and other authorities have no information on which to consider the likely employment generation at the store proposed. It is widely held, but has not been satisfactorily demonstrated, that non-food superstores employ far fewer staff than food superstores and that these are more likely to be male and to work full-time than would be the case in food superstores. Figures to illustrate this belief are not readily available. In some cases the question has revolved around employment densities either by acre or by some measure of floorspace [e.g., Whysall, 1981; Portsmouth City Council, 1987]. Are the employment opportunities generated sufficient, for example, to offset the 'loss' of industrial land and thus industrial jobs? Again, the base data available are insufficient to consider such questions.

At a more complex level there is the question of competitive impact and job gain and loss over a wider area. Initially with the earlier DIY stores it could perhaps be argued that there were few competitive impacts

TABLE 1

STORE AND EMPLOYMENT CHARACTERISTICS OF DIY SUPERSTORES

	No. of stores	No. of employees (FTE)	Av. sales area (sq. ft.) per store	Av. No. of FTE employees per store	Av. sales area (sq. ft.) per employee
B and Q	239	9,635	38,900	40	965
Texas	183	7,300	31,150*	40	781*
Wickes	44	1,046	20,750	24	873
Payless	98	3,475	25,568	35	721
Great Mills	74	2,050	30,400	28	1,097*
Homebase	48	2,535	47,000	53	906
Do-It-All	105	3,726	31,600	35	890

Source: DIY Week, 23 June 1989, Retail Leaders 1989 Supplement.
Notes: The FTE calculations here take a non-full-time worker as being equivalent to 0.5 of a full-time employee.

* Gross floorspace.

as a new and expanding market was being created or tapped. In such cases jobs created at a new store were seen as all gains. With many non-food superstores today, however, there is a real competitive impact on both existing town centres and other non-food superstores. The number of jobs created at a new store has therefore to be deflated by the jobs lost elsewhere. This is a very complicated issue that probably depends on local circumstances, but again without the base data, little real progress in assessing effects can be made. It is hoped that this article begins to shed light on this area.

The levels at which published data are avilable on employment in DIY superstores are shown in Table 1. This table provides details of store profile and basic employment numbers for the seven leading DIY superstore retailers, including companies participating in this survey. Care has to be taken with this table as it is based on a study for a trade magazine, which itself indicated that estimates had been made and companies had provided the data at varying levels of accuracy. Nevertheless, the table contains some interesting points. Chief among these is the variation of both the employee levels per store and also the sales area per employee figures. These columns suggest that staffing levels vary by operator as well as in accordance with turnover, etc. The variation between B and Q and Texas in floorspace per worker is quite marked given the identical figures for the average number of employees per store. The table, however, is at an insufficient level to allow more detailed considerations of DIY superstore employment. This is the focus of the survey results presented below.

EMPLOYMENT IN FOOD AND DIY SUPERSTORES

The data obtained from the current survey into employment in DIY stores can be compared with the base data obtained from three food superstore operators in an earlier survey [Dawson, Findlay and Sparks, 1986]. It is accepted that there is a time-lag between the two surveys and that this might affect the results, but it is believed that this effect is not substantial. As will be seen, the magnitude of differences between the two types of superstore is sufficient to reduce the importance of this time-lag. The summarised, averaged data obtained from the DIY superstores are compared in Table 2 with comparable data from the earlier food superstore survey. In Table 2 the attributes compared are those of gender and hours worked, as well as total and full-time-equivalent (FTE) employment. It should be noted that in this and subsequent tables the FTE calculation has treated a part-time worker as 0.5 of a full-time worker, and a casual worker as 0.2 of a full-time worker.

The basic differences between the employment structure of food and DIY superstores are well marked by the data in Table 2. The average employment in the DIY superstores is only approximately 15 per çent of that of food superstores, with DIY superstores employing on average only 46 people. This figure of 46 is deflated to 34 when a FTE calculation is made. Within this employment total there are marked differences between food and DIY superstores with respect to employment composition. The DIY superstore labour force comprises both more full-time employees and more male employees that are found in the food superstores. Full-time workers comprise half of the DIY superstore workforce, while male employees are just under half of the work-force. The contrast to the food superstore is marked, where the labour force employed is predominantly part-time and overwhelmingly female.

It has been argued for food superstore employment that there is a clear correlation between female and part-time work and that female, part-time workers, comprising half the food superstore work-force, are crucial to retail operations of this form. For DIY stores this category of employee remains important, but the main category is in fact male, full-time workers. It would appear that in DIY superstores the female, part-time employees found in the food superstores are replaced by male, full-time workers. It can be suggested that the reasons for this more male orienta-

TABLE 2

EMPLOYMENT IN FOOD AND DIY SUPERSTORES: MEAN NUMBER OF
EMPLOYEES PER STORE BY GENDER AND HOURS WORKED

	Food Superstores	DIY Superstores
No. of stores	175	336
Av. floorspace (m^2)	3,650	3,415
Standard deviation	847.9	N.A.
Av. total employees	285	46
Av. FTE employees	195	34
Full-time	108(38)	23(50)
Part-time	170(60)	20(44)
Casual	7(2)	3(7)
Male	80(28)	21(46)
Female	204(72)	25(54)
Male		
Full-time	52(18)	14(31)
Part-time	27(9)	6(13)
Casual	2(1)	1(3)
Female		
Full-time	56(20)	9(19)
Part-time	143(50)	14(31)
Casual	3(2)	2(4)

Source: Food Superstores – Dawson, Findlay and Sparks, [1986]. DIY Superstores –
Author Survey.

Notes: 1. Figures in parentheses are the percentage of total store employment within each
category.
2. Figures may not sum due to rounding.
3. The floorspace for DIY superstores is taken from IGD (1988), p. 13 and is based
on their analysis and does not refer to the 336 superstores in this study.

tion revolve around perceptions of male employees knowing more about
the products sold in DIY outlets and being more physically competent to
handle the products. It is also probably true, however, that in smaller
labour forces, as in DIY superstores, managers become proportionately
more important. The managerial category is often dominated by male,
full-time workers. This issue is examined in more detail later. Despite this
more male composition however, the DIY superstore sector is still an
important employment destination for female workers and they are in the
majority in the work-force, as shown in Table 2. It is also clear that the
female, full-time component is approximately the same in both food and
DIY superstores, reinforcing the importance of female workers to both
operations.

The lower reliance on part-time labour in DIY superstores also requires some consideration. While part-time employment is still a major element of the DIY workforce, it is less strong numerically than in the food superstore sector. This may be the result of the lower volume of customer flow in DIY superstores which requires, for example, fewer checkout operators and may also result from variations in the flow of these customers over the trading week. The operating hours of the stores may also be different between the two sectors, with the more extensive DIY hours, including possibly Sunday trading, permitting a more flexible pattern of full-time working. It is also possibly a function of the size of the store in that it can be argued that retail units require a core of full-time workers supplemented by part-time workers to cover peak customer flows, etc. In smaller units, whether by floorspace or by number of employees, this core of full-time workers is proportionately larger than in, for example, a large food superstore. It has also to be considered whether the different physical distribution systems in food and DIY superstores affect the labour composition. In food superstores most delivery is from a central warehouse whereas in DIY superstores the trend is still for direct-to-store delivery from suppliers. In labour terms, the centralisation of distribution can both reduce the labour requirement and, more relevantly here, change the labour used from full-time to part-time. This is an area that is clearly a focus for further research.

Table 3 provides a similar form of comparison as Table 2, but in this case considers the job category within the superstore. It has to be noted that Company D was unable to supply data at this level and so is omitted from Table 3. This has the effect of making the DIY category in the table almost wholly comprised of Company B. The results here may therefore be less respresentative of all DIY stores than in the previous table. As might perhaps be expected, the data in Table 3 show that the bulk of the DIY work-force, as with food superstores, is found in the sales category. This category, which includes checkout operators and shelf-fillers, is the category that deals primarily with the public. The main differences between the food superstores and DIY superstores lie in the higher levels of managers, supervisors and clerical staff in DIY superstores at the expense of the 'other' category. The higher level of managers and supervisors may be a function of the size of the store as argued above. With a smaller work-force, the managerial proportion remains high as such managerial staff are needed in all shop units. This may also be associated with the higher level of clerical staff. As a generalisation, DIY superstores are more decentralised than their food equivalents, and process more of the retail activity at the store level, e.g., direct-to-store delivery. This would necessitate not only more clerical staff, but probably also more managerial/supervisory staff.

TABLE 3

EMPLOYMENT IN FOOD AND DIY SUPERSTORES: MEAN NUMBER OF
EMPLOYEES PER STORE BY JOB CATEGORY

	Food Superstores	DIY Superstores
No. of stores	175	247
Managers	10(4)	3 (6)
Supervisors	14(6)	5 (9)
Prof. & Tech.	2(1)	0 (0)
Sales	167(73)	35 (70)
Clerical	10(4)	5 (10)
Trainees	3(2)	0.4(1)
Others	25(11)	2 (3)

Sources: Food Superstores – Dawson, Findlay and Sparks [1986].
            DIY Superstores – Author Survey.

Notes: Figures in parentheses are the percentage of total store employment within each
         category. Figures may not sum because of rounding.
            The difference in the number of DIY superstores in the sample compared with the
         previous table is because Company D did not provide job-category data. This
         reduces the number of stores to 247 and increases the average total employment to
         50.

The category that is reduced in DIY superstores when compared to
food superstores is that of 'other'. This is a 'catch-all' category that
comprises elements of the labour force such as cleaners, cafeteria staff,
drivers and warehousemen. It is possible that the lack of cafeterias in
many DIY superstores accounts for these differences, but also that cleaning of much of the store is carried out by sales staff as part of the job as
opposed to specialists as often occurs in food superstores. Again, more
details on exact job tasks in stores would be needed to come to categoric
conclusions.

This analysis can be taken further by considering the relationship of
gender and hours worked by job category. This is presented in Table 4
which provides details of the average employment per category for DIY
superstores. Again it has to be noted that this table excludes Company D
and is based on 247 stores, mainly those from Company B. This table
reinforces the comments earlier about gender differences in terms of
hours worked. Male workers work mainly full-time while female workers
are concentrated in the part-time category. The distinction by gender is
well marked in the sales category where male workers are more evenly
divided between full- and part-time work, with more in the former category, while female workers are concentrated in the part-time positions.

TABLE 4

AVERAGE EMPLOYMENT PER DIY SUPERSTORE

	Male				Female				
	Full-time	Part-time	Casual	Total men	Full-time	Part-time	Total Casual	Grand women	Total
Managers	2.6	–	–	2.6	0.4	–	–	0.4	3.0
	(5.3)	(–)	(–)	(5.3)	(0.8)	(–)	(–)	(0.8)	(6.1)
Supervisors	2.9	–	–	2.9	1.7	0.0	–	1.7	4.6
	(5.8)	(–)	(–)	(5.8)	(3.4)	(0)	(–)	(3.4)	(9.2)
Prof. & Tech.	0.0	–	–	0.0	0.0	0.0	–	0.0	0.0
	(0)	(–)	(–)	(0)	(0)	(0)	(–)	(0)	(0)
Sales	7.7	6.0	1.3	15.1	4.0	13.6	2.3	19.9	34.9
	(15.5)	(12.1)	(2.6)	(30.2)	(8.1)	(27.2)	(4.5)	(39.8)	(70.0)
Clerical	0.1	0.1	–	0.2	2.5	2.4	–	4.9	5.1
	(0.2)	(0.1)	(–)	(0.3)	(5.0)	(4.9)	(–)	(9.8)	(10.2)
Trainees	0.3	–	–	0.3	0.2	0.1	–	0.4	0.6
	(0.6)	(–)	(–)	(0.6)	(0.5)	(0.2)	(–)	(0.7)	(1.3)
Others	1.3	0.1	–	1.4	0.1	0.1	–	0.2	1.6
	(2.7)	(0.1)	(–)	(2.8)	(0.2)	(0.2)	(–)	(0.4)	(3.2)
Totals	15.0	6.1	1.3	22.5	8.9	16.3	2.3	27.5	50.0
	(30.1)	(12.3)	(2.6)	(45.0)	(17.9)	(32.5)	(4.5)	(54.9)	(100)

Note: Figures in parentheses are the percentage of total employment in store in category.

Gender separation can also be noted in terms of job categories as a whole. Female workers are dominant in the managers', supervisors' and 'others' categories. In particular, male workers in the managers' and supervisors' categories are entirely full-time. There would thus seem to be a gender bias in the DIY superstore work-force. These distinctions between female and male job categories and full-time and part-time working by gender mirror the findings of a similar exercise for food superstores [Dawson, Findlay and Sparks, 1987a].

The overall conclusions from these comparisons between food superstores and DIY superstores are that DIY superstores employ far fewer people, more full-time workers and more male workers than food superstores. Overall, however, the occupational composition is broadly similar between the two superstore groupings with gender distinctions in employment common to both forms of superstore retailing. Despite these differences in male and full-time employment, however, DIY superstore employment is still an important sector for female and part-time employment, with part-time working being 50 per cent of the total jobs and female workers being in the majority (54 per cent).

DIY SUPERSTORE EMPLOYMENT: COMPANY ANALYSIS

In addition to the comparisons with another form of superstore retailing presented above, it is also important to consider employment within the DIY superstore category and to consider whether this varies by company. The data that allow this are presented in Table 5. It can be seen from the table that variance among the companies does in fact occur. At the simple level of average total number of employees, the level varies from 35 to 50 with the highest figure being produced by the company with the largest number of stores in the survey. This suggests that the average figures used in the earlier analysis may be somewhat too large if all the smaller DIY companies are similar to each other. In other respects, however, the level of employment in a market leader in the sector is obviously of more interest and importance than in a number of much smaller companies.

When the employment figures are disaggregated by gender and hours worked it can be seen from Table 5 that the data for Company B fall in the mid-part of the ranges of the four companies. Thus while male employment as a proportion of total employment varies across the companies from 37 per cent to 59 per cent, the figure for Company B is neither of these two extremes. A broadly similar position is found in term of hours worked. Appendix 1 which provides brief details of the companies involved in the study indicates that Company A, which is one of the 'extreme' companies in both the categories of gender and hours worked, has other stores (excluded here from the analysis) located at the 'heavy' end of the DIY market. This company has its roots more towards the traditional builders' merchant rather than the DIY householder. These origins and the remaining orientation may help explain why the company is different from the others in terms of the gender composition of its work-force. The use of male workers at the builders' merchant 'end' of the market is not particularly surprising. It is possible that this orientation 'spills' over into the main superstore sector, and may also be a relict feature of previous strategies. Even here, however, it must be noted that over 40 per cent of the work-force in this company's stores are female.

Much less clear is the difference among the companies in terms of the hours worked. The broad pattern across all the companies is approximately the same, with smaller variations in the level of part-time working than by gender. These variations in part-time employment do not appear to be explained by the types of markets in which the companies trade, and must therefore at this stage be put down to company policy. These

TABLE 5

EMPLOYMENT IN DIY SUPERSTORES: MEAN NUMBER OF
EMPLOYEES PER STORE

	Company A	Company B	Company C	Company D
No. of stores	13	229	5	89
Av. total employees	43	50	42	35
Av. FTE employees	33	36	30	27
Full-time	24(55)	24(48)	17(41)	20(56)
Part-time	20(45)	22(44)	25(59)	14(39)
Casual	(–)	4 (8)	– (–)	2 (5)
Male	25(59)	2(45)	16(37)	17(48)
Female	18(41)	2(55)	26(63)	18(52)
Male				
Full-time	15(36)	15(30)	10(24)	11(32)
Part-time	10(23)	6(12)	6(13)	5(14)
Casual	– (–)	1 (3)	– (–)	1 (3)
Female				
Full-time	8(19)	9(18)	7(17)	9(24)
Part-time	10(22)	16(33)	19(46)	9(24)
Casual	– (–)	2 (5)	– (–)	1 (3)
Managers	3 (6)	3 (6)	3 (7)	N.A.
Supervisors	3 (7)	5 (9)	4 (9)	N.A.
Prof. & Tech.	1 (2)	– (–)	– (–)	N.A.
Sales	29(67)	36(71)	23(54)	N.A.
Clerical	4 (8)	5(10)	3 (6)	N.A.
Trainees	1 (2)	0 (1)	1 (2)	N.A.
Others	3 (8)	1 (3)	9(22)	N.A.

Note: Figures in parentheses are the percentage of total store employment within each category.

Figures may not sum because of rounding.

distinctions are carried over into the data on the gender and hours worked comparisons which show that the two groups of male full-time workers, and female part-time workers, form the bulk of the DIY superstore workforce in all cases but that the balance between these two groups varies by company.

The data in Table 5 also allow some comparisons to be made in terms of job category, although as indicated earlier Company D has to be excluded from this. A very similar pattern is found in the main across all three companies, with the exception being Company C where the sales category is deflated at the expense of the 'other' category. This may be due to a misunderstanding of the category, or may be due to a much clearer demarcation of the warehouse category in this company. Broadly, however, the data by job category by company follow similar patterns.

COMPARISON WITH OTHER NON-FOOD SUPERSTORES

It has been anticipated that the project would have had more support from other non-food superstore operators and thus a more comprehensive analysis of non-food superstore employment as a whole could have been undertaken. In the event, however, data from only two other companies were made available and these are presented in Table 6. Table 6 follows the same pattern of presentation of data as in the earlier tables. What must be noted is that the electrical superstore chain (F) operates much smaller units in the main than other superstore companies and that this has an effect on the employment levels generated.

The results from Table 6 make interesting comparisons with the results presented earlier. Company E has an employment composition that is more similar to the food superstore profile than to the DIY superstore profile, although the total number of people employed per store is not of the order of magnitude of a food superstore. The pattern for Company E is one that shows more emphasis on part-time employment and female employment than is found in the DIY superstore results shown above. This perhaps is not surprising given the product mix of the company and the role of women consumers in purchasing the household products sold in these stores. The part-time nature of the employment may be a function of the consumer flow.

For Company F, the results are much more like the DIY superstore profile although in this case the number of employees is even smaller than in DIY superstores. There is a dominance of full-time and male workers in the stores reflecting probably both the role of the product and also the need for a core of workers when store size is small. With the employment level being so low in Company F, it is difficult to draw any meaningful conclusions from the data in Table 6, in terms of this paper, although there is clearly a need to better understand employment composition and possibilities in smaller shop units in general.

Disaggregation by company for the six companies in the survey has not really revealed any unexpected results. Variations occur among the companies, as might be expected, but the broad pattern for DIY superstores holds across the four companies. It is interesting to speculate, however, that other non-food superstores exhibit different employment patterns, although the data are not sufficient here to enable such a conclusion to be formally drawn. Company variation in DIY superstores seems to focus on the gender balance, and may therefore be associated

TABLE 6

EMPLOYMENT IN NON-FOOD SUPERSTORES:
HOME FURNISHINGS AND ELECTRICALS

	Company E	Company F
No. of stores	8	170
Av. total employes	47	15
Av. FTE employees	32	12
Full-time	19(41)	10(62)
Part-time	24(52)	6(38)
Casual	3 (6)	– (–)
Male	14(30)	10(66)
Female	32(70)	5(34)
Male		
Full-time	7(15)	8(49)
Part-time	6(12)	3(17)
Casual	2 (4)	– (–)
Female		
Full-time	13(27)	2(12)
Part-time	18(40)	3(21)
Casual	1 (3)	– (–)
Managers	3 (8)	2(13)
Supervisors	3 (6)	– (–)
Prof. & Tech.	– (–)	– (–)
Sales	34(74)	9(61)
Clerical	2 (3)	– (–)
Trainees	1 (2)	1 (5)
Others	3 (7)	3(21)

Note: Figures in parentheses are the percentage of total store employment within each category.

Figures may not sum because of rounding – this is particularly the case with Company F owing to the small numbers involved.

with the product mix of each individual company. Again, further work is needed in this area.

DIY SUPERSTORE EMPLOYMENT AND STORE SIZE

Table 1 illustrated that many of the figures discussed with respect to superstore employment often also consider floorspace. In many cases this is because of the lack of availability of accurate sales data. Obviously it would be much more informative to examine employment patterns of the store level in terms of turnover figures and customer flow but this is not possible in the vast majority of cases. Companies quite rightly would also view these data as commercially confidential and are not willing to sanction publication. Instead, sales or gross floorspace have in the past been used as surrogates for turnover (e.g., Dawson, Findlay and Sparks, 1986; Sparks, 1983). It has to be accepted, however, that there are a number of problems with this. First, floorspace is in fact a very poor surrogate as floorspace and turnover are unlikely to be perfectly related. Floorspace is an inadequate measure. Second, there is a question over whether it is better to use gross or net floorspace in the analysis. Finally, there is a problem over both the accuracy and availability of the data. There are often wide discrepancies between sources (if available) on the floorspace figures, and these in any case often change over time. While sources for food superstores are now fairly common, equivalent directories for non-food superstores do not have a very good coverage of floorspace figures. For example, the analysis below is limited to only a percentage of the stores in one company and then for sales area alone. The sources are not good enough at present to allow this analysis in other companies or on gross floorspace as well.

The earlier work on food superstores has demonstrated a variety of relationships between floorspace and employee numbers [Dawson, Findlay and Sparks, 1986; Sparks, 1983]. The strength of these relationships varied considerably, including by company. From the present survey it is possible only to analyse floorspace and employment relationships for 195 stores taken from one company. For these stores, the employment data are available by gender, hours worked and job category at the individual store level and net sales area floorspace data are available for each store from published sources [IGD, 1988]. The accuracy or otherwise of the floorspace data is not known but it is believed to be derived from that company, so at least the method of calculation should be standard across the stores.

The results of simple linear regressions using floorspace as the predictor variable and the various employment categories as the independent variable are given in Table 7. The table provides the R^2 value and an indication of whether or not the relationship is statistically significant at the 99 per cent level. The regression equations are not shown in the table but are available from the author. What the regression co-efficients in Table 7 show is that at best, only 41 per cent of the variation in any relationship is 'explained' by the floorspace figures. It is true, however, that the majority of the relationships in the table are statistically significant. The exception is that of casual workers. The R^2 value for full-time workers compared with the other hours-worked categories reinforces

TABLE 7

REGRESSION CORRELATIONS BETWEEN SALES FLOORSPACE
AND EMPLOYEES FOR COMPANY B

(n = 195 stores)

Category	R^2	Significance (99% level)
Total	.333	*
FTE	.395	*
Male	.286	*
Female	.305	*
Full-time	.414	*
Part-time	.190	*
Casual	.081	N.S.

Note: * denotes statistically significant.

comments about a core of full-time workers being required in retail stores. In the main there is a positive relationship between floorspace and employment levels. When disaggregated by gender and hours worked the strongest relationships are found with male, full-time workers (R^2= 0.424) and female, part-time workers (R^2=0.227). These are the two largest groups in the DIY superstore work-force and the relationships found emphasise the importance of these categories of employment to the retail operation. The weakness of the majority of relationships, however, equally emphasises the poor nature of sales floorspace as an indicator measure.

With the restriction of the floorspace data to one company and the weakness of the relationships, it is not possible to extend the analysis any further. The conclusions from this brief analysis is that there is a relationship between sales floorspace and employment numbers and types, but that it would be unwise to extend the relationships found into any predictor tool for employment numbers in all DIY or non-food superstores.

CONCLUSIONS

The main aim of this study, set out at the start, was the procuring and analysis of more detailed data on employment in non-food superstores. The project was needed to inform and educate about the employment characteristics of these stores and this retail format. To a considerable extent this aim has been met and the article has produced data and analysis of these data to a level that was not available before. Knowledge has been extended and one hopes, understanding improved.

Before the survey it was generally felt, though unproved, that non-food superstores employed far fewer people than would food superstores and that of these more would be male workers. The results of the study demonstrated that such feelings were indeed based in reality. For DIY superstores it was shown that average employment was 46 and that male, full-time workers formed the numerically most important category. Managers and supervisors tend to be male, mainly full-time workers. Sales staff and clerical workers, on the other hand, are mainly female and mostly part-time workers. The sales category is numerically by far the most dominant category.

The results, disaggregated by company, show variations among the companies, but in general the broad pattern of employment composition is quite standard. Store operator is an important variable in employment composition, but the broad pattern is similar.

These conclusions and summarised results have broadened understanding of the nature and composition of the DIY superstore workforce. The figures shown here should be of use in understanding the employment role of new and existing DIY superstores and be of particular interest to planners, business managers and service industry researchers. The non-food superstore sector has been shown to be a major employment sector with perhaps 100,000 people employed. There is a clear need, however, to extend the scope of the work presented here.

The survey presented here has a number of limitations which future research needs to overcome. The data collection and analysis process needs to be extended beyond the DIY superstore sector to permit a full understanding of the employment characteristics in the broader non-food superstore sector. The data-base needs to be widened. It is also necessary to go beyond the numbers of employees in each category, useful as this is at this stage, and consider the way in which employees are used within the stores, the methods of setting job numbers and types and the personal characteristics of the employees. The last heading would include study of journey-to-work, previous job history, etc., as has been done for food superstores [Dawson, Findlay and Sparks, 1987b]. A further development would be the consideration of employment in DIY superstores in a local area to look at the employment effects of competition and the introduction of new stores. There is also need to consider the employment levels and implications of support services in such companies, such as head offices, distribution centres and computer centres.

The survey results presented here have developed a numerical consideration of employment in DIY superstores. While important and informative, much more detailed work needs to be done.

The assistance of Mr Alan Elder in initial data aggregation and calculations is gratefully acknowledged. I would also like to thank the companies which particiapted in the study for their assistance and data provision.

APPENDIX 1

Data Collection
The basic information requested for each store can be seen from the grid below. This disaggregates store employment by gender, hours worked and job category. The definitional terms used are also noted below. All store managers involved received this information to help completion of the tables. For centrally derived information, completion of the tables for individual stores was undertaken at Stirling.

STORE EMPLOYMENT TABLE

	Male				Female				
	Full-time	Part-time	Casual	Total men	Full-time	Part-time	Casual	Total women	Grand Total
Managers									
Supervisors									
Prof. & tech.									
Sales									
Clerical									
Trainees									
Others									
Total									

The following definitions are used in completing the table.

Occupational level	*Example of specific occupation covered*
1. Managers	Store manager
2. Supervisors	Sales supervisor, foremen
3. Professional & technical	Personnel officers, buyers, accountants
4. Sales	Sales assistants, cashiers, shelf- fillers, display staff
5. Clerical	Typists, secretaries, telephonists, payroll clerks
6. Trainees	Apprentices, management trainees
7. Others	Craftsmen, drivers, warehouse staff, catering.

Full-time employee – works 30 hours or more per week.
Part-time employee – works between 8 and 30 hours per week.
Casual employee – works fewer than 8 hours per week.

Company Participation

The companies involved in the project are described briefly below, with details of their participation.

Company A is a superstore operator with outlets at both the standard and the 'heavier' end of the DIY market. This company participated in a postal survey of store managers and 19 stores completed returns from a base of 44, i.e., a response rate of 43 per cent. Of these 19 replies, 6 were from the 'heavier' builders' merchants style of operation and have been excluded from the analysis on the basis that they are not really DIY superstores. These stores employed on average 10 people each.

Company B is one of the market leaders in the DIY sector and provided central information on 229 of their stores. Of these 229 stores, it was possible to obtain floorspace data for only 195, and so these 195 stores are used in the section on floorspace and employment.

Company C is a company from the second rank (numerically) of companies in the DIY market. This company would only allow information to be obtained from a sample of their stores. The sample number was five which is approximately eight per cent of their stores trading at this time.

Company D is another company from the second rank (numerically) of the DIY market. This company provided details of employment by gender and hours worked but *not* job category for 89 of their stores. The hours-worked data for this company enforces a 29-hours-per-week cut-off for part-time/full-time work. It is not believed that this (compared with 30 hours for all other data analysis here) is significant in this context.

Company E is a company that is involved in the home furnishings and furniture business from both in-town and out-of-town locations. Details were provided by the company for their eight off-centre locations.

Company F is an electrical retailer that operates from a variety of formats and locations. The data reported here relate to the 170 off-centre locations. Some of these are stand-alone whereas others are shared buildings.

REFERENCES

Bernard Thorpe and Partners, 1985, *Retail Warehouse Parks*, London: Authors.

Dawson, J. A., A. M. Findlay and L. Sparks, 1986, 'The Importance of Store Operator on Superstore Employment Levels', *The Service Industries Journal*, Vol. 6 No. 3.

Dawson, J. A., A. M. Findlay and L. Sparks, 1987a 'Opportunities for Female Employment in Superstore Retailing', *Equal Opportunities International*, Vol. 6, No. 1.

Dawson, J. A., A. M. Findlay and L. Sparks, 1987b, 'Employment in British Superstores: summary of project findings', *Institute for Retail Studies, Working Paper 8701, University of Stirling.*

Dawson, J. A., A. M. Findlay and L. Sparks, 1988, 'The Employment Implications of Locational Decision-Making: the case of in-town and out-of-town superstores', *Inter-*

national Journal of Retailing, Vol. 3 No. 2.
Distributive Trades EDC, 1985, *Employment Perspectives and the Distributive Trades*, London: HMSO.
Driver, Jonas, 1987, *West Midlands Shopping Survey*, London: Authors.
Gibbs, A., 1987, 'Retail Innovation and Retail Planning', *Progress in Planning*, 27.
GLC, 1986, 'Retailing Employment: the impact of large new stores', *GLC Department of Transportation and Development, Retail Working Paper*, London: Authors.
Institute of Grocery Distribution, 1988, *DIY Superstores*, Watford: Authors.
Jones, P., 1984a, 'Retail Warehouse Developments in Britain', *Area*, Vol. 6, No. 1.
Jones, P., 1984b, 'The Retailing of DIY and Home Improvement Products', *Service Industries Journal*, Vol. 4, No. 1.
London Research Centre, 1986, Retail Warehouses in London, *Reviews and Studies Series Number 30*, London: Authors.
Portsmouth City Council, 1987, *Estimating the Employment Effects of Discount Retail Warehouses*, Portsmouth: Authors.
Scottish Office, 1982, *Retail Employment Change in Scotland*, Edinburgh: HMSO.
Sparks, L., 1983, 'Employment Characteristics of Superstore Retailing,' *The Service Industries Journal*, Vol. 3, No. 1.
Whysall, P., 1981, 'Retail Competition and the Planner – some Reflections', *Retail and Distribution Management*, Vol. 9, No. 3.

This study first appeared in *The Service Industries Journal*, Vol. 11, No. 3 (1991).

9
Labour Productivity, Economies of Scale and Opening Time in Large Retail Establishments

by

A. Roy Thurik*

Differences in labour productivity are dealt with for large French retail establishments. Influences of scale, weekly opening time, assortment composition, wage rate and share of counter service are considered. The relationship used is a result of analyses in the field of small retail establishments.

INTRODUCTION

The aim of this study is two-fold. First, to test whether economies of scale can be obtained with respect to labour productivity for large French retail establishments (*magasins populaires*,[1] hypermarkets and supermarkets). Second, to analyse the influence of weekly opening time on labour productivity. As far as we are informed, no detailed studies have been conducted yet on the explanation of differences in labour productivity of these shop types, which play an important role in French retailing.[2] The emphasis on the role of opening time is induced by the fact that recently the French press[3] devoted much attention to the problem of establishing weekly opening time, and by a recent article on trading hours and economies of scale in retailing.[4] In addition, the roles of assortment composition, wage rate and share of counter service are studied. The data used for our exercises stem from the French weekly *Libre Service Actualités*.

LABOUR PRODUCTIVITY IN RETAILING

In this study we shall use a relationship between volume of labour and value of annual sales for retail establishments which offer essentially the same product mix and service level. Such a group of establishments will be called shop type. This relationship was developed by Nooteboom

*This article is part of a large research programme on productivity differences in retailing. This programme is a combined effort of the Research Institute for Small and Medium-Sized Business in The Hague and the Econometric Institute of the Erasmus University, Rotterdam. The author would like to thank Professor Dr J. Koerts of the Erasmus University, Rotterdam and Dr B. Nooteboom of the Research Institute for Small and Medium-Sized Business in The Hague for their useful comments on an earlier draft of this article.

[1982: 163-86] for small retail establishments. The basic elements of his analysis are:

(a) There is a linear non-homogeneous relationship between volume of labour and value of annual sales for establishments belonging to a certain shop type.

(b) The intercept of this relationship is associated with threshold labour, i.e. a minimum capacity of labour which must be present during opening hours. The amount of this labour is assumed to be equal to the sum of opening times of all independently staffed departments in the shop. Per department the minimum capacity of one attendant must always be present.

(c) Theoretically, this relationship can be derived noting that there are two types of labour: labour to serve customers and labour for other activities (administration, stock-keeping etc.), and using a very narrow definition of a shop type.[5]

(d) Empirically, however, promising results are obtained for shop types having the practical definition given above.

(e) The precise theoretical definition of a shop type does not leave room for a significant possibility for substitution of capital for labour. Consequently, the relation between volume of labour and value of annual sales can be studied disregarding the use of capital.

In mathematical form, the relationship reads for a certain shop type:

(1) $L_i = \alpha_o + \alpha_{1i}Q_i$ with $\alpha_o > o$ and $\alpha_{1i} > o$ for all i,

where L_i : volume of labour in establishment i;

Q_i : value of annual sales in establishment i;

α_o : threshold coefficient. Its value is independent of i, if it is assumed that the number of independently staffed departments and annual opening time are equal for all i;

α_{1i} : scale adjusted labour intensity. This terminology becomes clear after rewriting equation (1): $L_i/Q_i = \alpha_{1i} + \alpha_o/Q_i$. The variable L_i/Q_i, volume of labour per value unit of annual sales, contains two parts: scale independent α_{1i} and scale dependent α_o/Q_i. L_i/Q_i decreases and approximates α_{1i} with increasing scale, if $\alpha_o > o$. The value of α_{1i} depends on specific properties of establishment i within the shop type. We shall return to these properties in the next section.

FRENCH SUPERMARKET-LIKE ESTABLISHMENTS

In applying relationship (1) to French *magasins populaires*, hypermarkets and supermarkets, we have to bear in mind that these establishments are sometimes very large. In Table A2 of the Appendix to this paper, an indication of the range of some variables is given. Also, there is considerable variation in the assortment composition per shop type. For instance, the non-food sales share usually increases with increasing scale. Therefore, the establishments are assumed to consist of two smaller establishments: a food and a non-food establishment. This is done to facilitate our analysis of differences in labour intensities, because they depend largely on the type of products. Two relationships result from this approach:

(2) $L_{ki} = \alpha_{ok} + \alpha_{1ki}Q_{ki}$ with k = 1,2,

where k = 1 refers to food sales and k = 2 to non-food sales; Clearly,

(3) $L_{1i} + L_{2i} \triangleq L_i$ and $Q_{1i} + Q_{2i} \triangleq Q_i$,

where L_i: total volume of labour in establishment i;
       Q_i: total value of annual sales in establishment i.

Summation of equation (2) gives:

(4) $L_i = \alpha_o + \alpha_{11i}Q_{1i} + \alpha_{12i}Q_{2i}$,

where

(5) $\alpha_o \triangleq \alpha_{o1} + \alpha_{o2}$.

We are forced to confront equation (4) instead of equation (3) with the data because L_{1i} and L_{2i} are not available separately and because α_{o1} and α_{o2} cannot be estimated separately.

SPECIFIC PROPERTIES

We shall now introduce hypotheses on the influence of specific properties per establishment on the relationship between volume of labour and value of annual sales:

Opening Time

The intercept of the relation between volume of labour and value of annual sales increases, if opening time increases. In addition, opening time may influence scale adjusted labour intensity. If opening time increases:

(a) intensity of competition decreases, because an increasing number of competing establishments is assumed to be closed. This may imply that customers have to accept longer waiting time. Then labour intensity decreases;
(b) fluctuations in the requirement of labour increase, because an increasing number of opening hours comprises more 'odd hours'. The average discrepancy between required and available labour increases and labour intensity increases.

We have no a priori hypothesis about the resulting 'sign' of the influences of opening time on scale adjusted labour intensity.

Wage Rate

Firstly, it is assumed that the average wage rate per establishment is an indicator of the quality of labour. Secondly, it is assumed that the motivation to use available labour efficiently is induced by the height of the wage rate. Thus, we assume that scale adjusted labour intensity decreases if the wage rate of the establishment increases.

Mode of Service

The mode of service depends on whether counter service or self-service is used to sell the products. Obviously, there is a difference in labour intensity between these types of service. We assume that scale adjusted labour intensity increases if the percentage of shop space used for counter service increases.

TEST SPECIFICATION

Combining equation (4) with the hypothesis of the previous section, we propose the following test specification:

$$(6) \qquad L_i = \alpha_o \left(\frac{DO_i}{\bar{D}\bar{O}}\right) + (\alpha_{11}Q_{1i} + \alpha_{12}Q_{2i})\left(\frac{DO_i}{\bar{D}\bar{O}}\right)^{\alpha_2}\left(\frac{FL_i}{\bar{F}\bar{L}}\right)^{\alpha_3} \exp \alpha_4(CS_i - \bar{C}\bar{S}),$$

where L_i : volume of labour in establishment i (in full-time equivalents);
  DO_i : weekly opening time (in hours);
  Q_{1i} : value of annual food sales (in 10^6 French francs of 1976);
  Q_{2i} : value of annual non-food sales (in 10^6 French francs of 1976);
  FL_i : wage rate per man-year (in 10^3 French francs of 1976);
  CS_j : share of counter service area in total selling area;
  $\bar{D}\bar{O}, \bar{F}\bar{L}, \bar{C}\bar{S}$: sample averages.

Equation (6) needs some explanation:

(a) We restrict ourselves to a multiplicative specification of the influences (DO_i, FL_i and CS_i) on the scale adjusted labour intensities. This is done because it accounts for interaction between variables. An exponential specification is chosen for CS_i, because this variable can take zero value.

(b) The effect of these influences is taken to be symmetric regarding both assortment groups. This is assumed for the sake of convenience.

(c) α_{11} and α_{12} are called partial 'average' scale adjusted labour intensities, because they refer to one assortment group (partial) and to an establishment with $DO_i = \bar{D}\bar{O}$, $FL_i = \bar{F}\bar{L}$ and $CS_i = \bar{C}\bar{S}$ ('average').

(d) α_o is called 'average' threshold coefficient, because it expresses the threshold labour of an establishment with $DO_i = \bar{D}\bar{O}$. Strictly, $\alpha_o = \bar{N}\bar{D} \times \bar{D}\bar{O} \div \bar{D}\bar{T}$, where $\bar{N}\bar{D}$ is sample average number of independently staffed departments and $\bar{D}\bar{T}$ is sample average working time per full-time employee.

(e) the hypotheses of the previous section say that $\alpha_3 < o$, $\alpha_4 > o$, whereas no a priori sign for α_2 is given.

TESTS

The coefficients of equation (6) are estimated for French *magasins populaires* of 1975–79 (MP), French hypermarkets of 1975–77 (HYP) and French supermarkets of 1975–79 (SUP).[7] This estimation is performed by minimising the sum of squares of a disturbance variable which is added to the right hand side of equation (6) and which is assumed to have zero expectation and constant variance. Marquandt's algorithm [1963: 431-41] is used for this numerical minimisation. The results are given in Table 1.

TABLE 1

ESTIMATES OF THE COEFFICIENTS OF EQUATION (6) FOR FRENCH SUPERMARKET-LIKE ESTABLISHMENTS

Shop type		MP	HYP	SUP
Threshold	$\hat{\alpha}_0$	2.76	39.12	3.65
		(1.63)*	(8.89)	(1.12)
Foods	$\hat{\alpha}_{11}$	1.64	.89	1.85
		(.14)	(.25)	(.10)
Non-foods	$\hat{\alpha}_{12}$	3.70	2.15	.98
		(.20)	(.26)	(.20)
Opening time	$\hat{\alpha}_2$	−.20	.33	−.14
		(.09)	(.19)*	(.07)
Wage rate	$\hat{\alpha}_3$	−.87	−.86	−.65
		(.07)	(.11)	(.06)
Counter service	$\hat{\alpha}_4$	.30		
		(.05)		
Number of observations	I	86	82	131
Goodness of fit	ϱ^2	.975	.938	.929

Note: Estimated standard errors ($\hat{\sigma}$) are printed beneath the estimated coefficient. They are assumed to be asymptotically normally distributed. An asterisk (*) is printed next to the standard error of coefficient η if $(\hat{\eta}) < 2\ \hat{\sigma}(\hat{\eta})$, i.e. if $\hat{\eta}$ is significantly different from zero at a 5 per cent level of significance. The square of the correlation coefficient between the vectors of L_i and its estimation is taken as a measure of goodness of fit.

The following conclusions can be drawn from Table 1:

(a) As expected· $\hat{\alpha}_0 > o$ and significantly in case of hypermarkets and supermarkets: economies of scale can be obtained with respect to labour productivity for large French supermarket-like establishments. 'Average' threshold labour is approximately 2.8 full-time equivalents for *magasins populaires*, 39 for hypermarkets and 3.7 for supermarkets. Sample average weekly opening times of these three shop types are 47, 70.4 and 49.2 hours, respectively. Under the assumption that average weekly working time per full-time employee is 36 hours and that one full-time equivalent is needed per independently staffed department, the calculated number of independently staffed departments becomes approximately 2 ($\approx 2.8 \times 36 \div 47$), 20 ($\approx 39.12 \times 36 \div 70.4$) and 3 ($\approx 3.7 \times 36 \div 49.2$), respectively.

(b) As expected $\hat{\alpha}_{11}>0$ and $\hat{\alpha}_{12}>0$ and significantly. Foods are less labour intensive than non-foods for *magasins populaires* and hypermarkets, whereas they are more labour intensive than non-foods for supermarkets.
(c) Weekly opening time has a negative influence on scale adjusted labour intensity for *magasins populaires* and supermarkets. It has a positive influence for hypermarkets, though here $\hat{\alpha}_2>0$ and significantly only at a 10 per cent level of significance.
(d) As expected $\hat{\alpha}_3<0$ and significantly.
(e) As expected $\hat{\alpha}_4>0$ and significantly. Unfortunately, the variable CS_i is not available for hypermarkets and supermarkets.

Finally, we see that the explanation obtained with relationship (6) is extremely high for cross-section samples. Examination of residual values computed with equation (6) does not reveal any structure. There is no reason at all to be suspicious about the use of equation (6) to explain differences in labour productivity.

INTERPRETATION

In the previous section, the results are discussed from a statistical point of view. In this section, these results will be interpreted from an economic point of view:

(a) The calculated number of independently staffed departments seems realistic for *magasins populaires* and supermarkets: one department consists of a series of cash desks and the second and third consist of service counters for specialised goods (for example, fresh foods). The calculated number of cash desks for hypermarkets seems rather large. However, one has to bear in mind that most hypermarkets have a cafeteria, petrol station, garden centre or hobby centre, which are undoubtedly independently staffed.
(b) Probably, *magasins populaires* and hypermarkets have a high degree of specialisation (deep assortment composition) in non-foods, whereas supermarkets specialise in foods. This may cause the differences in labour intensities between the assortment groups per shop type. On the whole, *magasins populaires* are more labour intensive than hypermarkets and supermarkets, which may explain the decrease of the market share of *magasins populaires* in the *grand commerce* in France.[8]
(c) Specification (6) assumes that threshold labour increases with increasing opening time. We learn from the results in Table 1 that this effect is partially offset by a negative influence of opening time on scale adjusted labour intensity for *magasins populaires* and supermarkets. This counterforce is scale dependent; the elasticity of L_i with respect to $\frac{DO_i}{\overline{DO}}$, E, reads:

$$(7) \qquad E = \frac{\mathrm{dlog}L_i}{\mathrm{dlog}\frac{DO_i}{\bar{D}\bar{O}}} = \left[\alpha_o \frac{DO_i}{\bar{D}\bar{O}}[1-\alpha_2] + \alpha_2 L_i \right] /L_i.$$

Now, $E>o$ if $L_i<L^*$ with $L^* = (1 - \frac{1}{\alpha_2})\alpha_c\frac{DO_i}{\bar{D}\bar{O}}$. For *magasins populaires* and supermarkets $L^*(DO_i = \bar{D}\bar{O}) = 17$ and 30, respectively. The sample minimum volumes of labour for *magasins populaires* and supermarkets are 20 and 12 respectively. See Table A2 of the Appendix to this article. From this we conclude that only for very small establishments $E>o$ and that for the major part of the sales range an increase of relative weekly opening time appears to favour labour productivity.

For hypermarkets, however, there is a positive influence of relative opening time on scale adjusted labour intensity: $E>o$ for all values of L. Our hypothesis concerning the difference between *magasins populaires* and supermarkets on the one hand and hypermarkets on the other is the following: generally, hypermarkets have a stronger competitive position than *magasins populaires* and supermarkets. They cannot improve this position by increasing relative weekly opening time, whereas *magasins populaires* and supermarkets can, motivating customers to accept longer waiting time and hence, decreasing labour intensity. Another hypothesis is based on the fact that, generally, hypermarkets have longer opening times than *magasins populaires* and supermarkets, and are not in a position to improve their competitive position by varying their already long opening time.

We refer to Nooteboom [1983: 57-62] for a discussion of the influence of opening time under the assumption that $DO_i/\bar{D}\bar{O}$ is constant, in other words, there is a structural shift in opening time. Then

$$(8) \qquad \frac{\mathrm{dlog}L_i}{\mathrm{dlog}DO_i} = \left[\alpha_o \frac{DO_i}{\bar{D}\bar{O}} \right] /L_i >o$$

(d) The influence of the wage rate is approximately equal for all three shop types. The values found for $\hat{\alpha}_3$ are comparable to, or somewhat higher than those found in earlier studies concerning small retail establishments.[9]

(e) Labour productivity decreases if the share of counter service increases at the expense of the share of self-service. It would be interesting to study its influence on floorspace productivity and margin.

CONCLUSIONS

The main conclusions of the exercises with large French supermarket (-like) establishments are:[10]

(a) The relationship between volume of labour and value of annual sales, discussed in the section on labour productivity in retailing , serves its

purpose very well in the case of large retail establishments, because:
  (i)   according to what is expected, a positive threshold coefficient is
        found, implying economies of scale regarding the use of labour;
  (ii) the value of the threshold coefficient can quite well be explained
        in terms of expected number of independently staffed depart-
        ments;
  (iii) differences in labour productivity can very well be explained
        using variables such as assortment composition, wage rate,
        weekly opening time and share of counter service;
  (iv) the explanation of the relationship used is extremely high for a
        cross-section sample.
(b) Assuming that weekly opening time has a positive influence on
    threshold labour (labour which is independent of scale), we find that
    it has a negative influence on scale dependent labour in the case of
    magasins populaires and supermarkets. The latter influence offsets
    the former up from a certain (rather small) scale. Consequently, for
    the major part of the sales range, an increase of relative weekly
    opening time appears to favour labour productivity. This is not the
    case for hypermarkets.

NOTES

1. *Magasins populaires* can be associated with English variety stores, but they have an integrated supermarket.
2. The market share of *magasins populaires*, hypermarkets and supermarkets in total retailing sales grew from 17.9% in 1975 to 21.7% in 1979. See Marenco and Quin [1981:23].
3. See Laresse [1980:30-3], 'Libre Service Actualités' [1980a:22], [1980b:21-2], [1980c:17-19], and [1981:32-5], and Vié [1980].
4. Nooteboom [1983], who analyses the influence of average opening time on average labour productivity per shop type. This article deals with the influence of different opening times on labour productivity per shop.
5. See Nooteboom [1982:163-86].
6. See Nooteboom [1981].
7. In the Appendix to this article, definitions of the shop types are given as well as the sources of the data used.
8. See Marenco and Quin [1981:23].
9. See Nooteboom [1982] and Thurik and Van der Wijst [1982].
10. Further results concerning influences on labour productivity for these establishments are reported by Thurik [1982]. Differences in floorspace efficiency are discussed in Thurik and Koerts [1982].

REFERENCES

Laresse, A., 1980, 'Horaires: Entre le Ras-le-bol et le Service', *Points de Vente*, No. 196, 1 February.
Libre Service Actualités, 1980a, '78% des Supermarchés Américains Ouverts le Di-manche', No. 740, 11 January.
Libre Service Actualités, 1980b, 'Le Dimanche qui n'est pas Sacré', No. 741, 18 January.

Libre Service Actualités, 1980c, 'Ouverture du Dimanche, Vers un Cadre Juridique Nouveau', No. 755, 25 April.
Libre Service Actualités, 1981, 'Les Français Plébiscitent les Nocturnes', No. 812, 11 September.
Marenco, C. and C. Quin, 1981, *Structures et Tendances de la Distribution Française*, Paris: Ministère du Commerce et de l'Artisanat/Université Paris 9 Dauphine.
Marquardt, D. W., 1963, 'An Algorithm for Least Squares Estimation of Non-Linear Parameters, *Journal of the Society for Industrial and Applied Mathematics*, Vol. 11.
Nooteboom, B., 1981, *Productivity Growth in the Grocery Trade*, Research paper 8103, The Hague: Research Institute for Small and Medium-Sized Business in the Netherlands.
Nooteboom, B., 1982, 'A New Theory of Retailing Costs', *European Economic Review*, Vol. 17.
Nooteboom, B., 1983, 'Trading Hours and Economy of Scale in Retailing', *European Small Business Journal*, Vol. 1, No. 2.
Thurik, A. R., 1982, *Labour Productivity in French Supermarkets*, Report 8210/S, Rotterdam: Econometric Institute, Erasmus University.
Thurik, A. R. and J. Koerts, 1982, *On the Use of Supermarket Floorspace and its Efficiency*, Report 8225/S, Rotterdam: Econometric Institute, Erasmus University. Also E.I.M.-Research-paper 8206.
Thurik, A. R. and D. van der Wijst, 1982, *Part-time Labour and Labour Productivity in Retailing*, Report 8244/S, Rotterdam: Econometric Institute, Erasmus University. Also E.I.M.-Research-paper 8205.
Vié, J. E., 1980, 'Repos Hebdomadaire et Travail Dominical', *Le Monde*, 6 April.

APPENDIX

The source of the data and the partitioning of our samples over the years of observation is given in Table A1. A further description of the data is given in Table A2. The definitions of the shop types are:

Supermarché: magasin d'alimentation (autonome) atteignant 400 m2 de surface de vente (ne dépassant pas 2500 m2) en libre service ou réalisant au moins 7.5 millions de francs de chiffre d'affaires annuel, grâce à un assortiment de 2500 à 5000 références, comprenant 500 à 1500 références non alimentaires.

Hypermarché: libre-service de 2500 m2 de surface de vente minimale, présentant un assortiment complet (20000 à 35000 références), avec des rayons alimentaires (3500 à 5000 références) et non alimentaires (16000 à 30000 références) et offrant un parking à sa clientèle.

Magasin populaire: point de vente limitant son assortiment (7000 à 10000 références) aux articles de grande vente et offrant généralement, en plus des secteurs nouveauté et bazar, des rayons alimentaires (1500 à 4000 références). Le plus souvent exploités en libre-service, ces derniers peuvent constituer, selon la surface qui leur est consacrée et leur propre chiffre d'affaires, un supermarché intégré au magasin populaire.

TABLE A1

SOURCE OF DATA AND PARTITIONING OVER THE YEARS OF OBSERVATION

Code	Year of observation	Number of establish-ments	Average sales (in 10⁶ French francs of the current year)	Average volume of labour (in full-time equivalents)	Source of the data
MP	1975	18	25.1	70.6	P.d.R., 1975, Magasins Populaires, *L.S.A.*, No. 595 (7-10-1976)
	1976	24	23.1	65.7	P.d.R., 1976, Magasins Populaires, *L.S.A.*, No. 631 (24-6-1977)
	1978	19	30.2	70.1	P.d.R., 1978, Magasins Populaires, *L.S.A.*, No. 722 (13-7-1979)
	1979	25	30.5	60.1	P.d.R., 1979, Magasins Populaires, *L.S.A.*, No. 757 (9-5-1980)
		86			
HYP	1975	22	132.7	257.6	P.d.R., 1975, Hypermarchés, *L.S.A.*, No. 593 (15-9-1976)
	1976	36	120.8	214.2	P.d.R., 1976, Hypermarchés, *L.S.A.*, No. 629 (10-6-1977)
	1977	24	180.8	276.7	P.d.R., 1977, Hypermarchés, *L.S.A.*, No. 676 (30-6-1978)
		82			
SUP	1975	42	17.8	36.8	P.d.R., 1975, Supermarchés, *L.S.A.*, No. 593 (19-6-1976)
	1976	56	20.8	37.4	P.d.R., 1976, Supermarchés, *L.S.A.*, No. 629 (10-6-1977)
	1978	23	22.0	36.4	P.d.R., 1978, Supermarchés, *L.S.A.*, No. 720 (29-6-1979)
	1979	10	26.3	34.0	P.d.R., 1979, Supermarchés, *L.S.A.*, No. 764 (27-6-1980)
		131			

Note: P.d.R. = 'Points de Repère', *L.S.A.* = 'Libre Service Actualités'.

TABLE A2
FURTHER DESCRIPTION OF THE DATA

Code	$minL_i$ L $maxL_i$	$minQ_{1i}$ Q_1 $maxQ_{1i}$	$minQ_{2i}$ Q_2 $maxQ_{2i}$	$minDO_i$ $\bar{DO}$ $maxDO_i$	$minFL_i$ $\bar{FL}$ $maxFL_i$
MP	20.0	5.87	2.41	40.0	25.2
	66.1	14.57	10.12	47.0	40.5
	207.0	69.06	38.67	65.0	53.4
HYP	65.0	24.27	11.95	52.0	28.3
	244.1	78.48	62.26	70.4	40.2
	517.0	162.66	154.72	79.0	56.9
SUP	12.0	4.31	.51	40.0	20.2
	36.8	15.40	4.56	49.2	38.6
	105.0	51.17	21.62	78.0	70.0

Note: L_i is volume of labour (in full-time equivalents), Q_{1i} and Q_{2i} are value of annual sales of foods and non-foods, respectively (in 10^6 French francs of 1976), DO_i is weekly opening time (in hours) and FL_i is wage rate per man year (in 10^3 French francs of 1976).

This study first appeared in *The Service Industries Journal*, Vol.4, No.1 (1984).

10
Female and Male Earnings Differentials in Retailing

ADELINA BROADBRIDGE

Female sales assistants and checkout operators in the retail sector earned 79.7 per cent of the male sales assistants and checkout operators' gross weekly wage in 1992. This article examines some of the reasons put forward by Robinson and Wallace in the 1970s for pay differences between men and women in retailing. By using data from the New Earnings Survey this paper compares pay differentials in retailing in 1992 by kind of retail business and examines in particular pay differentials of sales assistants and checkout operators. The paper suggests that differentials between men and women's earnings in retailing remain and that explanations for these differences are not dissimilar to those found by Robinson and Wallace in the 1970s.

INTRODUCTION

There were 2.1 million employees in retailing in Great Britain at June 1992. This represents 9.9 per cent of employees in employment in Great Britain [Department of Employment, 1993]. In the past 20 years there has been a substantial decline in the number of businesses and outlets in retailing, with an increase in the market share of multiple retailers. Employment in large multiple retail businesses now accounts for 53 per cent of all employees in retailing [Business Monitor SDA25, 1990]. Eight of the top ten retail companies in the UK employed over 35,000 staff in 1992 [Times Books, 1993]. From these figures it is apparent that employment in retailing is large and economically crucial to Great Britain.

Robinson and Wallace [1974a] argued that the characteristics of retail employment relied on a concentration of women, and a high proportion of youths and part-time workers; while as an industry, retailing was charac-

terised by a fragmentation of employing units and limited incidence of collective bargaining. Wage councils, responsible for determining statutory minimum wage levels, were additionally regarded as symptomatic of a low-pay
industry. Almost 20 years later retailing is still dominated by these characteristics. Nearly two-thirds of employees in retailing are female and of these
two-thirds work part-time. Females comprise 82 per cent of part-time employees in retailing [Department of Employment, 1993]. Furthermore, a fifth of all
employees in retailing in 1989 were under 18 years old. The very nature of
retailing has meant that it has traditionally been regarded as a low pay industry.

     This article examines the pay differentials between male and female
employees in the retail sector. The aim of the paper is to enlarge on the work
of Robinson and Wallace. Their findings will form a basis to compare pay differentials between males and females in retailing in the 1990s. The IRRR
[1991] have argued that the last 20 years have seen some improvements in the
economic and legal position of women within the labour market, yet women
remain disadvantaged in terms of the pay they receive and the jobs which they
are given.

     The article begins by examining the findings of Robinson and Wallace.
Using data from the New Earnings Survey (NES), the study then compares
pay differentials between men and women in 1992. The New Earnings Survey
is a 1 per cent sample of employees except top management (gathered each
April) paying tax through PAYE and is the largest pay survey in Great Britain.
Perhaps its limitation in the retail context is that the data mainly relate to full-
time males and females on adult rates whose earnings are not affected by
absence. It is also limited in that details such as length of service, entry qualifications and labour turnover levels of the groups are unavailable. Although
wage payment systems are not available at the level of the firm, the NES is
widely regarded as the most comprehensive source of earnings data available.
Specifically the paper reveals that retailing remains a low pay industry for
both men and women by comparing it to the rest of the economy. In the third
section the paper compares pay differentials between men and women by kind
of business. This allows a comparison and consideration of pay differentials
in the retail sector. The New Earnings Survey data by kind of retail business
does not provide a detailed analysis of the various occupations and pay levels. To examine whether pay differentials between men and women exist
within the *same* occupational category, the fourth section considers a more
detailed examination of the occupational category 'sales assistants and checkout operators'. This occupational category was investigated by Robinson and
Wallace in the 1970s, is numerically large in retailing, characterised by the
secondary labour market and dominated by female workers.

PREVIOUS RESEARCH

The work of Robinson and Wallace during the 1970s, which concentrated on wage payment systems of sales assistants at the level of the firm, is seminal to the discussion of pay in retailing in the 1990s. In this section a review of some of their findings provides a backdrop to the present investigation.

Using data from the 1972 New Earnings Survey, Robinson and Wallace [1974a] found that the job of sales assistant is one of the lowest paid in Britain. They reported that only gardeners, farm workers, general catering workers, waiters and barmen earned less than salesmen; while only kitchen hands, hairdressers and barmaids earned less than saleswomen. Furthermore, they claimed that if gratuity payments were included in earnings, the relative position of sales assistants could have been even worse than is indicated in the NES. In another article, they [1973c] additionally argue that the earnings of both male and female sales assistants were significantly below those of other retail categories.

Total earnings in retailing comprise a basic wage, overtime and incentive payments; and wages may be determined by collective bargaining, unilateral decisions, and/or observance of a statutory minimum wage [Robinson and Wallace, 1973a]. Craig and Wilkinson [1985] found hardware and menswear retailers were more likely to pay all their shop assistants above the statutory minimum rate than grocers and CTNS (who both employ a higher proportion of women working part-time). They also found that nearly all (83 per cent) multiple retailers aimed at pay rates which were above the statutory minimum. This compared to 58 per cent of independent retailers, who are less likely to belong to a trade union and have no collective bargaining. It was only the large retailers who had any significant collective bargaining, but trade union activity was still limited because of the fragmentation of units and high proportion of female part-time staff. Robinson and Wallace [1973c] argue that it is reasonable to expect small retail businesses generaly to pay lower wages than multiple organisations, but this does not necessarily preclude multiples from any consideration of low pay, particularly among their female staff. Conducting research into wage payments of sales assistants in three department stores [1972], a department store and co-op society [1973a] and department store [1974b], Robinson and Wallace found male and female full-time workers were paid at different weekly rates according to age and sex. Very few, if any, men received only the minimum wage rate, whereas female earnings in the same firm were heavily concentrated at the lower end of the distribution, with many receiving the minimum wage rate. This, argue Robinson and Wallace [1973a], indicates the generally high grading of men's occupations.

The make-up of average earnings is important to understanding wage differences between men and women in retailing. As well as basic pay, incentive wage components exist. These consisted of merit awards, commission on sales, consolidation payments, spiffs and long service increments, each of which are paid according to different criteria. There were clear differences between the types of additional payments received, according to the sex of the worker. Merit awards, consisting of a fixed weekly payment to individual sales assistants on the recommendation of the head of department, were the principal source of incentive payments for most sales assistants [Robinson and Wallace, 1973a].

Commission payments were of most monetary value, far more significant for men than women, and formed a substantial part of the differential earnings of the higher paid men. Although commission on sales was reported by Robinson and Wallace [1972] as declining as a form of wage payment, it had been retained in departments selling goods of high unit value such as furniture, carpets and major household appliances. Furthermore, Robinson and Wallace [1974b] found that commission was highest in departments employing men only. Robinson and Wallace [1973a] also found that men had the opportunity to earn nearly twice the amount of consolidation payments than women. Staff employed after commission payments had ended did not qualify for consolidation pay. Because of women's more fragmented participation in the labour force, this system possibly further disadvantaged them. Women's incentive payments were found by Robinson and Wallace [1972, 1973a] to consist almost exclusively of spiffs (paid to approximately 25 per cent of all adult women). The amounts earned from spiffs, however, were comparatively small and their removal would not affect women's earnings distribution to any extent.

Robinson and Wallace [1972] claim that the nature and value of goods sold, together with the method of selling have an important bearing on the duties and production knowledge required of sales assistants – hence a generally wider distribution of earnings may be expected in department stores than in stores where both the merchandise and display techniques are more uniform. In department stores more autonomy existed in individual departments, which gave rise to greater scope for maintaining internal wage differentials. The widest gap between male and female earnings was found to be in departments where the goods sold are heavy or bulky [Robinson and Wallace, 1973d]. This gave rise to women being paid at a lower basic wage or at reduced rates of commission because of their alleged inability to cope with the physical demands of handling the merchandise. The majority of retailers were reluctant to employ women in such departments at all, stressing the greater need for product knowledge as a further reason for the employment of salesmen only.

This was not uncommon: widespread views on which jobs belong to men and women were found across a variety of firms by the Office of Manpower Economics [Robinson and Wallace, 1975]. The exclusion of women from these sectors of retail employment is not covered by the Equal Pay Act. There appeared to be loopholes to get around the 'like work' aspect of the Equal Pay Act, and so may be of limited value to sales assistants. The other determination of equal pay is via the concept of 'work evaluated as equivalent'. As there was no obligation on employers to carry out job evaluations (and women cannot claim equal pay unless the work of the man has been evaluated), it too was limited in its nature.

The average earnings of part-time sales assistants were found by Robinson and Wallace [1973b, 1974a] to be considerably lower than average earnings of full-time male and female assistants. In all instances full-time employees were better treated in respect of the size and frequency of increases in their basic pay, in merit awards and increments based on length of service. Lower wage levels were found to be justified because of employers' assumptions that part-time employment reflects a lower degree of attachment to the labour market. Therefore Robinson and Wallace [1974a] concluded that an increase in part-time employment may exacerbate the problems of low pay in retailing.

Such variations in wage differentials led Robinson and Wallace [1972] to conclude that there appeared to be no consistent narrowing of pay differentials between men and women, and in some cases they were widening. The composition of earnings, they claimed [1973d], may differ considerably in the part played by additional earnings from commission on sales, bonus payments or service increments.

RETAIL DIFFERENTIALS COMPARED WITH THE REST OF THE ECONOMY

In April 1992 the average gross weekly earnings of all full-time employees in Great Britain was £305 [New Earnings Survey]. Retailing has traditionally been associated with low pay. A comparison of the average earnings index for the whole economy with distribution and repairs [SIC (1980) classes 61, 62, 64, 65, 67] shows that the average earnings index of the whole economy was 129.3 in 1991 against an average earnings index for distribution and repairs of 124.7 [Department of Employment, 1993]. Tables 1 and 2 detail earnings for full-time male and female non-manual workers in 1992.

TABLE 1
FULL-TIME MALE WORKERS EARNINGS – 1992

Industry	Average Gross Weekly Earnings (£)	Average Gross Hourly Earnings (£)	Average Weekly Hours (total)
All occupations	340.1	8.10	41.4
All non-manual occupations	400.4	10.23	38.6
All manual occupations	268.3	5.89	44.5
Retail distribution 64/65 (non manual)	297.2	7.15	39.4
Retail distribution (manual) - 64/65	219.3	5.06	40.3

Source: Department of Employment [1992].

TABLE 2
FULL-TIME FEMALE WORKERS EARNINGS – 1992

Industry	Average Gross Weekly Earnings (£)	Average Gross Hourly Earnings (£)	Average Weekly Hours (total)
All occupations	241.1	6.38	37.3
All non-manual occupations	256.5	6.88	36.8
All manual occupations	170.1	4.21	39.8
Retail distribution 64/65 (non manual)	187.2	4.83	38.4
Retail distribution (manual) - 64/65	152.7	3.85	39.2

Source: Department of Employment [1992].

Male earnings statistics from the New Earnings Survey for 1992 describe the retail sector as below average for both manual and non-manual workers. Where average male hourly rates for all manual workers are £5.89, retail manual workers earn 86 per cent of this figure; and where average male hourly rates for all non-manual workers are £10.23, retail non-manual workers earn 74 per cent of this figure. Similar trends are apparent for female retail workers. The pay of both male and female non manual retail workers is significantly better than their respective manual counterparts. Male non-manual retail workers receive on average £77.90 more weekly pay than their manual counterparts, while female non-manual retail workers receive on average

£34.50 more weekly pay than retail manual female workers.

For both men and women, a comparison of the NES data shows that the job of sales assistant and checkout operator is one of the lowest paid in Great Britain. In 1992, only male waiters, bar staff and launderers, dry cleaners and pressers earned less than a full-time male sales assistant and checkout operator. This represents just three occupational categories from a listing of 140 non-manual occupations. Perhaps more surprising is that of the 140 male manual occupations listed, only three (clothing cutters, milliners, furriers, hotel porters, and kitchen porters and hands) earned an average gross weekly salary less than the sales assistant and checkout operator (classified as a non-manual occupation). Hospital porters and cleaners and domestics command a lower hourly rate of income, but obviously other payments such as overtime, shift, etc brings their gross weekly salary to above that of sales assistants and checkout operators.

With regard to female non-manual workers, only bar staff, dental nurses, hairdressers and beauticians and launderers, dry cleaners and pressers earn less than the average gross weekly earnings of full-time sales assistants and checkout operators. This represents five occupational categories from a listing of 119 non-manual occupations. Waitresses and domestic staff earned a lower hourly rate of income but their average gross weekly salary was above the female sales assistants and checkout operators. Even from the 29 manual occupations listed, only three occupations earn less than female sales assistants and checkout operators (catering assistants, kitchen porters and hands, shoe repairers, leather cutters and sewers, etc.).

It should be noted, however, that in practice, there is a wide range of pay levels in retailing which vary according to the type of store, location and type of job performed. The range of earnings in the retail sector is very large, with senior retail management commanding very high salaries while very many sales assistants receive low wages. This is confirmed by Howe [1992], who notes one major food retail company estimating that over 70 per cent of its full-time staff employed in stores were in receipt of state family income support. At the other extreme, the chief executive of a company may earn 470 times the amount of his average checkout operator.

EARNINGS BY RETAIL SECTOR

Figure 1 shows that women's gross weekly and hourly earnings are below those of men throughout the retail industry (in sectors where comparisons are available). In non manual retail distribution, women on average earn two thirds that of their male counterparts, while the differential is slightly narrower in manual occupations. Throughout the various sectors of retailing, male employees' average weekly earnings vary from £217.2 to £305.5, while the corresponding range for women is only £152.7 to £198.8.

FIGURE 1
PAY DIFFERENTIALS IN RETAIL DISTRIBUTION: FULL-TIME PAY AS A
PERCENTAGE OF MALE EARNINGS

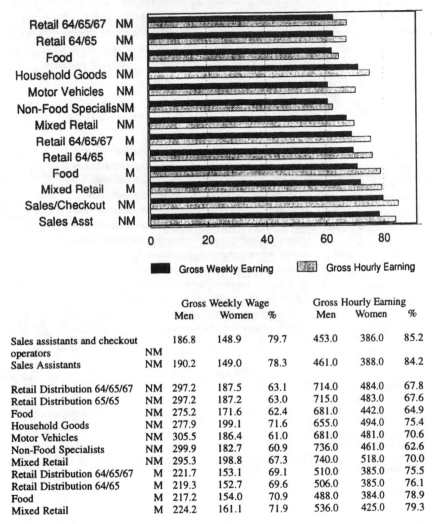

	Gross Weekly Wage			Gross Hourly Earning		
	Men	Women	%	Men	Women	%
Sales assistants and checkout	186.8	148.9	79.7	453.0	386.0	85.2
operators NM						
Sales Assistants NM	190.2	149.0	78.3	461.0	388.0	84.2
Retail Distribution 64/65/67 NM	297.2	187.5	63.1	714.0	484.0	67.8
Retail Distribution 65/65 NM	297.2	187.2	63.0	715.0	483.0	67.6
Food NM	275.2	171.6	62.4	681.0	442.0	64.9
Household Goods NM	277.9	199.1	71.6	655.0	494.0	75.4
Motor Vehicles NM	305.5	186.4	61.0	681.0	481.0	70.6
Non-Food Specialists NM	299.9	182.7	60.9	736.0	461.0	62.6
Mixed Retail NM	295.3	198.8	67.3	740.0	518.0	70.0
Retail Distribution 64/65/67 M	221.7	153.1	69.1	510.0	385.0	75.5
Retail Distribution 64/65 M	219.3	152.7	69.6	506.0	385.0	76.1
Food M	217.2	154.0	70.9	488.0	384.0	78.9
Mixed Retail M	224.2	161.1	71.9	536.0	425.0	79.3

Non-Manual Occupations (NM) include sales assistants and checkout operators, petrol pump
forecourt attendants, sales representatives, buyers, managerial and supervisory grades, merchan-
disers, window-dressers, floral arrangers, telephone sales persons and mobil door to door sales
persons and street traders.
Manual Occupations (M) include shelf-fillers, catering assistants, lift and car park attendants.

Source: New Earnings Survey, 1992.

With the exception of food and household goods retailing, the average gross weekly wage for non-manual men is close to the average gross weekly earnings for all full-time employees of £305 (see Figure 2). The highest paying sector is motor vehicles, which matches the average gross weekly earnings for all full-time employees of £305. Manual male retail workers, however, do earn considerably less than the average weekly full-time wage, with those in the food sector earning the least at £217.2 – just 71.2 per cent.

FIGURE 2
MALE AND FEMALE RETAIL EARNINGS AS A PERCENTAGE OF THE AVERAGE
GROSS WEEKLY EARNINGS FOR ALL FULL-TIME EMPLOYEES

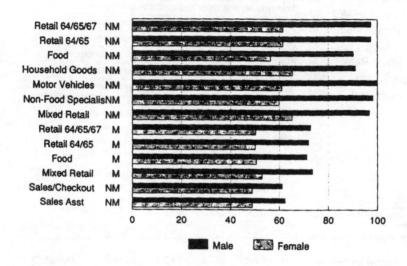

		Men	Women
Retail Distribution 64/65/67	NM	97.4	61.5
Retail Distribution 64/65	NM	97.4	61.4
Food	NM	90.2	56.3
Household Goods	NM	91.1	65.3
Motor Vehicles	NM	1.00	61.1
Non-Food Specialised	NM	98.3	59.9
Mixed Retail	NM	96.8	65.2
Retail Distribution 64/65/67	M	72.7	50.2
Retail Distribution 64/65	M	71.9	50.1
Food	M	71.2	50.5
Mixed Retail	M	73.5	52.8
Sales assistants and checkout operators	NM	61.2	48.8
Sales assistants	NM	62.4	48.9

Source: New Earnings Survey, 1992.

None of the male weekly earnings (manual or non-manual), however, falls below what would be constituted as low pay. There are two methods by which low pay is defined. The Low Pay Unit define low pay as two-thirds of the median male earnings, which in 1992 was £197.30 or £5.26 per hour; The Council of Europe defines low pay as 68 per cent of the mean national earnings, which in 1992 was £207.13 or £5.52 per week.

In contrast, Figure 2 shows that the average gross weekly wage for non manual women in retailing does not match the average gross weekly earnings for all full-time employees. For sectors in which a comparison between men and women's pay is possible, the highest paying sector of retailing for women is the mixed retail sector with an average gross weekly wage of £198.8. As well as being only 65 per cent of the average gross weekly earnings for all full-time employees, it falls below the lowest wage for men. As with male manual workers, female manual workers earn considerably less than their non manual counterparts. The lowest wage for women is for manual workers in retail distribution (SIC codes 64/65) who receive just half the earnings of the average weekly earnings for all full-time employees.

FIGURE 3A
MALE AND FEMALE GROSS WEEKLY PAY AS PERCENTAGE OF LOW PAY UNIT
DEFINITION

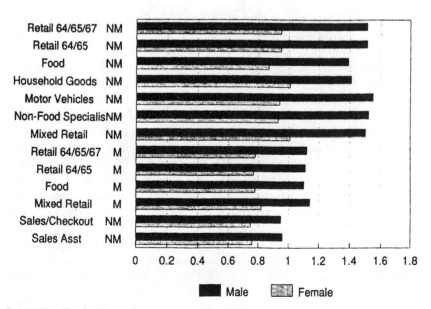

Source: New Earnings Survey.

FIGURE 3B
MALE AND FEMALE GROSS WEEKLY PAY AS PERCENTAGE OF COUNCIL OF EUROPE
DEFINITION

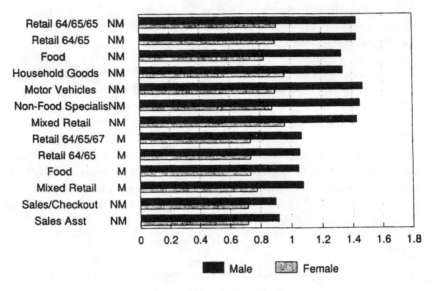

Source: New Earnings Survey.

Furthermore, with the exception of non-manual household goods and mixed retail, all manual and non-manual female gross weekly earnings fall below what would be considered low pay by the Low Pay Unit; while all fall below the Council of Europe's definition. Figures 3a and 3b show male and female retail earnings as a percentage of definitions of low pay.

The position is slightly different if the comparison is made on average hourly earnings. All male manual workers in the retail sector earn less than the hourly rates considered to be low pay by the Council of Europe, although non manual workers earn more than the low pay rate. Females, however (both manual and non-manual), all receive an gross hourly earning below the low-pay definition. As hourly earnings exclude overtime, shift work and payment by results, the implication is that women working in the household goods and mixed retail sector, and men working in the manual retail sectors rely on such payments to supplement their basic wage.

Table 3 reveals that differential pay between men and women is narrowest in the household sector with women earning 71.6 per cent of male gross weekly earnings but widest within the non-food specialist retail sector where women earn only 60.9 per cent of gross male weekly earnings.

There may be several possible reasons why such differentials exist in retailing. First, many sectors and departments within retail distribution have been traditionally gender segregated [Holcombe, 1973; Game and Pringle 1983; Robinson and Wallace, 1973d]. This helps to maintain the barriers between men and women over several issues, pay being one of them.

TABLE 3
PAY DIFFERENTIALS IN RETAILING BY GENDER – 1992

Pay differentials for non manual occupations by gross *weekly* wage is highest in:

Non-food specialised retailing	60.9%
Motor Vehicles	61.0%
Food	62.4%
Retail Distribution 64/65	63.0%
Retail Distribution 64/65/67	63.1%
Mixed Retail	67.3%
Household Goods	71.6%

Pay differentials for non manual occupations by gross *hourly* wage (except overtime) is highest in:

Non-food specialised retailing	62.6%
Food	64.9%
Retail Distribution 64/65	67.9%
Retail Distribution 64/65/67	67.8%
Motor Vehicles	69.3%
Mixed Retail	70.0%
Household Goods	75.4%

Source: Department of Employment [1992].

The data provided in Figures 1 to 3 and Table 3 do not categorise the various retail sectors by occupation. A second possibility for the existence of pay differentials in table 3 is based on Doeringer and Piore's [1971] labour segmentation theory which suggest that employees concentrated into a primary and secondary sector. Primary sector jobs which are characterised by job security, well-defined promotional ladders, good fringe benefits, better working conditions and good pay, while secondary sector jobs are characterised by low pay, poor fringe benefits, poor working conditions, limited promotion prospects, job insecurity and a high turnover rate. Barron and Norris [1976] suggested that men occupy the primary sector while women occupy secondary sector positions, while Blau and Jusenius [1976] suggest it is likely that a higher proportion of women then men occupy secondary jobs. This was reinforced more recently by Freathy [1993], who applied labour segmentation theory to the superstore labour market.

Table 4 tends to support a labour segmentation theory. From Table 4 we see that within each occupational category there appears to be a clear distinction between male and female jobs, with one gender predominating in each category. Although the 1981 census is outdated this distinction is also supported by Craig and Wilkinson [1985]; Dawson, Findlay and Sparks [1987]; Sparks [1991]; and Freathy [1993] across various types of retailing. Men dominate the professional and managerial retail occupations (primary sector) while the data from Robinson and Wallace [1972] showed that women in department stores clearly dominated selling occupations (secondary sector). This is not to suggest that women may not be found in primary sector occupations (nor men in the secondary sector). Women do hold some managerial positions in retailing but many women are further segregated in those positions, such as personnel, administration and supervisory posts. Many women occupy the lower tier of these primary sector occupations [a distinction made by Piore, 1975] and seldom make it to senior management and board level. This was reinforced by Freathy's [1993] findings of a gender breakdown in food superstores.

TABLE 4
PERCENTAGE COMPOSITION OF JOB TYPES IN RETAIL DISTRIBUTION BY
GENDER, 1981

Job Type	Male	Female
Professional[1]	6.2	3.8
Managerial[2]	42.2	15.2
Selling[3]	22.4	52.5
Clerical & related[4]	2.8	19.7
Catering[5]	1.2	4.4
Material Processing/Skilled[6]	7.8	1.4
Processing[7]	6.5	0.1
Transport[8]	8.0	1.4
Others[9]	2.6	1.2
Total	100.0	100.0

1. Including marketing, sales, purchasing managers, accountants, finance specialists, pharmacists.
2. Wholesale and retail distribution managers, transport and warehouse managers.
3. Salesmen, sales assistants, shop assistants, shelf fillers, sales representatives, sales supervisors.
4. Clerks, retail shop cashiers, checkout and cash and wrap operators, secretaries, receptionists.
5. Counterhands and assistants, cleaners.
6. Butchers, bakers, dressmakers and other clothing workers, window dressers.
7. Motor vehicle mechanics, electronic mechanics.
8. Store keepers, warehouse and other porters, lorry drivers, materials moving and storage foremen.
9. Security workers, painters, french polishers and general labourers.

Source: HMSO Census 1981 Great Britain, Economic Activity.

Given that occupational segregation by gender continues to exist in retail distribution, with a dominance of men in primary sector jobs, this may also partially explain the pay differentials between men and women in the various sectors of retail distribution. To examine pay differentials between men and women more closely requires a comparison within the same occupational category.

PAY DIFFERENTIALS BY OCCUPATION

The Equal Pay Act [1970], aimed to eliminate wage differentials between men and women employed in the 'same' or 'like' work. It would be expected that male and female wages within the category 'sales assistants and checkout operators' would be the same. NEDO [1974] suggested that equal pay had been introduced into several sectors of retailing, (particularly in supermarket groups) in response to the Equal Pay Act, but claimed that in retail organisations where women are clustered at the bottom of the occupational hierarchy, the direct impact of the Equal Pay provisions was small.

One would expect that with the introduction of Equal Pay that pay differentials by gender in the same occupational category would no longer exist. If this is not the case, an investigation into the make up of pay will be undertaken, as this was found by Robinson and Wallace [1972, 1973a, 1973d, 1974b] to influence the pay differentials received by men and women sales assistants.

If we were to accept that pay differentials between men and women in retailing are the result of their concentration in particular occupational categories, one would expect that an analysis of earnings between men and women within the same occupational grouping, (that is, sales assistants and checkout operators) would show that earnings as a whole would be lower than for retail distribution in general, because this category of workers is in the secondary sector characterised by low pay. It would also show that pay differentials between men and women would be narrower or non existent, as the same occupation is being compared. If pay differentials do exist this may support the argument that men and women are further segregated even within the same occupation, and points to some shortcomings in using a labour segmentation theory alone to explain gender differentiations in the labour market.

In sectors where men and women do similar work however, NEDO [1974] claimed that women's rates would be increased. A trend analysis over the last 20 years indeed suggests that although fluctuations have occurred, the pay differentials between male and female sales assistants have narrowed (Figure 4). In 1992, however, female sales assistants and checkout operators average gross weekly wages was still only 79.7 per cent of men's.

The New Earnings Survey provides data by occupational category for sales assistants and sales assistants and checkout operators. Both are classified as

FIGURE 4
FEMALE EARNINGS AS A PERCENTAGE OF MALE

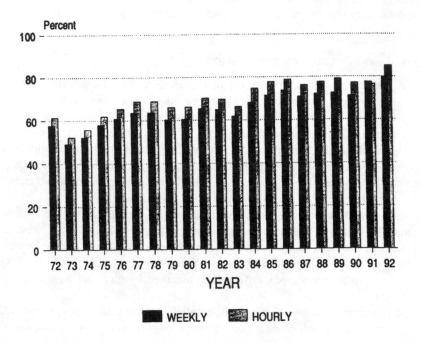

Source: New Earnings Survey.

non-manual occupations. Part D of the New Earnings Survey provides analysis of earnings between men and women by occupation. It must be noted that the occupations of employees from the 1991 New Earnings Survey were coded using the new occupational classification (SOC). Hence, occupational categories provided in the 1992 edition are not strictly comparable to previous years.

Sales occupations are divided into several categories by the New Earnings Survey data. Four of these categories provide data for male and female earnings (buyers, brokers and related agents; sales representatives; sales assistants and checkout operators; sales occupations – mainly telephone salespersons). For the purposes of this article the category 'sales assistants and checkout operators' was selected for comparison because the sample size of this category was largest (4,020) and provided a more balanced number of men and women employed in retailing generally. It also allows a comparison with the work of Robinson and Wallace who specifically examined this category of workers. A comparison of buyers was also considered but rejected as the sample size of 380 was considered to be too low for relevant conclusions to be drawn (while 72 per cent of the sample were male buyers).

An examination of both the gross weekly and hourly earnings of male and female sales assistants and checkout operators in 1992 reveals that their earnings are lower than those of the various non-manual sectors of retail distribution. Their earnings are closer to the manual occupations in retail distribution, which may be expected owing to the secondary nature of the occupation. The gross weekly earnings for male and female sales assistants and checkout operators in 1992 were £186.80 and £148.90 respectively, while their hourly earnings were 453p and 386p respectively. Comparing these earnings to those regarded as low pay, male sales assistants and checkout operators' gross weekly earnings are 95 per cent of the Low Pay Unit's definition and 90 per cent of the Council of Europe's definition (while male hourly earnings are 86 per cent of the Low Pay Unit, and 82 per cent of the Council for Europe definition). Female sales assistants and checkout operators earn 75 per cent of the Low Pay Unit's gross weekly pay definition and 72 per cent of the Council of Europe's definition of low pay (while female hourly earnings are 73 per cent of the Low Pay Unit, and 70 per cent of the Council for Europe definition).

These findings clearly show that differentials between men and women in the same occupational category do exist. Female sales assistants and checkout operators earn, on average, 79.7 per cent of male gross weekly earnings; while the hourly earning differential is 85.2 per cent. However, comparing this differential to that of gender differentials of non manual earnings by sector (Figure 1), they are indeed narrower than that for the various sectors of retailing as a whole.

COMPONENTS OF PAY

To explain the differential earnings of men and women between their gross weekly and hourly earnings requires an examination of the make-up of their total weekly earnings. This is split by the New Earnings Survey data between their basic pay and other components, such as shift work, overtime payments and payment by results (including commission).

One reason the average gross weekly earnings of female sales assistants and checkout operators are lower than those of their male counterparts is because women have a shorter working week (this also explains why hourly differentials are narrower). Full-time female sales assistants and checkout operators worked on average 2.2 fewer hours per week in 1992 than male sales assistants and checkout operators. This is because women work less overtime than men (0.8 to 1.8 respectively); however, the normal basic hours for women are also lower than for men (37.7 and 38.9 respectively). These basic and overtime hourly trends have remained the same since 1972.

Given that trends for average weekly hours have not changed appreciably for two decades, it is encouraging to find that gross weekly pay differentials between male and female sales persons have narrowed over the last 20 years (Figure 4), and it would appear that the Equal Pay Act is partly responsible. However, women's gross weekly earnings are just over three-quarters those of men. One explanation for this is that total earnings do not only depend on hours worked but also on other pay which is not directly affected by the wage rate. As weekly overtime hours are low (1.8 for men and 0.8 for women), a closer analysis of the components of total gross weekly earnings is necessary to understand the differentials in pay. Table 5 shows a trend analysis of the make up of male and female sales assistants pay as a percentage of their total weekly earnings.

TABLE 5

PAY COMPONENTS OF TOTAL GROSS WEEKLY EARNINGS – SALES ASSISTANTS AND CHECKOUT OPERATORS (%)

Year	Overtime pay		PBT etc pay		Shift Pay etc premium		All Other pay	
	M	F	M	F	M	F	M	F
1973	2.8	2.1	16.0	2.3	0.2	–	81.1	95.6
1977	1.9	1.0	15.7	2.2	0.3	0.5	82.0	96.4
1982	2.7	1.0	13.4	2.1	0.4	0.5	83.5	96.4
1987	3.7	1.6	13.9	2.1	1.1	0.8	81.3	95.4
1988	4.0	2.0	13.6	2.7	0.8	0.5	81.7	94.9
1989	4.5	2.9	12.5	2.8	0.8	0.6	82.1	93.7
1990	4.5	2.0	11.2	2.6	1.7	0.8	82.6	94.6
1991	5.6	3.4	10.9	2.6	1.4	0.7	82.1	93.3
1992	5.4	2.5	8.8	2.5	1.8	0.7	84.1	94.2
1992 non-manual occ.	3.0	1.9	3.3	1.3	0.7	1.0	93.1	95.9
1992 all	7.0	2.4	4.1	1.9	1.8	1.2	87.1	94.5

Source: Department of Employment [1992].

From Table 5 we see that basic pay comprises most of the female sales assistants and checkout operators gross weekly earnings in 1992 (94.2 per cent), although they rely very slightly more on overtime pay and PBR (payment by results) than in the past. Female sales assistants and checkout operators rely less than men on such additional payments however. The basic pay for male sales assistants and checkout operators has remained fairly static over the years, and makes up only 84.1 per cent of their gross weekly pay. Shift pay does not significantly affect gross weekly earnings for either men or women, although males do receive slightly more shift pay, as is the case with overtime pay. It is the category of payment by results (PBR) payments which shows the widest differentials between male and female sales assistants and checkout operators. Whilst this makes up 2.5 per cent of women's gross weekly earnings, it contributes towards 8.8 per cent of men's.

Compared to the average for all non-manual occupations, overtime and PBR as components of gross weekly earnings are more important to sales persons of either gender, but most notably PBR is a significant element of the pay of male sales assistants and checkout operators. This begs the question 'Why do male sales assistants and checkout operators appear to have more opportunity to earn commission than women?'

The fact that the various components of pay between male and female sales assistants and checkout operators differ, and that female hourly earnings (which exclude overtime and shift hours) remain below those of men, suggests that although the Equal Pay Act may have helped the relative position of male and female sales persons earnings, it has not eliminated the differentials. This suggests a sectoral difference does exist, with men and women employed in different departments or sectors of retailing with men more likely to be employed in departments or sectors which are based on payment by results schemes. This confirms the work of Robinson and Wallace [1973d] and was also found by Robinson and Wallace [1984] within a manufacturing establishment where the highest bonus earnings were in a department staffed by 48 men. They also found, within a retail establishment, that approximately two-thirds of the men employed as sales assistants earned commission on individual sales, compared with four full-time and two part-time female assistants.

PART-TIME EMPLOYEES IN RETAILING

Although comparable data are unavailable for male and female part-time sales assistants and checkout operators, some reference should be made to the pay of females working part-time in retailing, as they comprise 39 per cent of the retail workforce. The NES data reveal that all women working on a part-time basis in retailing earn comparably less than their full-time counterparts. At a sector level, women working part-time receive an hourly earning which is just over three quarters of female full-time employees, and just over half the male full-time employees.

Many part-time workers in retailing are employed as sales assistants and checkout operators. Differentials also exist in this category although they are narrower. Female sales assistants working part-time receive an hourly earning which is 95 per cent of female full-time and 85 per cent of male full-time sales assistants and checkout operators.

DISCUSSION AND CONCLUSIONS

This article has examined the 1992 earnings of male and female employees in the retail sector, and found that not only do pay differentials exist between men and women across various sectors of retailing but that pay differentials also exist within the same occupational categories. In accordance with Robinson and Wallace's [1973c, 1974a] findings, this article reveals that not only are the earnings of sales assistants and checkout operators still significantly below those of other retail categories, but that retailing remains one of the lowest paid jobs in the economy.

Limitations in the NES data mean that wage comparisons are not available for multiple and small businesses. Anecdotal evidence in 1992, however, would support Craig and Wilkinson [1985] and Robinson and Wallace's [1973c] suggestions that the rates of pay of multiple retailers are more likely to be above the statutory minimum.

Pay differentials between men and women still exist within retailing. These differences were found to be greater at the sector level. Evidence from Robinson and Wallace [1973d, 1975] suggests that gender segregation remains in certain departments, which helps to maintain wage differentials between men and women, while firms often categorise occupations as being masculine or feminine. This is still in evidence today and market segmentation theory may partially help to understand why wage rates are different across various sectors of retailing.

Robinson and Wallace implied that loopholes in the Equal Pay Act would mean the continuation of wage differentials for male and female sales assistants. This article found that wage differentials continue to exist within the same occupational category, with female sales assistants and checkout operators in 1992 earning an average gross weekly wage of just 79.7 per cent of the male wage. These differentials have, however, narrowed considerably since 1972 when they stood at 58 per cent. Retail organisations, particularly multiple organisations, have been addressing equal pay issues over the past few years, acknowledging cases of 'like work' and conducting job evaluation exercises. So some progress has been made. However, the author remains unconvinced that wage differentials between men and women in retailing will erode completely over time.

As Robinson and Wallace found in the 1970s, this article discovered that incentive payments are still more important (yet to a lesser degree) to male as opposed to female sales assistants and checkout operators. This was partially attributed by Robinson and Wallace to skill levels being used against women and the existence of sex segregated departments to encourage the maintenance of gender wage differentials. This could be one explanation of differences in incentive payments in 1992, and is worthy of further research.

Another explanation could lie with another limitation of the NES data, which provides no data on employees' length of service. If employees are paid the minimum rate on joining a company, length of service may be a contributory factor to women's lower pay. This is directly related to their dual domestic–work role and thus fragmented participation in the labour force.

This article also demonstrates that female part-time sales assistants and checkout operators earn considerably less than their full-time counterparts. This supports Robinson and Wallace's [1974a] assertion that an increase in part-time employment would exacerbate the problems of low pay in retailing.

Although current research draws on secondary data, which has various limitations, it appears the nature of pay differentials between men and women in retailing have not changed considerably since the 1970s. Reference to labour segmentation theory may help in understanding differentials across various sectors of retailing if, as it appears, men and women are concentrated into different occupational groupings. It does not, however, explain why differentials continue to exist within the same occupational category, nor why men and women should occupy particular segments of the market. Witz [1993] claims that such a theory, although useful in offering insights into the structuring of labour markets, does not provide an exhaustive explanation of either the operation of labour markets nor gender segregation at work.

Rather, tracing the history of women's involvement in the retail trade, it is more likely that an explanation for women's lower earnings must be more complicated than labour segmentation theory alone. It would appear that women's lower earnings, as posited by Joseph [1983], cannot be divorced from their position in the labour market which serves to reinforce the existing sex inequality in the home, work and society. This is worthy of further consideration and will be taken up elsewhere.

ACKNOWLEDGEMENT

The author would like to thank Professor Leigh Sparks for his valuable suggestions on an earlier draft of this paper.

REFERENCES

Blau, F. D. and C. L. Jusenius, 1976, 'Economists' Approaches to Sex Segregation in the Labor Market: An Appraisal', *Signs: Journal of Women in Culture and Society*, Vol. 1, No. 3, Pt. 2, pp. 181-99.
Barron, R. D. and G. M. Norris, 1976, 'Sexual Divisions and the Dual Labour Market', in Barker, D. L. and S. Allen (eds.), *Dependence and Exploitation in Work and Marriage*, London: Longman.
Business Monitor SDA25, *1990, Retailing*, Central Statistical Office, London: HMSO.
Craig, C. and F. Wilkinson, 1985, 'Pay and Employment in Four Retail Trades', *Research Paper No 51 Department of Employment*, London: HMSO.

Dawson, J. A., A. Findlay, and L. Sparks, 1987, 'Opportunities for Female Employment in Superstore Retailing', *Equal Opportunities International*, Vol. 6, No. 1.

Department of Employment, 1992, *New Earnings Survey*, London: HMSO.

Department of Employment, 1993, *Employment Gazette*, Vol. 101, No. 2.

Doeringer, P. and M. Piore, 1971, *Internal Labour Markets and Manpower Analysis*, Massachusetts: D. C. Heath.

Freathy, P., 1993, 'Developments in the Superstore Labour Market', *Service Industries Journal*, Vol. 13, No 1, pp. 65-79.

Game, A. and R. Pringle, 1983, *Gender at Work*, Hemel Hempstead: George Allen and Unwin.

Holcombe, L., 1973, *Victorian Ladies at Work*, Newton Abbott: David and Charles.

Howe, W.S., 1992, *Retailing Management*, London: Macmillan.

IRRR, 1991, 'Twenty Years of Increasing Opportunities for Women?', *Industrial Relations Review and Report*, Vol. 22, Nov., pp. 7-9.

Joseph, G., 1983, *Women at Work: The British Experience*, Oxford: Philip Allan.

NEDO, 1974, *Manpower and Pay in Retail Distribution*, Distributive Trades EDC, National Economic Development Office.

Poire, M. J., 1975, 'Notes for a Theory of Labour Market Stratification', in Edwards, R. C., M. Reich and D. Gordon (eds.), *Labour Market Segmentation*, Massachusetts, Lexington Heath.

Robinson, O. and J. Wallace, 1972, 'Pay in Retail Distribution: Wage Payment Systems in Department Stores', *Industrial Relations Journal*, Vol. 3, No. 3, pp. 17-28.

Robinson, O. and J. Wallace, 1973a, 'Wage Payment Systems in Retailing', *Retail and Distribution Management*, Vol. 1, No. 3, pp. 24-8.

Robinson, O. and J. Wallace, 1973b, 'Earnings of Part-Time Workers in Retailing', *Retail and Distribution Management*, Vol. 1, No. 4, pp. 12-17.

Robinson, O. and J. Wallace, 1973c, 'Measurement and Problems of Low Pay in Retail Distribution', *Retail and Distribution Management*, Vol. 1, No. 5, pp. 33-9.

Robinson, O. and J. Wallace, 1973d, 'Equal Pay in Retailing', *Retail and Distribution Management*, Vol. 1, No. 6, pp. 28-31.

Robinson, O. and J. Wallace, 1974a, 'Part-time Employment and Low Pay in Retail Distribution in Britain', *Industrial Relations Journal*, Vol. 5, No. 1, pp. 38-57.

Robinson, O. and J. Wallace, 1974b, 'Prospects for Equal Pay in Britain: Retail Distribution and the Equal Pay Act 1970', *International Journal of Social Economics*, Vol. 1, No. 3, pp. 243-60.

Robinson, O. and J. Wallace, 1975, 'Equal Pay and Equality of Opportunity', *International Journal of Social Economics*, Vol. 2, No. 2, pp. 87-105.

Robinson, O. and J. Wallace, 1984, 'Part-time Employment and Sex Discrimination Legislation in Great Britain: A Study of the Demand for Part-time Labour and of Sex Discrimination in Selected Organizations and Establishments', *Research Paper No 43 Department of Employment*, London: HMSO.

Sparks, L. 1991, 'Employment in DIY Superstores', *Service Industries Journal*, Vol. 11, No. 3, July, pp. 304-23.

Times Books, 1993, '*The Times 1000 1992-1993: The Indispensable Annual Review of the World's Leading Industrial and Financial Companies, London*: Times Books (A Division of Harper Collins Publishers).

Witz, A., 1993, 'Women at Work' in Richardson, D. and V. Robinson (eds.), *Introducing Women's Studies: Feminist Theory and Practice*, London: Macmillan.

This study first appeared in *The Service Industries Journal*, Vol.15, No.1 (1995).

11
Flexibility, Skill and Technical Change in UK Retailing

ROGER PENN

This article examines employment patterns in British retailing during the 1980s. It focuses on two debates central to contemporary economic sociology: the flexibility thesis and theories of skill and technical change. The data derive from the ESRC's Social Change and Economic Life Initiative and represent a sample of 72 retailing establishments from six localities in Britain. The article reveals that technological change had not produced much in the way of deskilling: rather, it had enskilled the work of already qualified and trained employees. Whilst part-time employment had increased in many stores, there was little evidence of any significant growth of other kinds of peripheral labour.

INTRODUCTION

The purpose of this article is to examine changing patterns of employment in contemporary retailing. The analysis is based on a random sample of 72 retailing establishments investigated as part of the ESRC's Social Change and Economic Life Initiative which ran between 1985 and 1990. The data were collected in 1988 by the PSI for the Initiative by means of a telephone survey conducted in Aberdeen, Coventry, Kirkcaldy, Northampton, Rochdale and Swindon. Whilst not strictly a national sample, the results of the survey can be taken as broadly representative of current trends in retail employment in Britain [Gallie, 1987]. The analysis is organised around an examination of the two dominant theories of employment change in contemporary economic sociology: the deskilling thesis and the theory of flexibility [Gallie, 1988; Wood, 1989].

THE DEBATE ABOUT CHANGING PATTERNS OF WORK

Flexibility

There has been a burgeoning of research about flexibility in the last decade [see Pollert, 1991, and Gilbert *et al*, 1992]. In particular, Atkinson and Meager

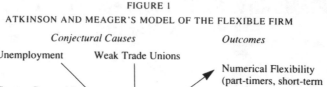

FIGURE 1

ATKINSON AND MEAGER'S MODEL OF THE FLEXIBLE FIRM

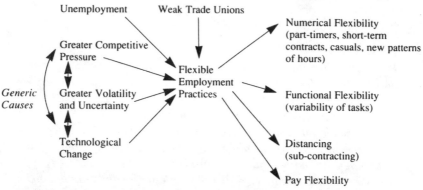

[1986] have suggested that there is a generic trend towards increased flexibility of employment within contemporary organisations. They argued that increasing competitive pressures, greater uncertainty and accelerating technological change have produced a more uncertain environment for contemporary employers (see Figure 1). In Britain, increased levels of unemployment and weakened trade unions since 1979 have enabled employers to develop a range of innovative responses to such broad structural and conjunctural changes. According to Atkinson and Meager [1986] a 'rational' response to such factors involved a strategy of 'flexibility'. They suggested that such flexibility took a variety of forms. The first involved *numerical flexibility*, which signified the capacity of employers to adjust the number of workers or the number of hours worked in line with variations in the level of demand. This could include the employment of part-time, temporary and casual employees or the organisation of flexible shift patterns during the working day. This was complemented by *distancing,* which involved the use of contract labour to undertake what were seen as peripheral activities to the organisation. These included such features as contract cleaning and catering. The third form of flexibility involved *functional flexibility* which indicated the ability of employers to deploy workers over a broader range of tasks. Functional flexibility was often synonymous with 'dual-' or 'multi-skilling'. The final form of flexibility was *pay flexibility*, which included both moves towards more individualized payment schemes and the realisation that functional flexibility often required parallel modifications to salary structures.

Atkinson and Meager [1986] examined four sectors of employment in their research, one of which was retailing. The other three were engineering, financial services and the manufacture of food and drinks. In their report Atkinson and Meager found that almost all retailing firms had increased their use of part-time workers between 1980 and 1984. A major reason for this was the lengthening opening times within such retail firms. Rather than paying overtime to their existing full-time staff to cope with such longer hours, retailing organisations had increased their use of part-time employees. Such economies could be made relatively easily since, according to Atkinson and Meager [1986], most jobs in retailing required very little training. Indeed, some retailing firms used nearly 80 per cent part-timers within their stores. Most part-time employees in retailing were female. Indeed, the growth of part-time employment in retailing had been a major factor in the overall growth of female part-time employment over the last twenty years [Elias, 1989]. In particular, retailing was a sector where married women had traditionally employed in very large numbers [Joshi, 1989].

Atkinson and Meager [1986] provided the following detailed explanation for the growth of part-time employment in retailing. They argued that 'intensive competition and squeezed margins, particularly in the retail food multiples, have meant that there is a strong need to match manning levels during the day and during the week to fluctuations in customer demand' (p.25). Retailers also mentioned the lower costs of part-timers, both in terms of lower hourly rates of pay and reduced employer contributions to national insurance. Two supermarket chains were cited as examples by Atkinson and Meager [1986] of how working patterns had become more flexible during the 1980s. 'ABC Foodstuffs' had increased the numbers of part-timers to match the peaks and troughs of customer demand. 'Everopen Ltd' had increased the proportion of part-time staff to 70 per cent since 1980. These findings were corroborated in a later research project undertaken by Penn and Wirth [1993] at five supermarkets in the Lancaster area.

Curson [1986] also emphasised the growth of part-time and temporary employment during the 1980s. In 1951 only 2.7 per cent of the workforce were employed for 30 hours or less per week, but by 1986 this had climbed to over 20 per cent of the workforce. Indeed, 46.5 per cent of all female workers were part-timers by the mid-1980s. Curson [1986] argued that part-timers had replaced full-timers to a larger degree in retailing than within any other sector of employment because staffing constituted such a very high proportion of overall costs. The hourly cost of a part-time employee within retailing stood at around 12 per cent less than that for a full-timer in the mid-1980s. Such views received additional support from Meager's [1985] report on Temporary Work, from Hakim's [1987] research at the Department of Employment and from Elger's [1987] article which suggested that numerical flexibility, and particularly the increasing use of part-time labour, were general features of retailing in Britain, whereas functional flexibility was more typical in manufacturing industry.

There has been widespread agreement, therefore, among researchers that part-time employment has increased in Britain over recent years. This growth is seen to be concentrated within specific sub-sectors of service industries. Retailing is seen as the major, and often the archetypical, example of these developments. Indeed, retailing employed over two million people in Britain by 1987: a figure that represented almost 10 per cent of the entire workforce. Most of the increase in such part-time employment affected women, many of whom were married with dependent children. Such a strategy of employment was a 'rational' response by retailers to increasing competition, longer opening hours, fluctuations in demand, high overall staffing costs and the relative cheapness of part-time employees. Women, and particularly married women with children, were seen as the main source of such a flexible workforce in retailing. This image of employment patterns in retailing was accepted by most social scientists. Indeed, there was strong *prima facie* evidence for the view that food supermarkets employed a high proportion of female, married, part-time employees.

TABLE 1

EMPLOYMENT IN RETAILING IN GREAT BRITAIN, 1981–90 (THOUSANDS)

	1981	1984	1987	1990	% Change 1981–87
Male Full-time	637	641	642	676	+ 6.1
Male Part-time	131	117	135	140	+ 6.4
Female Full-time	582	544	546	640	+ 10.0
Female Part-time	698	722	745	800	+ 12.8
TOTAL	2048	2024	2068	2256	+ 10.2

Source: Censuses of Employment

Pollert [1988], however, argued a counter case. She cited evidence from Casey [1987] which showed that there had been an 'absence of significant change' in the use of temporary work between 1983 and 1985. Pollert [1988] also cautioned against exaggerating the growth of part-time employment in the 1980s. She reported that, within the service sector, as a whole, the rise in part-time employment between 1979 and 1984 had only been from 40 per cent to 42 per cent. Likewise, the rise in part-time employment in retailing had only been from 34 per cent to 36 per cent over the same period. She criticised Atkinson and Meager [1986] for over-generalising from their own small sample of retailing firms. However, as is clear from Table 1, part-time employment did increase significantly within retailing during the 1980s, particularly among women. Interestingly, from this longer time perspective than the one adopted by Pollert [1988], the growth of female part-time employment had been accompanied by the growth of full-time female employment in retailing. This suggested that issues both of gender and of part-time employment remained of central importance within retailing. Indeed, Sparks [1982; 1983] demonstrated in a succession of articles that part-time employment for women had been increasingly significant within the retailing sector. This was confirmed by the reports of the Distributive Trades EDC's Part-Time Employment Group for NEDO in 1988 [NEDO, 1988a and 1988b].

This present research examined these various and competing claims made about employment and flexibility within the retailing sector. In particular, it assessed Atkinson and Meager's [1986] hypotheses about numerical, functional and pay flexibility and Curson's [1986] view that full-timers had been replaced by part-timers in retailing during the 1980s.

Technological Change and Skilled Work

There has also been a longstanding debate about the effects of technological change on levels of skill among the workforce. Advocates of the deskilling thesis [Braverman, 1974; Crompton and Jones, 1984; Martin, 1988] have suggested that computerisation has produced a general lowering of skill levels. Proponents of the skilling thesis, on the other hand [Bell, 1973], have argued that such technological changes required an increasingly skilled and trained workforce. At Lancaster University we have been engaged in a long-standing research project designed to examine these issues. Our analyses [Penn, 1990; Penn et al., 1992; Penn et al., 1994] suggested the following conclusions.

Firstly, there have been a wide range of technological changes underway over recent years. Some involved computerisation, others did not. These changes have had a variety of effects on occupational skills and training. In particular, within manufacturing industries, changes in production have not necessarily been paralleled by the same kinds of changes within machine maintenance work. Similarly, changes in clerical areas often have not mirrored those either on the shopfloor within manufacturing or in the sphere of service provision. Indeed, research into technical change and skill within establishments in Rochdale and Aberdeen [Penn et al., 1992] revealed that the skill levels of clerical workers had risen sharply during the 1980s within a wide range of service sector establishments, including those located in retailing. These conclusions led us to envisage – on an a priori basis – that computerisation of service provision and clerical activities within retailing would have followed asymmetric and divergent trajectories. For instance, the introduction of EPOS systems within food supermarkets at the checkouts may not have been paralleled by similar changes in the areas of ordering, salaries or stock-taking. These were all areas which warranted separate attention. These issues are probed further in this article, although the data could only support a general level of analysis. Nevertheless, they provide a useful benchmark for the kinds of future detailed analyses that would be required in this area.

METHODOLOGY

The data were collected by means of a telephone survey of 954 establishments in 1988.[1] The questionnaire was designed to elicit information on changes in employment patterns during the 1980s as part of the ESRC's Social Change and Economic Life Initiative (SCELI). These establishments all employed 20 or more at the time of the interview. The present article is based on our analysis of the 72 retailing establishments taken from the overall national sample.[2]

Most establishments (65) were PLCs. 55 establishments were also branches of a larger organisation. They covered a wide range of sizes (see Table 2).

TABLE 2

SIZE OF RETAILING ESTABLISHMENTS (NUMBERS OF EMPLOYEES)

20 – 49	18
50 – 99	17
100 – 249	19
250 – 499	15
500+	3

THE CONTEXT: TECHNOLOGICAL CHANGE, MARKET UNCERTAINTIES AND TRADE UNION POWER IN THE 1980s

There had been considerable technological change within the 72 retailing establishments in the sample during the preceding two years. Half had introduced new computer systems. A quarter had also introduced new equipment without microelectronics. Thirteen establishments had introduced word processors into their offices and the same number had installed new equipment that incorporated microelectronic technologies. Most firms (43) reported that less than a quarter of their workforces had experienced significant changes in their work as a result of these changes overall, but another ten reported that over 75 per cent of their employees had experienced changes in their working patterns.

There was also evidence of considerable increases in competitive pressures over the preceding five years. Almost all (62) reported that customers were more selective in terms of the quality of products purchased and the majority (56) reported that there had been an intensification of price competition. Such competitive pressures had led to greater efforts in service provision at 62 establishments and an increase in the range of products sold at 40. Respondents at 55 retailing firms reported that increased competition had led to far greater attention having to be paid to the rescheduling of work. Interestingly, most firms reported that the increase in competition came from other British firms. Only 9 stated that foreign competition was in any way significant.

TABLE 3

TRADE UNION INFLUENCE ON PAY AND ON WORK ORGANISATION OVER THE PRECEDING FIVE YEARS (NUMBER OF ESTABLISHMENTS)

	On Pay	On Work Organisation
Increased	9	7
Decreased	3	1
No change	23	27

Half the establishments recognized trade unions and half did not. This reflected the general bifurcation of unionisation within retailing nationally. Firms like Asda and the Coop operate quasi-closed shops, whilst Marks and Spencer do not recognise trade unions at all [Penn and Wirth, 1993]. There was little evidence that trade union influence had waned over the preceding five years (see Table 3). Most unionised retail establishments reported little change, therefore, in the power of unions during the 1980s. This reflected the general pattern of trade union power in Britain at this time [see Rose, Gallie and Penn, 1995, for the results of the SCELI research into trade unionism].

Overall, there was considerable *prima facie* support for the efficacy of Atkinson and Meager's [1986] generic causal model but far less for the salience of their conjunctural factors (see Figure 1). There had indeed been considerable technological change and increasing competitive pressures but there was little evidence of decreasing union influence within the establishments in the sample.

EMPLOYMENT PATTERNS

Numbers had increased in most establishments (38) over the preceding five years. There were fewer employed at 14 establishments and the same at another 10.[3] There were also more part-timers at 33 establishments, fewer at six outlets and the same at 17 other establishments. Overall the increase in the number of part-time employees in retailing had occurred simultaneously with the expansion of employment in these establishments. The main reasons given for the expansion of part-time employment was the drive for 'flexibility' (8), 'rationalisation' (7) and the 'desire to reduce unit wage costs' (7). 'Technology' (1), 'employees preference' (2) and the 'desire for improved productivity' (3) featured far less as reasons. There was also some evidence that the workforce was becoming more feminised as numbers expanded. The numbers of female employees increased in a third more establishments (32) than was the case for increases in males (24). However, it was a pattern of differential increase rather than one of widespread substitution of women for men within the sector. Such results were consistent with the Census of Employment data cited earlier in Table 1.

Just over half (38) the establishments provided special working hours designed to be convenient for women with school-age children. These were mainly special shifts (17), part-time hours fitting in with school times (13) and specific hours designed to suit individual's needs (9). Flexitime (4) and job sharing (1) were rarely used in these retailing establishments.

TABLE 4

PERIPHERAL LABOUR UTILISATION WITHIN RETAILING (%)

Agency Workers	30.6
Contractors Staff	55.6
Workers on Short-Term Contracts	45.8
Casual Workers	37.5

TABLE 5

LENGTH OF TRAINING PROVIDED BY RETAILERS FOR NEW STAFF (%)

	Routine Operatives	Skilled Operatives	Clerical
Up to a week	18.3	1.6	3.3
Up to a month	40.0	30.0	25.0
Up to six months	38.3	43.4	65.0
More than six months	3.3	25.0	6.6

There was considerable use of various types of peripheral labour (see Table 4). However, despite such *prima facie* support for Atkinson and Meager's theses, there were two features of such labour utilisation which, upon closer inspection, served seriously to weaken their claims. Firstly, very few establishments were using a total of more than ten peripheral workers at the time of the survey. Twenty-five establishments utilised none and a further 29 establishments employed ten or *less*. When we controlled for size of establishment it became clear that such peripheral labour, whilst widespread, accounted for a very small proportion of overall employment. Indeed, the numbers of peripheral employees had decreased at 12 establishments and increased at only 8 during the preceding *five* years. Overall, it was clear that peripheral labour was both a small and declining part of total employment within contemporary retailing.

QUALIFICATIONS AND TRAINING

Few qualifications were required by most establishments for their routine operatives. Only 7 required any qualifications for sales staff. Only slightly more than half (35) of the establishments required qualifications for entry into skilled occupations. These were generally either apprenticeship credentials for bakers and butchers or HGV licences for drivers. Almost half of the establishments (30) did not require such credentials for entry into skilled retailing jobs. Only 39 establishments required formal qualifications for entry into clerical work. Overall the general impression was one of relatively low demands for qualified personnel within this sector.

All establishments provided some degree of training for new employees. However, as was clear from Table 5, most routine operatives such as check-out staff and shelf-fillers received a month or less training. Furthermore, most had no formal qualifications either. The general picture here was one of lowly qualified, minimally trained workers in the main. The length of training received by skilled operatives and clerical workers was not that much longer on average. Whether such relatively low levels of qualification and training are appropriate within contemporary retailing remains an open question.

TECHNOLOGICAL CHANGE AND THE DIVISION OF LABOUR

Virtually no respondents (5) stated that technological change had produced less skilled work. Furthermore, such deskilling was concentrated entirely among routine operatives such as checkout personnel. On the other hand, respondents often identified enskilling processes at work as a result of technological changes. Interestingly, managers were seen as the group whose skills were most likely to have been upgraded. They were followed by clerical workers and, to a lesser extent, by skilled retail employees. Routine operatives were seen as the least likely to have been enskilled. However, these results should not be exaggerated. In a majority of cases there were no perceived effects on skill as a result of the technological changes introduced during the preceding two years.

TABLE 6

TRAINING REQUIREMENTS OF TECHNOLOGICAL INNOVATIONS IN RETAILING
(NUMBER OF ESTABLISHMENTS RESPONDING POSITIVELY)

	Some Need	Most Need
Routine Operatives	10	4
Skilled Operatives	18	13
Clerical	23	12
Managerial	34	15

These asymmetric patterns were re-emphasised by responses to questions concerning the training effects of these technical innovations (see Table 6). Once more, managers were seen to have required the most training and routine workers relatively little training to operate these new technologies. It was clear from these overall findings on qualifications, training and recent technological change that there had been something of a process of polarisation within retailing organisations in recent years. Skilled operatives, clerical employees and managers required both qualifications and a degree of training. Routine operatives, on the other hand, in the main required no qualifications and minimal training. Technological changes had reinforced and exacerbated this bifurcated structure of employment opportunities. This process of polarisation closely parallels the findings of the NEDO investigation into part-time working [NEDO, 1988a and 1988b; Robinson, 1990].

TABLE 7

CHANGES IN WORKING PATTERNS IN RETAILING (% OF ESTABLISHMENTS RESPONDING POSITIVELY)

Increased shift working	27.8
Increased use of collective pay incentives	30.6
Increased use of individual performance assessment	57.8
Increased use of work measurement/method study	29.2
Training of employees to cover jobs other than their own	54.2
Replacement of some full-time employees by part-timers	31.9
Replacement of some employees by peripheral employees	12.5
Reduction of numbers	30.6

CHANGING WORKING PATTERNS

As was evident from Table 7, there had been a wide range of changes in working practices over the preceding two years. The most common change involved a degree of functional flexibility as a result of employees being trained for jobs other than their own. Whether this involved job enrichment or an intensification of work remained open to interpretation. Interestingly, whilst individualised forms of payment had increased at 58 per cent of retail establishments, collective pay incentives had increased in use at 31 per cent of the establishments in the sample. Whilst these results are rather paradoxical, it was clear that there had been widespread changes in payment systems within retailing during the 1980s.

In almost one third of the establishments there had been substitution of part-timers for full-time employees. Whilst the overall numbers were clearly small – as was shown earlier in this article – such results provided considerable support for Curson's [1986] arguments on this score.

EMPLOYEE RELATIONS

Establishments in retailing reported a marked improvement in the willingness of their employees to work well over the preceding five years. Forty reported an improvement and only ten reported a deterioration. There was a rather different picture with regard to time-keeping by employees during the same five year span. Only 15 establishments reported an improvement whilst 12 reported a deterioration. Most reported no significant change.

Although only half the firms recognised unions, many of the other establishments utilised a range of alternative means of involvement of employees. These were most likely to entail a works council or a Joint Consultative Committee. There was little evidence of the array of new managerial strategies of involvement so popular with contemporary management pundits. There were no examples of quality circles, there was merely one example of team briefing and profit-sharing only existed at three firms.

Whilst trade unions were recognised at half of the establishments, their influence on decision-making appeared minimal. Salaries were generally determined away from the establishment in company-wide bargaining systems. Only 12 firms reported that they engaged in discussions with employees or their representatives locally over pay. Negotiations over other issues were also infrequent. During the preceding two years, nine establishments had negotiated with unions over changes in numbers employed. Only six had discussed either the introduction of new technology or changes in the use of part-time employees with their unions.

CONCLUSIONS

The SCELI data on retailing establishments provided a good test for Atkinson and Meager's [1986] flexibility thesis. There had been widespread technological change and also considerable increases in competitive pressures during the preceding period. Trade unions had not become markedly weaker but the data revealed them to be relatively marginal during this period. This may not have been a new phenomenon but it was consistent with the overall logic of the Atkinson and Meager [1986] model.

Most retailing establishments reported increased levels of employment in the 1980s. This had partly, but not exclusively, involved an expansion in the numbers of part-time employees. However, this trend was by no means specific to the 1980s. As is clear from Table 8, part-time employment in retailing rose dramatically during the 1970s.[4] Indeed, it rose much faster in that decade than in the succeeding one. On closer inspection it also becomes clear that the period between 1971 and 1975 witnessed the most rapid rise in part-time employment in retailing in Britain. The decline of full-time female employment dates from that period at the very least. The aggregate patterns in the 1980s are therefore part of a much longer structural transformation of employment within retailing. Atkinson and Meager [1986] identified the phenomena reasonably correctly but their causal model is inadequate – none of the mechanisms at work can be compressed exclusively into the 1980s. Given such long-term structural shifts in employment patterns, it was perhaps even more surprising that almost half of the retailing establishments in the survey made no special arrangements in terms of hours of work for women with school-age children.

TABLE 8

EMPLOYMENT IN THE DISTRIBUTIVE TRADES IN THE 1970S

	1971	1975	1978	1981	% Change 1971–81
Male Full-time	1044	1052	1068	1055	+ 1.1
Male Part-Time	107	144	147	137	+ 18.7
Female Full-Time	812	752	745	733	– 9.7
Female Part-Time	591	761	756	758	_ 28.3
TOTAL	2554	2709	2716	2683	+ 5.1

Source: Censuses of Employment.

There was evidence of widespread utilisation of peripheral labour in retailing establishments. However, the data do not square with any notion that such forms of employment were the brave new pattern for the 1980s. Such employees accounted for a very small proportion of overall employment within retailing and more establishments revealed that the numbers of such workers had fallen over the preceding two years than reported an increase. Furthermore, 25 establishments used no peripheral labour at all! We conclude, therefore, that overall employment patterns in retailing embodied significant aspects of flexibility but that these patterns were *neither specific to the 1980s nor an accelerating trend.*

The data revealed an increasingly bifurcated, polarised workforce. Routine retail employees had few qualifications and little training. Technological change had not produced much in the way of deskilling – rather, it had *enskilled the work of already qualified and trained employees.* The higher up the occupational hierarchy within retailing, the more likely it has been that technological change in recent years would have resulted both in significant retraining and the enskilling of job tasks.

What are the likely developments in the 1990s? It would seem probable that the growth of part-time female employment in retailing will continue. The emergence of discount-club stores and the advent of Sunday trading and longer hours of opening will sustain this trend. However, it seems unlikely that there will be a major growth in the use of peripheral labour such as contract workers or temporary employees. This will continue to be marginal to retail employment.

Technology will continue to affect jobs. It remains an open question, and one which merits further research, whether the present tendency for technological change to enhance mainly managerial and clerical jobs will continue or whether a wider, more pervasive set of changes will envelop retailing organisations.

NOTES

1. See M. White, 1987, 'The Employers' Telephone Survey', London: Policy Studies Institute, The questionnaire itself is available from Michael White at the PSI and the data is now lodged with the ESRC Data Archive at the University of Essex.
2. The distribution of retail establishments across the six localities was as follows: Aberdeen (14), Coventry (9), Kirkcaldy (10), Northampton (13), Rochdale (8) and Swindon (18).
3. Ten did not respond.
4. The data for the period 1971–81 cover 'distributive trades' which is a broader definition than that used for 'retailing' in the period since 1981.

REFERENCES

Atkinson, J. and N. Meager, 1986, *Changing Working Patterns: How Companies Achieve Flexibility to Meet New Needs*, London: National Economic Development Office.

Bell, D., 1973, *The Coming of Post-Industrial Society*, London: Basic Books.

Braverman, H., 1974, *Labor and Monopoly Capital*, New York: Monthly Review.

Casey, B., 1987, 'The extent and nature of temporary employment in Great Britain', *Policy Studies*, Vol. 8, No. 1, July, pp.64-75.

Crompton, R. and G. Jones, 1984, *White-Collar Proletariat: Deskilling and Gender in Clerical Work*, London: Macmillan.

Curson, C., 1986, *Flexible Patterns of Work*, London: Institute for Personnel Management.

Elger, T., 1987, 'Flexible Futures? New Technology and the Contemporary Transformation of Work', *Work. Employment and Society*, Vol. 1, No. 4, pp.528-40.

Elias, P., 1989, 'A Study of Trends in Part-time Employment, 1971-86', *Institute for Employment Research*, Warwick University, February.

Gallie, D., 1987, 'The Social Change and Economic Life Initiative', *ESRC Social Change and Economic Life Initiative*, Working Paper 1, Oxford: Nuffield College, pp.1-32.

Gallie, D. (ed.), 1988, *Employment in Britain*, Oxford: Basil Blackwell.

Gilbert, N., R. Burrows, and A. Pollert (eds.), 1992, *Fordism and Flexibility: Division and Change*, London: Macmillan.

Hakim, C., 1987, 'Trends in the Flexible Workforce', *Employment Gazette*, November, pp.549-60.

Joshi, H. (ed.), 1989, *The Changing Population of Britain*, Oxford: Basil Blackwell.

Martin, R., 1988, 'Technological Change and Manual Work', in D. Gallie (ed.), *Employment in Britain*, Oxford: Basil Blackwell.

Meager, N., 1985, *Temporary Work in Britain: Its Growth and Changing Rationales*, Brighton: Institute of Manpower Studies.

National Economic Development Office, 1988a, *Part-Time Working in the Distributive Trades: Volume 1, Training Practices and Career Opportunities*, London: NEDO.

National Economic Development Office, 1988b, *Part-Time Working in the Distributive Trades: Volume 2, Evidence from Company Case Studies and an Employee Attitude Survey*, London: NEDO.

Penn, R.D., 1990, *Class, Power and Technology*, Oxford: Polity.

Penn, R.D., A. Gasteen, H. Scattergood and J. Sewel, 1992, 'Technical Change and the Division of Labour in Rochdale and Aberdeen', *British Journal of Sociology*, Vol. 43, No. 4, pp.657-80.

Penn, R.D., M.J. Rose and J. Rubery (eds.), 1994, *Skill and Occupational Change*, Oxford: Oxford University Press.

Penn, R.D. and B. Wirth, 1993, 'Employment Patterns in Contemporary Retailing: Gender and Work in Five Supermarkets', *Service Industries Journal*, Vol. 13, No. 4 (Oct.), pp.252-66.

Pollert, A. (ed.), 1991, *Farewell to Flexibility?*, Oxford: Basil Blackwell.

Pollert, A., 1988, 'The 'Flexible Firm': Fixation or Fact?', *Work, Employment and Society*, Vol. 2, No. 3, pp.281-316.

Robinson, O., 1990, 'Employment Policies in the Service Sector: Training in Retail Distribution', *Service Industries Journal*, Vol. 10, No. 2, pp.284-305.

Rose, M.J., D. Gallie and R.D. Penn (eds.), 1995, *Trade Unionism and Local Labour Markets*, Oxford: Oxford University Press.

Sparks, L., 1982, 'Female and Part-Time Employment within Superstore Retailing', *European Journal of Marketing*, Vol. 16, No. 7, pp.16-29.

Sparks, L., 1983, 'Employment Characteristics of Superstore Retailing', *Service Industries Journal*, Vol. 3, No. 1 (March), pp.63-78.

Wood, S. (ed.), 1989, *The Transformation of Work*, London: Hutchinson.

This study first appeared in *The Service Industries Journal*, Vol.15, No.3 (1995).

12

Contemporary Developments in Employee Relations in Food Retailing

PAUL FREATHY and LEIGH SPARKS

Over the past decade considerable attention has been focused upon the changing nature of the retail food sector. While some attempts have been made to detail the implications for employee relations, the majority of studies have chosen in-depth qualitative research. While all such study is to be welcomed, it is necessary to place such focused research into the context of sectoral change. This article provides an overview of the major developments within food retailing and details their impact upon contemporary employment relations.

Retailing has become the focus of increased study. The economic changes of the 1980s forced acknowledgement of the role of the service sector. Academics are finally realising the scope for research into this important area. In many cases such studies are undertaken by non-sector specialists, who bring a different perspective and approach to bear. It is important that these examinations take account of the individual sector and that the sector context is sufficiently apparent and understood. If this is achieved, then there is considerable merit in combining such functional expertise with sector specific studies. The dangers lie in insufficiently understanding the business context within which the study is placed.

It is recognized and welcomed that there are a variety of methodological approaches to the study of employee relations in food retailing. Some commence from the standpoint of detailed cases, whilst others begin by seeking an understanding of the general context. To develop fully the study of employee relations in retailing, we would argue that both approaches are necessary. Some, such as Marchington and Harrison [1991] and Penn and Wirth [1993], have provided detailed case material. Here, we address some of the broad issues and focus in particular on food superstores, as these represent the leading edge of food retailing and, we contend, employment practices and developments.

The aim of this article, therefore, is to provide a review of contemporary developments in employee relations in food retailing. The article is divided into four main sections. First, an analysis of the recent changes in food retailing is provided. Secondly, a theoretical framework is used to help the discussion before reviews of employee relations in food retailing are examined in the third section, including consideration of employment change and the way in which food retailers are reconciling the supply of, and demand for, labour. Finally, the basic premises of the article are summarised and conclusions are drawn.

RECENT CHANGES IN FOOD RETAILING

There are a considerable number of commentaries on the changing food retailing sector in Great Britain [Akehurst, 1983; 1984; Baden Fuller, 1986; Beaumont, 1987; Burt, 1991; County NatWest, 1992; Davies et al., 1986, Davis and Kay, 1990; Dawson, 1987; Duke, 1991; Lewis and Thomas, 1990; McClelland, 1990; McGoldrick, 1984; Manchester Business School, 1987; Mintel, 1992; Moir, 1990; Shaw et al., 1989; Sparks, 1992a; Wrigley, 1988; 1991; 1993]. What they all illustrate is that the food sector is one where change has been dramatic and concentration ratios have increased strongly. The sector is seen as being at the forefront of change and the leading food retailers are amongst the largest companies in the United Kingdom.

Growing concentration has been associated with the increasing power of multiple retailers and a decline in the strength of the co-operatives and independents. The rise of the multiple retailers particularly through economies of scale and replication has produced a situation where only a handful of companies dominate food retailing. Currently the leading food retailers are Sainsbury and Tesco with Safeway in third place. These are followed by the troubled chains of Gateway and Asda. The Co-operative Movement as a whole is large, accounting for approximately 7 per cent of the total grocery market share, but the individual societies differ widely in their performance. In the discount sector the dominant player is Kwik Save, with recent interest from companies such as Aldi, Netto and Shoprite. There are also a small number of regional multiples such as Wm Low and Wm Morrison.

Strategically, food retailing has become a highly competitive industry increasingly answerable to the City and shareholder pressure. Labour represents the second largest financial outlay for the retailer after merchandise costs. The most efficient means of labour utilisation are therefore a strategic priority. Attempts to improve market share and increase profitability have resulted in operational changes that have influenced the structure of the retail food labour market. These are summarised in Table 1.

TABLE 1
FOOD RETAILING CHANGE AND EMPLOYMENT

Food Retailing Changes and Trends	Employment Implications
a: Sector Trend	
Concentration	Centralisation of functions; loss of store autonomy.
b: Operational Changes	
Increasing Size of Store	Number of workers employed at one site; Scale economies in employment; Specialist functions.
Decentralisation of Store Locations	Types of workers employed; Travel to work patterns.
Retail Branding	Specialists needed at 'head office'.
Finance	Capital/Labour balance; Specialists at 'head office'; De-skilling at store level.
Service/Value Competition	Types of store staff needed; Inter-personal skills; Training; Reward bases.
Technology Introduction	De-skilling; Labour replacement; Centralisation tendencies; Management skills requirement.
Logistics	Less store staff; Balance of store staff; Timing of work.

Table 1, which is based on the work cited above and a wide range of other sources, points to the employment implications of the changing retail context [Davies and Sparks, 1989; Thorpe, 1991; Dawson, 1988; Dawson et al., 1986a; 1986b; 1988; Ogbonna and Wilkinson, 1988; 1990; Sparks, 1991a, Sparks, 1992b]. As retailing has changed, so too have the employment inputs, both at store level and elsewhere in the company. There are also employment implications stemming from the changing relationships amongst retailers and their suppliers. It is therefore important in discussions about contemporary employment changes that this wider perspective is understood.

It is possible, therefore, to see how a transformation in the nature of food retailing has implications for the structure and composition of the workforce. One can compare the post-war 'idyll' of small retail outlets, run mainly by independents and co-operatives, based on a corner shop model where counter service dominated (or was just being replaced by self-service) and where daily shopping trips were predominant, to food retailing today which is focused on large scale, off-centre, self-service based food superstores operated primarily by multiples. Quality, value and choice have become the by-words. The rationing and utility of the 1950s have been replaced by the choice and quality of the 1980s and 1990s with an intermediate stage of price consciousness in the 1960s and 1970s. As these changes outlined above have taken place and the transformation has been undertaken, so there have been major effects on store and head office employment. Prior to considering how these changes have influenced the structure of the food labour market, it is useful to provide a conceptual framework for understanding such developments.

UNDERSTANDING EMPLOYEE RELATIONS : A THEORETICAL
FRAMEWORK

The polarisation of operating scale and the transformation of the retail
food sector has accentuated the process of change within the labour
market. The imperatives of flexible response and consumer supremacy
has led to a restructuring of employment relations.

One means by which this change may be conceptualised is through
segmentation theory. While this approach has been criticised on the
priority it accords to demand rather than supply side factors [Hamilton
and Hirszowicz, 1993], it represents an adequate means for understanding retail labour market change.

Much academic debate has focused upon the segmented nature of
labour markets [Ashton and Snug, 1992; Atkinson, 1985; Edwards,
1979; Peck, 1989a; 1989b; Rubery, 1989; Gordon et al., 1982; Tanner et
al., 1992]. Some, such as Gordon et al. [1982] and Edwards [1979], see
labour market segmentation as constituting a barrier to the development of a unified anti-capitalist movement. Through the
development of dual economies, working-class consciousness is defused
and the formation of class-wide solidarity removed. Others have viewed
segmentation as the outcome of a relationship based upon asymmetric
power relations. The influence of both supply and demand side factors
are fundamental to understanding empirical events. Whilst capital remains the dominant partner in this relationship, the role of the labour
supply cannot be ignored.

Focusing upon the dynamic nature of this power relationship is a
means of conceptualising retail change in the grocery labour market. It
has been argued that labour markets are both hierarchical and segmented and can be divided broadly into primary and secondary forms of
employment [Doeringer and Piore, 1971]. Primary employment conditions are characterised by having secure terms of employment, high
wages and good working conditions. The primary sector could be
further divided between the upper and lower primary sectors. What dis-
tinguishes each element is the control exercised over the job. The upper
primary tier comprises professional and managerial positions where individuals have control and autonomy over their working environment.
In contrast, the lower primary tier consists of jobs where individuals
have little control over their working environment [Piore, 1975].

While the nature of this relationship may change, a distinction has
been drawn between the different terms and conditions applying to
each. An integral element to understanding the nature of the retail
labour market is the concept of the internal labour market. Based on
work originally undertaken in the 1950s, internal labour markets were
seen as methods of sheltering specific groups of workers from the open

market [Kerr, 1954; Lester, 1952; Slichter, 1950]. Entry into the internal market can be governed by both the organisation and trade unions and, once achieved, the pricing and allocation of labour is not affected by the market but is governed through a series of institutional rules and procedures [Glynn and Gospel, 1993]. The internal market is distinguished from the external when labour is no longer controlled by economic variables.

Access into an internal labour market is through a 'port of entry'. Entry at a specific port provides access to higher positions through an internal promotion system. It is argued that the existence of a defined career structure for individuals provides benefits for both employer and employee. Internal labour markets offer employers greater flexibility. Employees are given a range of specific company skills which makes it difficult (though not impossible) for them to transfer to comparable positions elsewhere. Once a worker has begun to move up the career ladder, switching to another firm becomes less attractive as they may be relegated to a lower port of entry. The internal labour market is therefore seen as placing a voluntary tie upon the individual by making it unattractive to leave the firm. The practice of restricting entry in this way also allows firms to use their internal markets as screening devices against opportunistic labour. Those workers who were hired in error can either be dismissed or the firm can minimise its losses by halting the progression of an individual on the career ladder [Williamson, 1975; Wachter, 1974].

Glynn and Gospel's [1993] review of quality and productivity maintains that in the UK internal labour markets have been slow to develop relative to other countries. Emphasis has been placed on the recruitment of external labour with insufficient attention given to the development of company-based training systems.

In contrast, the secondary sector generally comprises jobs with little security, poor wages and high turnover. It is possible for some elements of the secondary workforce to have both responsibility and specific skills [Rubery, 1989]. Like the primary, therefore, the secondary sector is also seen as being hierarchical with terms and conditions differing between different job categories. The secondary sector is seen as providing employers with a series of material benefits. It represents a method of externalising costs while at the same time maintaining flexibility [Atkinson, 1985; Michon, 1987]. In periods of economic downturn secondary workers may be removed from the labour force without affecting the employment conditions of primary workers. Conversely, in periods of expansion they may be drawn in as demand requires.

The boundaries between the primary and secondary are not fixed and are drawn and redrawn as employers respond to product market conditions or labour market changes. Some have argued that employers will seek to reduce the size of their core workforce during periods of economic uncertainty [Atkinson, 1985]. Others have maintained that the development of labour market dualism represents a more fundamental process of institutional reform. While wholesale deregulation of the labour market remains impractical, employers seek to attach less stringent conditions of employment protection to new appointments [Deakin and Mückenberger, 1992]. Flexibility of response takes precedence over traditional labour market rigidities. The use of sub-contractors, temporary workers and part-timers provides firms with increased flexibility.

The supply of labour within the labour market is also segmented by factors such as gender, age, race and residential location. Particular forms of labour are considered to occupy particular market segments or niches. The allocation of groups to positions within the labour market may result from external pressures, internal organisational decisions or general market failure [Ashton et al., 1982; Ashton and Snug, 1992; Crompton et al 1990]. The inequitable treatment of different groups within the labour market allows wider pay differentials for workers of comparable jobs. Identifying broad trends therefore obfuscates the highly complex nature of labour market allocation. For example, it was suggested that women as a whole represent a secondary labour force [Barron and Norris, 1976]. This, we maintain, ignores sectoral, locational and organisational differences in the interaction between labour and capital.

The remainder of this paper seeks to examine the structure of supply and demand within the retail food industry to identify the imperatives behind retail labour market allocation. There are limitations to segmentation theory [Rubery, 1989]. Its weaknesses when applied to the retail sector have been detailed elsewhere [Freathy, 1993]. We will, however, argue that this concept still provides an appropriate means for understanding the structure of the retail food labour market.

EMPLOYEE RELATIONS IN FOOD RETAILING

The structural changes that have occurred within the retail sector have influenced directly the nature of the employment relationship within food retailing [DTEDC 1985]. The discussion below concentrates on the current situation in food retailing and particularly food superstore retailing. Detailed quantitative analysis of the employment structure of the food superstore has been provided elsewhere and is not repeated here [Dawson, Findlay and Sparks, 1987; Freathy, 1993; Marchington and Harrison, 1991].

There has been a long-term decline in the total food retail workforce, associated with structural changes in the industry and in the replacement of labour by capital. The long-term decline has been particularly acute in terms of working owners and there has been a proportionately larger reduction in the self-employed than in employees. The rise of the large multiple food retailers has affected not only sales but also employment. The changes that have stemmed from the developments within the retail sector have not been confined to the shop-floor. Some of the most significant developments within the retail labour market have occurred at the *managerial level*.

Managers within the food sector have seen a number of changes to their method of working. We would maintain that one of the most influential mechanisms prompting this change has been advances in technology. Much research has focused upon how technology has helped produce in-store productivity gains and more cost effective and responsive re-ordering and stock control systems [Burt and Dawson, 1991; Dawson and Sparks, 1986]. However, a concentration upon operational efficiency ignores the impact such changes have had upon employment relationships.

For the large multiples, the ability to collect sales data through EPOS means that store performance and thus individual performance can be monitored and controlled both continuously and effectively. The centralisation of control has turned the store into a cost centre. Many decisions that would have been made by managers at the store level are now taken elsewhere in the company [Smith, 1988]. Decisions over pricing, promotion, space allocation and budgeting are in the majority of instances taken at head office. The use of real time or rapid response data means a better matching of performance to actual demand. For the firm, control can be vested in head office while the responsibility for meeting the targets remains with the individual store manager. The separation of conception from execution has been a key element in retail restructuring but its implementation has raised a dilemma for both retailers and store managers.

Food retailing has become an increasingly sophisticated and technologically demanding industry. Consequently these demands have led to the recruitment and selection of an increasing number of graduate managers to run superstores. The process of centralisation however has led to a situation where retailers require a more professional managerial workforce in store, to cover a reduced number of store based decisions. This decline in responsibility and autonomy has the potential to affect

TABLE 2

FINANCIAL PACKAGE FOR GENERAL MANAGER IN MEDIUM/LARGE FOOD SUPERSTORE

Category 8 (Band from £39,000–£49,000, performance rated)

Salary:	£45,000 per annum consolidated (no Premiums)
Overtime:	Double time for Sundays
	Fixed payment of £100 for Bank Holidays
Benefits:	Employee Profit Sharing – average 6% P.A.*
	Executive Share Options
	Annual Bonus of up to 30% of Annual Salary†
	Private Medical Insurance
	Annual Medical (Harley Street)
	Company car, ranges from BMW 520-Audi Coupe, Volvo 960-Senator, includes all costs including petrol.
	Staff Discount Card – 10% off over £3.00
	28 days paid holiday per annum
	26 weeks Company Sick Pay
	PEP's Schemes
	Company Pension Scheme (including Life Insurance)
	Subsidised Staff Restaurant
	5% discount at Hogg Robinson Travel Agents

*Dependent on Company Profit Performance.

the morale of store management and has been an issue that retailers have sought to address. One way in which this has been tackled has been to increase the remuneration package available. Table 2 illustrates the typical package available to a food superstore manager (in 1992) with approximately 10 years' experience running a medium/large store. Retailers have sought to remedy the problem of declining autonomy through financial and status related compensation.

Quantitative research confirms these points, revealing a highly segmented labour market which reflects the primary/secondary divide identified earlier. In an examination of food and non-food superstore employment it was shown that managerial and supervisory staff enjoyed terms and conditions that closely corresponded to primary sector employment. Positions were relatively secure and turnover averaged just over 5 per cent per annum [Freathy, 1993].

Within the management structure of food retailing it is also possible to identify a gender division. Research into food superstores has highlighted the high proportion of male store managers. Research being conducted at the Institute for Retail Studies to update this previous work shows that of 481 randomly selected stores from four multiple food retailers there were 469 male store managers (97.5 per cent) and only 12 (2.5 per cent) female. This gender bias continues at the level of deputy and assistant store manager. Only in superstores large enough to warrant a personnel department were women more fully represented with the majority of personnel officers being female [Freathy, 1993; Sparks, 1982].

At the *shop-floor level* food retailing has also undergone major structural changes. The most visible trend is that of increasing part-time working, with more than 45 per cent of all employees in retailing now being part-time workers. When FTE employment figures are calculated, a fundamental restructuring of retail employment is revealed rather than 'simply' a labour to capital exchange [NEDO, 1988]. The increase of part-time labour is related to retailers' need for greater flexibility in the working day. While this is undoubtedly true, it does represent only one demand side factor determining the structure of employment relations. The use of part-time labour has suited the industry well. Part-timers are less likely to receive wage bonuses, commissions, shift allowances or overtime payments. Societal conditions and practices also condition the level of part-time working in retailing [Gregory, 1991].

Much of the increase in part-time working has been made possible by advances in technology. In a way similar to managerial employment, technology has facilitated a rescheduling of labour deployment. Systems such as EPOS have been used to identify the peaks and troughs of the working day both for the store as a whole as well as for individual departments. Staff scheduling has been increasingly based upon the improved flow of information now available [Smith, 1988; Whitmore, 1990]. Employees can be tracked from till to till and their performance monitored closely throughout their working period. The data collected provide better understanding of the consumer demand on the store and also allows better utilisation of staff as they are matched to extended (12+hours and 7-day) demand. At its extreme form, this has resulted in so called 'flexible contracts' where the hours worked are left open and the staff brought in as consumer demand requires.

Shop-floor workers experience many of the conditions identified earlier as characterising the secondary labour market. For example, the skill level required to work as a sales assistant is low. Related to this is the low level of training that sales assistants are given. Reflecting an industry wide characteristic [Craig and Wilkinson, 1985], priority is placed upon ensuring that individuals reach the minimum level of competence required to undertake the work. Further training for many sales assistants is not an integral part of employment and is provided only in relation to specific changes in operation (such as the introduction of EPOS or EFTPoS).

The concept of the shop floor as a form of secondary labour market is further reinforced by the low level of demarcation that exists between jobs. Individuals are expected to undertake a range of duties such as shelf filling, check-out operations and dealing with customer inquiries. The ability to deploy staff wherever necessary provides superstores with an opportunity to respond flexibly to changes in customer flow during the working day, week and year.

The low level of skill required for shop-floor work combined with the requirement to be flexibly deployed has compounded the high rate of labour turnover. This is concentrated in certain jobs and with certain types of employee. Explanations vary, but the easy entry into the sector, the low skill level required, the routine and the low pay are all con-tributory factors. Traditionally many food retailers have considered high turnover as an integral part of the employment relationship and turnover rates in excess of 120 per cent were not uncommon. More re-cently, there has been a recognition that high turnover has a direct effect upon store productivity. Research reveals that the multiple retailers have been successful in reducing this figure by more than half, although it is debateable how much of this gain will be maintained post-recession.

Many retailers are placing greater effort on the areas of shop-floor re-cruitment, retention and training [Jarvis and Prais, 1989; Reynolds and Brue, 1991; Robinson, 1990; Freathy, 1991; Broadbridge and Davies, 1993]. Sophisticated interview and pre-entry techniques are being used more widely for shop-floor staff and more concern is being devoted to staff retention issues. Advances in technology have allowed a more detailed examination of leavers and a more accurate determination of the true costs of turnover.

TABLE 3
FINANCIAL PACKAGE FOR SHOP FLOOR STAFF IN FOOD SUPERSTORES, 1991-92

General Assistant at age 18+:	£7,374.54 per annum
Cashier at age 18+:	£7,743.21 per annum
Benefits: 10%	
Staff Discount Full-time and Part-time Pension Scheme	
Save As You Earn Scheme	
Profit Sharing	
Subsidised Staff Restaurant	
5% discount Hogg Robinson Travel Agents	
4 weeks and 2 days paid holiday as soon as joining Company	
Full uniform provided	
Staff Social Club	

Despite these efforts by individual retailers, retailing is generally con-sidered to be a low status, low pay sector [Craig and Wilkinson, 1985].

Until their recent abolition, two Wages Councils set minimum rates of pay for more than 1.2 million shopworkers, highlighting the large number of retail employees at the lower end of the pay scale. The large food multiples offer rather higher wages and ancillary benefits. Table 3 provides an example of the typical package received by a shop-floor worker in one large food multiple. The basic salary is above the Retail Food and Allied Trades Wages Council minimum rate for 1991 of £115.245 per week. There has been a recognition by the multiples that the shop-floor pay rates need to be more attractive to obtain and retain sufficient staff. In the late 1980s there have therefore been a series of substantial pay increases by major retailers. These have been driven both by the need to keep staff in difficult employment areas and by the threat of equal pay and value legislation in Europe. Whatever the cause, there has been a substantial improvement in the pay rates in many large companies.

In contrast to the managerial positions the overwhelming majority of sales floor positions are occupied by women. In food superstores women form the largest proportion of the secondary workforce comprising around 73 per cent of sales positions [Sparks 1991b]. Males working on the shop floor were mainly (though not exclusively) confined to specialist areas such as the butchery, bakery or storeroom. It is notable that these are the very areas of stores being affected by current changes to company operating practices.

Food retailing is also an important employer of young people, both at shop-floor level and also in management [NIESR, 1986]. Estimates suggest that over a quarter of all employees in retailing are aged 24 or under and that retailing is an important first destination for school leavers. At the shop floor level the relative lack of skill required means that entry barriers are minimal. A comparison of the age structure of J Sainsbury plc and IBM (UK) Ltd shows the youthful nature of the Sainsbury workforce, with 49 per cent of Sainsbury staff being under 30 compared to 25 per cent of IBM. Within this IBM have virtually no staff under 21 compared to 27 per cent for Sainsbury [NIESR, 1986; Sparks, 1992b].

The employment of such high numbers of young people for shop floor work further highlights the influence of supply side pressures upon labour market outcomers. The threat of the demographic time-bomb in the mid-to-late 1980s saw experiments in the utilisation of different forms of labour. Perhaps the best documented is B & Q. Although not a food retailer, B & Q demonstrates the way in which some retailers are beginning to move. For one of their stores in Macclesfield Cheshire, only people aged 50 or over were recruited for its opening. The company claims that the employees of this age provide better service and more commitment to the job [Hogarth and Barth, 1991].

Our research reveals a similar pattern by Tesco with its older employees. Whilst not staffing entire food superstores with older people, the proportion of older employees particularly in the 'more difficult' employment areas of the South of England has been increasing. Tesco have targeted such staff through leaflets and focused local advertising. Other retailers are beginning to follow suit as the value of such staff becomes more apparent and widespread.

CONCLUSIONS

The aim of this article has been to provide a commentary upon contemporary developments within food retailing. The retail sector has only recently begun to attract the level of academic attention devoted to other sectors. Such focus is obviously welcome; however, a clear understanding of the structure of the retail sector is necessary prior to any operational investigations. We have illustrated in this review some of the major strategies undertaken by food retailers and attempted to show how this basic framework is essential for understanding the changing nature of employment relationships.

This overview has also sought to highlight some theoretical considerations that help contextualise the retail food labour market. What remains apparent is the dynamic hierarchical and segmented nature, not only of employee relations but of the retail sector as a whole. The notion that food retailing is a secondary sector and consequently *all* employment relationships are also secondary is not sustainable.

It would appear that as the retail food sector has developed in complexity, contradictions have been highlighted in the traditional segmentation theory. Ports of entry into the internal labour market have become more rigorously defined. Increasingly a first degree is becoming a prerequisite for a store management position. At the same time, however, the notion of what constitutes a primary worker is becoming obfuscated. The centralised control characteristic of the industry seems to undermine many of the conditions of primary employment. The imperative for the changes witnessed within the primary sector seem to be related to the level of sophistication in the industry. As the retail food sector has become more complex, there has been a formalisation of job tasks, management development and career structure.

Many shop-floor workers remain in what is loosely classed as secondary employment. The notion of a hierarchical and segmented labour market is particularly valid in this context. Over the last 30 or so years, as retailers have become more adept at controlling their operations, so they have become clearer about the form of employment relationship they wish to foster. The asymmetry of the power relationship has led to the expansion of part-time employment and the movement towards more flexible working. Many of the employment conditions associated with the food retailing sector have traditionally been characteristic of the secondary sector; developments in employee relations have done little to rectify this. More recently, however, the dynamic nature of the consumer market and the increasing demand for value and service has created a dilemma between the issues of service provision and cost saving [Fuller and Smith, 1991]. Retailers are seeking to reconcile the need to train the secondary workforce in order to meet customer needs.

The traditional view of the labour market taken by segmentation theorists may therefore be seen to be static in its interpretation of labour market conditions (a factor that may account for criticisms of demand side bias). What has been illustrated here is that the labour market and consequently segmentation theory must be placed in a more dynamic framework that adequately accounts for contemporary employment changes.

REFERENCES

Akehurst, G., 1983, 'Concentration in Retail Distribution: Measurement and Significance', *Service Industries Journal*, Vol.3, No.2, pp.161–79.
Akehurst, G., 1984, 'Checkout: The Analysis of Oligopolistic Behaviour in the UK Grocery Retail Market', *Service Industries Journal*, Vol.4, No.2, pp.198–242.
Ashton, D. and J. Snug, 1992, 'The Determinants of Labour Market Transition: An Exploration of Contrasting Approaches', *Work Employment and Society*, Vol.6, No.1, pp.1–21.
Ashton, D., M. Maguire and V. Garland, 1982, 'Youth in the Labour Market', *Research Paper No.34, Department of Employment*, London: HMSO.
Atkinson, J., 1985, 'Flexibility: Planning for an Uncertain Future', *Manpower Policy and Practice*, Vol.1, pp.26–9.
Baden-Fuller, C. W. F., 1986, 'Rising Concentration in the UK Grocery Trade 1970–80', in K. Tucker and C. W. F. Baden-Fuller (eds.), *Firms and Markets*, London: Croom Helm.
Barron, R. and G. Norris, 1976, 'Sexual Divisions and the Dual Labour Market', in R. Barker and J. Allen (eds.), *Dependence and Exploitation in Work and Marriage*, London: Longman.
Beaumont, J., 1987, 'Trends in Food Retailing', in E. McFadyen (ed.), *The Changing Face of British Retailing*, London: Newman Books.
Broadbridge, A. and K. Davies, 1993, 'Management Education at a Distance and Its Effects upon Career Progression: The Case of MBA in Retailing and Wholesaling Students', *Distance Education*, Vol.14, No.1, pp.6–26.
Burt, S. L., 1991, 'Trends in the Internationalisation of Grocery Retailing: The European Experience', *International Review of Retail Distribution and Consumer Research*, Vol.1, No.4, pp. 487–515.
Burt, S. L. and J. A. Dawson, 1991, *The Impact of New Technology and New Payment Systems on Commercial Distribution in the European Community*, Commercial and Distribution Series Study No.17, Brussels, Commission of the European Communities.
County Natwest, 1992, *UK Food Retailing*, London: County Natwest.

Craig, C. and F. Wilkinson, 1985, 'Pay and Employment in Four Retail Trades', *Research Paper No 51 Department of Employment*, London: HMSO.

Crompton, C., L. Hautrais and P. Walters, 1990, 'Gender Relations and Employment', *British Journal of Sociology*, Vol.41, No.3, pp.329–50.

Davies, B. K. and L. Sparks, 1989, 'The Development of Superstore Retailing in Great Britain 1960–1986', *Transactions of the Institute of British Geographers*, Vol.14, No.1, pp.74–89.

Davies, B. K., C. Gilligan and C. Sutton, 1986, 'The Development of Own Label Product Strategies in Grocery and DIY Retailing in the UK', *International Journal of Retailing*, Vol.1, No.1, pp.6–19.

Davis, E. and J. Kay, 1990, 'Assessing Corporate Performance', *Business Strategy Review* (Summer), pp.1–16.

Dawson, J. A., 1987, 'The Evolution of UK Food Retailing: Inventory, Prospect and Research Challenges', Paper presented at the Twelfth Annual Macromarketing Conference, Montreal.

Dawson, J. A., 1988, 'Futures for the High Street', *The Georgraphical Journal*, Vol.154, No.1, pp.1–12.

Dawson, J. A. and L. Sparks, 1986, 'New Technology in UK Retailing: Issues and Responses', *Journal of Marketing Management*, Vol.2, No.1, pp.7–29.

Dawson, J. A., A. M. Findlay and L. Sparks, 1986a, 'The Importance of Store Operator on Superstore Employment Levels, *Service Industries Journal*, Vol.6, No.3, pp.349–61.

Dawson, J. A., A. M. Findlay and L. Sparks, 1986b, 'Defining the Local Labour Market: An Application of Log-linear Modelling to the Analysis of Labour Catchment Areas', *Environment and Planning A*, Vol.18, No.9, pp.1237–48.

Dawson, J. A., A. M. Findlay and L. Sparks, 1987, 'The Impact of Scanning on Employment in UK Food Stores: A Preliminary Analysis', *Journal of Marketing Management*, Vol.2, No.3, pp.285–300.

Dawson, J. A., A. M. Findlay and L. Sparks, 1988, 'The Employment Implications of Locational Decision Making: The Case of In-Town and Out-of-Town Superstores', *International Journal of Retailing*, Vol.3, No.2, pp.35–47.

Deakin, S. and U. Mückenberger, 1992, 'Deregulation and European Markets', in A. Castro, P. Mehant and J. Rubery (eds.), *International Integration and the Organisation of Labour Markets*, London: Harcourt Brace.

Doeringer, P. and M. Piore, 1971, *Internal Labour Markets and Manpower Analysis*, Massachusetts: D. C. Heath.

Duke, R., 1991, 'Post-Saturation Competition in UK Grocery Retailing', *Journal of Marketing Management*, Vol.6, pp.63–75.

Edwards, R., 1979, *Contested Terrain: The Transformation of the Workplace in the Twentieth Century*, London: Heinemann.

Freathy, J. P., 1991, 'Distance Learning and the Distributive Trades: Stirling's MBA', *Journal of European Industrial Training*, Vol.15, No.4, pp.21–4.

Freathy, J. P., 1993, 'Developments in the Superstore Labour Market', *Service Industries Journal*, Vol.13, No.1, pp.65–79.

Fuller, L. and V. Smith, 1991, 'Consumers Reports: Management by Customers in a Changing Economy', *Work, Employment and Society*, Vol.5, No.1, pp.1–16.

Glynn, S. and H. Gospel, 1993, 'Britain's Low Skill Equilibrium: A Problem of Demand?', *Industrial Relations Journal*, Vol.24, No.2, pp.112–25.

Gordon, D., R. Edwards and M. Reich, 1982, *Segmented Work, Divided Workers*, Cambridge: Cambridge University Press.

Gregory, A., 1991, 'Patterns of Working Hours in Large Scale Grocery Retailing in Britain and France: Convergence after 1992?', *Work, Employment and Society*, Vol.5, No.4, pp.497–514.

Hamilton, M. and J. Hirszowicz, 1993, *Class and Inequality*, Hemel Hempstead: Harvester Wheatsheaf.

Hogarth, T. and M. C. Barth, 1991, *Age Works: A Case Study of B & Q's Use of Older Workers*, Institute of Employment Research, University of Warwick.

Jarvis, V. J. and S. J. Prais, 1989, 'Two Nations of Shopkeepers: training for retailing in France and Britain', *National Institute of Economic Review*, No.128.

Kerr, C., 1954, 'The Balkanisation of Labour Markets', in E. W. Bakke (ed.), *Labour Mobility and Economic Opportunity*, New York: John Wiley.

Lester, R., 1952, 'A Range Theory of Wage Differentials', *Industrial and Labour Relations Review* (July).

Lewis, P. and H. Thomas, 1990, 'The Link Between Strategy, Strategic Groups and Performance in the UK Retail Grocery Industry', *Strategic Management Journal*, Vol.11, pp.385–97.

Manchester Business School 1987, *UK Grocery Retailing*, Manchester: Manchester Business School.

Marchington, M. and E. Harrison, 1991, 'Customers, Competitors and Choice: Employee Relations in Food Retailing', *Industrial Relations Journal*, Vol.22, No.4, pp.286–99.

McClelland, W. G., 1990, 'Economies of Scale in British Food Retailing', in C. Moir and J. A. Dawson (eds.), *Competition and Markets*, Basingstoke: Macmillan.

McGoldrick, P. J., 1984, 'Grocery Generics – An Extension of the Private Label Concept', *European Journal of Marketing*, Vol.18, No.3, pp.63–76.

Michon, F., 1987, 'Segmentation, Employment Structures and Productivity Structures', in R. Tarling (ed.), *Flexibility in Labour Markets*, London, Academic Press.

Mintel, 1992, Food Retailing, *Mintel Retail Intelligence*, Issue 1.

Moir, C., 1990, 'Competition in the UK Grocery Trades', in C. Moir and J. A. Dawson (eds.), *Competition and Markets*, Basingstoke: Macmillan.

NEDO, 1988, *Part-Time Working in the Distributive Trades* (two volumes), London: NEDO.

NIESR, 1986, *Young People's Employment in Retailing*, London: NEDO.

Ogbonna, E. and B. Wilkinson, 1988, 'Corporate Strategy and Corporate Culture: The Management of Change in the UK Supermarket Industry', *Personnel Review*, Vol.17, No.6, pp.10–14.

Ogbonna, E. and B. Wilkinson, 1990, 'Corporate Strategy and Corporate Culture: The View from the Checkout', *Personnel Review*, Vol.19, No.4, pp.9–15.

Peck, J., 1989a, 'Reconceptualising the Local Labour Market: Space, Segmentation and the State', *Progress in Human Geography*, Vol.13, No.1, pp.42–61.

Peck, J., 1989b, 'Labour Market Segmentation Theory', *Labour and Industry*, Vol.2, No.1, pp.119–44.

Penn, R. and R. Wirth, 1993, 'Employment Patterns in Contemporary Retailing: Gender and Work in Five Supermarkets', *Service Industries Journal*, Vol.13, No.4, pp.252–66.

Piore, M., 1975, 'Notes for a Theory of Labour Market Stratifications', in R. Edwards, M. Reich and D. Gordon (eds.), *Labour Market Segmentation*, Massachusetts: Lexington Heath.

Reynolds, J. and N. Brue, 1991, *Recruitment and Retention in Retailing*, Harlow: Longman.

Robinson, O., 1990, 'Employment Policies in the Service Sector', *Service Industries Journal*, Vol.10, No.2, pp.284–305.

Rubery, J., 1989, 'Employers and the Labour Market' in D. Gallie (ed.), *Employment in Britain*, Oxford: Blackwell.

Shaw, S. A., D. J. Nisbet and J. A. Dawson, 1989, 'Economies of Scale in UK Supermarkets: Some Preliminary Findings', *International Journal of Retailing*, Vol.4, No.5, pp.12–26.

Slichter, S., 1950, 'Note on the Structure of Wages', *Review of Economics and Statistics*, February.

Smith, S., 1988, 'How Much Change at the Store? The Impact of New Technologies and Labour Processes on Managers and Staff in Retail Distribution', in D. Knights and H. Wilmott (eds.), *New Technology and the Labour Process*, Basingstoke: MacMillan.

Sparks, L., 1982, 'Female and Part-Time Employment within Superstore Retailing', *European Journal of Marketing*, Vol.16, No.7, pp.16–29.

Sparks, L., 1991a, 'Retailing in the 1990s: Differentiation through Customer Service', *Irish Marketing Review*, Vol.5, No.2, pp.28–38.

Sparks, L., 1991b, 'Employment in DIY Superstores', *Service Industries Journal*, Vol.11, No.3, pp.304–23.

Sparks, L., 1992a, 'The Rise and Fall of Mass Marketing? Food Retailing in Great Britain Since 1960', in G. Jones and R. Tedlow (eds.), *The Rise and Fall of Mass Marketing*, London: Routledge, pp.58–92.

Sparks, L., 1992b, 'Restructuring Retail Employment', *International Journal of Retail and Distribution Management*, Vol.20, No.3, pp.12–19.

Tanner, J., S. Davis and B. O'Grady, 1992, 'Immanence Changes Everything: A Critical Comment on the Labour Process and Class Consciousness', *Sociology*, Vol.26, No.3, pp.439–53.

Thorpe, D., 1991, 'The Development of British Superstore Retailing – Further Comments on Davies and Sparks', *Transactions of the Institute of British Geographers*, Vol.16, No.3, pp.354–67.

Wachter, M. L., 1974, 'Primary and Secondary Labour Markets: A Critique of the Dual Approach', *Brookings Papers on Economic Activity*, No.3, pp.637–93.

Whitmore, M., 1990, 'The Influence of Management in Controlling Labour Retention in Tesco Stores' (unpublished MBA Dissertation, Unversity of Stirling).

Wrigley, N., 1988, 'Retail Restructuring and Retail Analysis', in N. Wrigley, *Store Choice, Store Location and Market Analysis*, London: Routledge.

Wrigley, N., 1991, Commentary: Is the 'Golden Age' of British Grocery Retailing at a Watershed?, *Environment and Planning A*, Vol.23, pp.1537–44.

Wrigley, N., 1993, 'Retail Concentration and the Internationalisation of British Grocery Retailing', in R. Bromley and C. Thomas (eds.), *Retail Change: Contemporary Issues*. London: UCL Press.

This study first appeared in *The Service Industries Journal*, Vol.14, No.4 (1994).

Further Reading

Bradley, K., and S. Estrin, 1992, 'Profit Sharing in the British Retail Trade Sector: The Relative Performance of the John Lewis Partnership', *Journal of Industrial Economics*, Vol.40, No.3, pp.291–304.

Collinson, D., 1987, '"Picking Women": The Recruitment of Temporary Workers in the Mail Order Industry', *Work, Employment and Society*, Vol.1, No.3, pp.371–87.

Dawson, J., 1985, 'The Costs and Returns of Sunday Trading', Working Paper 8502, *Department of Business Studies*, Stirling: University of Stirling.

Distributive Trades EDC, 1985, Employment Perspectives and the Distributive Trades, London: HMSO.

Ferris, J., 1991, 'On the Economics of Regulated Early Closing Hours: Some Evidence from Canada', *Applied Economics*, Vol.23, pp.1393–1400.

Flanders, A., R. Pomeranz and J. Woodard, 1968, *Experiment in Industrial Democracy: A Study of the John Lewis Partnership*, London: Faber.

Freathy, P., 1991, 'Distance Learning and the Distributive Trades: Stirling's MBA', *Journal of European Industrial Training*, Vol.15, No.4, pp.21–4.

Hogarth, T., and Barth, M., 1991, 'Age Works: A Case Study of B & Q's Use of Older Workers', *Institute of Employment Research*, Warwick: University of Warwick.

NEDO, 1988, *Part-time Working in the Distributive Trades*, London: NEDO, Vols. I & II.

NIESR, 1986, *Young People's Employment in Retailing*, London: NEDO.

Price, J., and Yandle, B., 1987, 'Labour Markets and Sunday Closing Laws', *Journal of Labour Research*, Vol.8, No.4, pp.407–14.

Reynolds, J., and N. Brue, 1991, *Recruitment and Retention in Retailing*, Harlow: Longman.

Robinson, O., and Wallace, J., 1976, *Pay and Employment in Retailing*, London: Saxon House.

Notes on Contributors

Gary Akehurst is at Portsmouth University Business School, Department of Business and Management, Locksway Road, Southsea, Hants PO3 8JF, UK.

Nicholas Alexander is in the School of International Business, University of Ulster, Coleraine, Northern Ireland, BT52 1SA.

Adelina Broadbridge is at the Institute for Retail Studies, University of Stirling, Stirling, FK9 4LA, UK.

John Dawson is in the Department of Business Studies, University of Edinburgh, William Robertson Building, 50 George Square, Edinburgh EH8 9JY, UK.

Anne Findlay is at the Institute for Retail Studies, University of Stirling, Stirling, FK9 4LA, UK.

Paul Freathy is at the Institute for Retail Studies, University of Stirling, Stirling, FK9 4LA, UK.

Roger Penn is in the Department of Sociology, University of Lancaster, Lancaster LA1 4YL, UK.

Jonathan Reynolds is at Templeton College, Oxford Institute of Retail Management, Kennington, Oxford OX1 5NY, UK.

Olive Robinson is formerly of the School of Management, University of Bath, Claverton Down, Bath, BA2 7AY, UK, currently Kingston University, Kingston upon Thames, Surrey, UK.

Leigh Sparks is at the Institute for Retail Studies, and School of Management, University of Stirling, Stirling, FK9 4LA, UK.

A. Roy Thurik is at the Centre for Advanced Small Business Economics, Erasmus University PO Box 1738, 3000 DR Rotterdam and EIM Small Business Research and Consultancy, PO Box 7001, 2701 AA, Zoetermeer, the Netherlands.

Betty Wirth is in the Department of Sociology, University of Lancaster, Lancaster LA1 4YL, UK.